COLLECTED PLAYS

SEAN O'CASEY

COLLECTED PLAYS

Volume One

JUNO AND THE PAYCOCK
THE SHADOW OF A GUNMAN
THE PLOUGH AND THE STARS
THE END OF THE BEGINNING
A POUND ON DEMAND

MACMILLAN
ST MARTIN'S PRESS

SBN Boards: 333 08037 8

First Edition 1949
Reprinted 1950, 1952, 1957, 1967, 1971

Published by
MACMILLAN LONDON LTD
London and Basingstoke
Associated companies in New York Toronto
Dublin Melbourne Johannesburg & Madras

Printed in Great Britain by
LOWE & BRYDONE (PRINTERS) LTD
London

CONTENTS

	PAGE
JUNO AND THE PAYCOCK	1
THE SHADOW OF A GUNMAN	91
THE PLOUGH AND THE STARS	159
THE END OF THE BEGINNING	263
A POUND ON DEMAND	293

JUNO AND THE PAYCOCK

A Tragedy in Three Acts

CHARACTERS IN THE PLAY

"CAPTAIN" JACK BOYLE
JUNO BOYLE, *his wife*
JOHNNY BOYLE } *their children*
MARY BOYLE
"JOXER" DALY   *Residents in*
MRS. MAISIE MADIGAN   *the Tenement*
"NEEDLE" NUGENT, *a tailor*
MRS. TANCRED
JERRY DEVINE
CHARLES BENTHAM, *a school teacher*
AN IRREGULAR MOBILIZER
TWO IRREGULARS
A COAL-BLOCK VENDOR
A SEWING MACHINE MAN
TWO FURNITURE REMOVAL MEN
TWO NEIGHBOURS

SCENE

ACT I.—The living apartment of a two-roomed tenancy of
the Boyle family, in a tenement house in Dublin.

ACT II.—The same.

ACT III.—The same.

A few days elapse between Acts I and II, and two months
between Acts II and III.

During Act III the curtain is lowered for a few minutes to
denote the lapse of one hour.

Period of the play, 1922.

Act I

The living-room of a two-room tenancy occupied by the Boyle family in a tenement house in Dublin. Left, a door leading to another part of the house; left of door a window looking into the street; at back a dresser; farther to right at back, a window looking into the back of the house. Between the window and the dresser is a picture of the Virgin; below the picture, on a bracket, is a crimson bowl in which a floating votive light is burning. Farther to the right is a small bed partly concealed by cretonne hangings strung on a twine. To the right is the fireplace; near the fireplace is a door leading to the other room. Beside the fireplace is a box containing coal. On the mantelshelf is an alarm clock lying on its face. In a corner near the window looking into the back is a galvanized bath. A table and some chairs. On the table are breakfast things for one. A teapot is on the hob and a frying-pan stands inside the fender. There are a few books on the dresser and one on the table. Leaning against the dresser is a long-handled shovel — the kind invariably used by labourers when turning concrete or mixing mortar. Johnny Boyle is sitting crouched beside the fire. Mary with her jumper off — it is lying on the back of a chair — is arranging her hair before a tiny mirror perched on the table. Beside the mirror is stretched out the morning paper, which she looks at when she isn't gazing into the mirror. She is a well-made and good-looking girl of twenty-two. Two forces are working in her mind — one, through the circumstances of her life, pulling her back; the other, through the influence of books she has read, pushing her forward. The opposing forces are apparent in her speech and her manners, both of which are degraded by her environment, and

3   A*

improved by her acquaintance — slight though it be — with
literature.   The time is early forenoon.

Mary [*looking at the paper*]. On a little bye-road, out
   beyant Finglas, he was found.
   [*Mrs. Boyle enters by door on right ; she has been shopping*
   and carries a small parcel in her hand.. She is forty-five
   years of age, and twenty years ago she must have been a
   pretty woman ; but her face has now assumed that look
   which ultimately settles down upon the faces of the
   women of the working-class ; a look of listless monotony
   and harassed anxiety, blending with an expression of
   mechanical resistance.   Were circumstances favourable,
   she would probably be a handsome, active and clever
   woman.]

Mrs. Boyle. Isn't he come in yet ?

Mary. No, mother.

Mrs. Boyle. Oh, he'll come in when he likes ; struttin'
   about the town like a paycock with Joxer, I suppose.   I
   hear all about Mrs. Tancred's son is in this mornin's
   paper.

Mary. The full details are in it this mornin' ;   seven
   wounds he had — one entherin' the neck, with an exit
   wound beneath the left shoulder-blade ;   another in
   the left breast penethratin' the heart, an' . . .

Johnny [*springing up from the fire*].   Oh, quit that readin',
   for God's sake !   Are yous losin' all your feelin's ?
   It'll soon be that none of you'll read anythin' that's
   not about butcherin' !
                              [*He goes quickly into the room on left.*

Mary. He's gettin' very sensitive, all of a sudden !

Mrs. Boyle. I'll read it myself, Mary, by an' by, when I come home. Everybody's sayin' that he was a Die-hard — thanks be to God that Johnny had nothin' to do with him this long time. . . . [*Opening the parcel and taking out some sausages, which she places on a plate*] Ah, then, if that father o' yours doesn't come in soon for his breakfast, he may go without any ; I'll not wait much longer for him.

Mary. Can't you let him get it himself when he comes in ?

Mrs. Boyle. Yes, an' let him bring in Joxer Daly along with him ? Ay, that's what he'd like, an' that's what he's waitin' for — till he thinks I'm gone to work, an' then sail in with the boul' Joxer, to burn all the coal an' dhrink all the tea in the place, to show them what a good Samaritan he is ! But I'll stop here till he comes in, if I have to wait till to-morrow mornin'.

Voice of Johnny inside. Mother !

Mrs. Boyle. Yis ?

Voice of Johnny. Bring us in a dhrink o' wather.

Mrs. Boyle. Bring in that fella a dhrink o' wather, for God's sake, Mary.

Mary. Isn't he big an' able enough to come out an' get it himself ?

Mrs. Boyle. If you weren't well yourself you'd like some-body to bring you in a dhrink o' wather.

[*She brings in drink and returns.*

Mrs. Boyle. Isn't it terrible to have to be waitin' this way ! You'd think he was bringin' twenty poun's a week into the house the way he's going on. He wore out the Health Insurance long ago, he's afther wearin' out the unemployment dole, an', now, he's thryin' to wear out me ! An' constantly singin', no less, when he ought always to be on his knees offerin' up a Novena for a job !

Mary [*tying a ribbon fillet-wise around her head*]. I don't like this ribbon, ma ; I think I'll wear the green — it looks betther than the blue.

Mrs. Boyle. Ah, wear whatever ribbon you like, girl, only don't be botherin' me. I don't know what a girl on strike wants to be wearin' a ribbon round her head for, or silk stockins on her legs either ; it's wearin' them things that make the employers think they're givin' yous too much money.

Mary. The hour is past now when we'll ask the employers' permission to wear what we like.

Mrs. Boyle. I don't know why you wanted to walk out for Jennie Claffey ; up to this you never had a good word for her.

Mary. What's the use of belongin' to a Trades Union if you won't stand up for your principles ? Why did they sack her ? It was a clear case of victimization. We couldn't let her walk the streets, could we ?

Mrs. Boyle. No, of course yous couldn't — yous wanted to keep her company. Wan victim wasn't enough. When the employers sacrifice wan victim, the Trades Unions go wan betther be sacrificin' a hundred.

Mary. It doesn't matther what you say, ma — a principle's a principle.

Mrs. Boyle. Yis ; an' when I go into oul' Murphy's to-morrow, an' he gets to know that, instead o' payin' all, I'm goin' to borry more, what'll he say when I tell him a principle's a principle ?   What'll we do if he refuses to give us any more on tick ?

Mary. He daren't refuse — if he does, can't you tell him he's paid ?

Mrs. Boyle. It's lookin' as if he was paid, whether he refuses or no.

> [*Johnny appears at the door on left.   He can be plainly seen now ; he is a thin, delicate fellow, something younger than Mary.   He has evidently gone through a rough time.   His face is pale and drawn ; there is a tremulous look of indefinite fear in his eyes.   The left sleeve of his coat is empty, and he walks with a slight halt.*

Johnny. I was lyin' down ; I thought yous were gone. Oul' Simon Mackay is thrampin' about like a horse over me head, an' I can't sleep with him — they're like thunder-claps in me brain !   The curse o' — God forgive me for goin' to curse !

Mrs. Boyle. There, now ; go back an' lie down again, an' I'll bring you in a nice cup o' tay.

Johnny. Tay, tay, tay !   You're always thinkin' o' tay. If a man was dyin', you'd thry to make him swally a cup o' tay !   [*He goes back.*

Mrs. Boyle. I don't know what's goin' to be done with him.   The bullet he got in the hip in Easter Week was bad enough, but the bomb that shatthered his arm in the fight in O'Connell Street put the finishin' touch on him.   I knew he was makin' a fool of himself.   God knows I went down on me bended knees to him not to go agen the Free State.

Mary. He stuck to his principles, an', no matther how you may argue, ma, a principle's a principle.

Voice of Johnny. Is Mary goin' to stay here ?

Mary. No, I'm not goin' to stay here ; you can't expect me to be always at your beck an' call, can you ?

Voice of Johnny. I won't stop here be meself !

Mrs. Boyle. Amn't I nicely handicapped with the whole o' yous ! I don't know what any o' yous ud do without your ma. [*To Johnny*] Your father'll be here in a minute, an' if you want anythin', he'll get it for you.

Johnny. I hate assin' him for anythin'. . . . He hates to be assed to stir. . . . Is the light lightin' before the picture o' the Virgin ?

Mrs. Boyle. Yis, yis ! The wan inside to St. Anthony isn't enough, but he must have another wan to the Virgin here !

> [*Jerry Devine enters hastily. He is about twenty-five, well set, active and earnest. He is a type, becoming very common now in the Labour Movement, of a mind knowing enough to make the mass of his associates, who know less, a power, and too little to broaden that power for the benefit of all. Mary seizes her jumper and runs hastily into room left.*

Jerry [*breathless*]. Where's the Captain, Mrs. Boyle, where's the Captain ?

Mrs. Boyle. You may well ass a body that : he's wherever Joxer Daly is — dhrinkin' in some snug or another.

Jerry. Father Farrell is just afther stoppin' to tell me to run up an' get him to go to the new job that's goin'

on in Rathmines ; his cousin is foreman o' the job,
an' Father Farrell was speakin' to him about poor
Johnny an' his father bein' idle so long, an' the foreman
told Father Farrell to send the Captain up an' he'd
give him a start — I wondher where I'd find him ?

Mrs. Boyle. You'll find he's ayther in Ryan's or Foley's.

Jerry. I'll run round to Ryan's — I know it's a great
house o' Joxer's.   [*He rushes out.*

Mrs. Boyle [*piteously*]. There now, he'll miss that job, or
I know for what ! If he gets win' o' the word, he'll
not come back till evenin', so that it'll be too late.
There'll never be any good got out o' him so long as
he goes with that shouldher-shruggin' Joxer. I killin'
meself workin', an' he sthruttin' about from mornin'
till night like a paycock !

[*The steps of two persons are heard coming up a flight of
stairs. They are the footsteps of Captain Boyle and
Joxer. Captain Boyle is singing in a deep, sonorous,
self-honouring voice.*

The Captain. Sweet Spirit, hear me prayer ! Hear . . .
oh . . . hear . . . me prayer . . . hear, oh, hear
. . . Oh, he . . . ar . . . oh, he . . . ar . . . me . . .
pray . . . er !

Joxer [*outside*]. Ah, that's a darlin' song, a daaarlin' song !

Mrs. Boyle [*viciously*]. Sweet spirit hear his prayer ! Ah,
then, I'll take me solemn affeydavey, it's not for a job
he's prayin' !

[*She sits down on the bed so that the cretonne hangings hide
her from the view of those entering.*

[*The Captain comes slowly in. He is a man of about
sixty ; stout, grey-haired and stocky. His neck is short,*

and his head looks like a stone ball that one sometimes sees on top of a gate-post. His cheeks, reddish-purple, are puffed out, as if he were always repressing an almost irrepressible ejaculation. On his upper lip is a crisp, tightly cropped moustache ; he carries himself with the upper part of his body slightly thrown back, and his stomach slightly thrust forward. His walk is a slow, consequential strut. His clothes are dingy, and he wears a faded seaman's-cap with a glazed peak.

Boyle [*to Joxer, who is still outside*]. Come on, come on in, Joxer ; she's gone out long ago, man. If there's nothing else to be got, we'll furrage out a cup o' tay, anyway. It's the only bit I get in comfort when she's away. 'Tisn't Juno should be her pet name at all, but Deirdre of the Sorras, for she's always grousin'.

    [*Joxer steps cautiously into the room. He may be younger than the Captain but he looks a lot older. His face is like a bundle of crinkled paper ; his eyes have a cunning twinkle ; he is spare and loosely built ; he has a habit of constantly shrugging his shoulders with a peculiar twitching movement, meant to be ingratiating. His face is invariably ornamented with a grin.*

Joxer. It's a terrible thing to be tied to a woman that's always grousin'. I don't know how you stick it — it ud put years on me. It's a good job she has to be so ofen away, for [*with a shrug*] when the cat's away, the mice can play !

Boyle [*with a commanding and complacent gesture*]. Pull over to the fire, Joxer, an' we'll have a cup o' tay in a minute.

Joxer. Ah, a cup o' tay's a darlin' thing, a daaarlin' thing — the cup that cheers but doesn't . . .

[*Joxer's rhapsody is cut short by the sight of Juno coming forward and confronting the two cronies. Both are stupefied.*

Mrs. Boyle [*with sweet irony — poking the fire, and turning her head to glare at Joxer*]. Pull over to the fire, Joxer Daly, an' we'll have a cup o' tay in a minute ! Are you sure, now, you wouldn't like an egg ?

Joxer. I can't stop, Mrs. Boyle ; I'm in a desperate hurry, a desperate hurry.

Mrs. Boyle. Pull over to the fire, Joxer Daly ; people is always far more comfortabler here than they are in their own place.

[*Joxer makes hastily for the door. Boyle stirs to follow him ; thinks of something to relieve the situation — stops, and says suddenly :* Joxer !

Joxer [*at door ready to bolt*]. Yis ?

Boyle. You know the foreman o' that job that's goin' on down in Killesther, don't you, Joxer ?

Joxer [*puzzled*]. Foreman — Killesther ?

Boyle [*with a meaning look*]. He's a butty o' yours, isn't he ?

Joxer [*the truth dawning on him*]. The foreman at Killesther — oh yis, yis. He's an oul' butty o' mine — oh, he's a darlin' man, a daarlin' man.

Boyle. Oh, then, it's a sure thing. It's a pity we didn't go down at breakfast first thing this mornin'— we might ha' been working now ; but you didn't know it then.

Joxer [*with a shrug*]. It's betther late than never.

Boyle. It's nearly time we got a start, anyhow ; I'm fed up knockin' round, doin' nothin'. He promised you —gave you the straight tip ?

Joxer. Yis. " Come down on the blow o' dinner," says he, " an' I'll start you, an' any friend you like to brin' with you." " Ah," says I, " you're a darlin' man, a daaarlin' man."

Boyle. Well, it couldn't come at a betther time — we're a long time waitin' for it.

Joxer. Indeed we were ; but it's a long lane that has no turnin'.

Boyle. The blow up for dinner is at one — wait till I see what time it 'tis.
    [*He goes over to the mantelpiece, and gingerly lifts the clock.*

Mrs. Boyle. Min' now, how you go on fiddlin' with that clock — you know the least little thing sets it asthray.

Boyle. The job couldn't come at a betther time ; I'm feelin' in great fettle, Joxer. I'd hardly believe I ever had a pain in me legs, an' last week I was nearly crippled with them.

Joxer. That's betther an' betther ; ah, God never shut wan door but He opened another !

Boyle. It's only eleven o'clock ; we've lashins o' time. I'll slip on me oul' moleskins afther breakfast, an' we can saunter down at our ayse. [*Putting his hand on the shovel*] I think, Joxer, we'd betther bring our shovels ?

Joxer. Yis, Captain, yis ; it's betther to go fully prepared an' ready for all eventualities.   You bring your
long-tailed shovel, an' I'll bring me navvy.   We
mighten' want them, an', then agen, we might : for
want of a nail the shoe was lost, for want of a shoe the
horse was lost, an' for want of a horse the man was
lost — aw, that's a darlin' proverb, a daarlin' . . .

[*As Joxer is finishing his sentence, Mrs. Boyle approaches
the door and Joxer retreats hurriedly.   She shuts the
door with a bang.*

Boyle [*suggestively*]. We won't be long pullin' ourselves
together agen when I'm working for a few weeks.

[*Mrs. Boyle takes no notice.*

Boyle. The foreman on the job is an oul' butty o'
Joxer's ; I have an idea that I know him meself.   [*Silence*]
. . . There's a button off the back o' me moleskin
trousers. . . . If you leave out a needle an' thread
I'll sew it on meself. . . . Thanks be to God, the
pains in me legs is gone, anyhow !

Mrs. Boyle [*with a burst*]. Look here, Mr. Jacky Boyle,
them yarns won't go down with Juno.   I know you an'
Joxer Daly of an oul' date, an' if you think you're
able to come it over me with them fairy tales, you're
in the wrong shop.

Boyle [*coughing subduedly to relieve the tenseness of the situation*].
U-u-u-ugh !

Mrs. Boyle. Butty o' Joxer's !   Oh, you'll do a lot o'
good as long as you continue to be a butty o' Joxer's !

Boyle. U-u-u-ugh !

Mrs. Boyle. Shovel !   Ah, then, me boyo, you'd do far

more work with a knife an' fork than ever you'll do
with a shovel ! If there was e'er a genuine job goin'
you'd be dh'other way about — not able to lift your
arms with the pains in your legs ! Your poor wife
slavin' to keep the bit in your mouth, an' you galli-
vantin' about all the day like a paycock !

Boyle. It ud be betther for a man to be dead, betther for
a man to be dead.

Mrs. Boyle [*ignoring the interruption*]. Everybody callin' you
" Captain ", an' you only wanst on the wather, in an
oul' collier from here to Liverpool, when anybody, to
listen or look at you, ud take you for a second Christo
For Columbus !

Boyle. Are you never goin' to give us a rest ?

Mrs. Boyle. Oh, you're never tired o' lookin' for a rest.

Boyle. D'ye want to dhrive me out o' the house ?

Mrs. Boyle. It ud be easier to dhrive you out o' the house
than to dhrive you into a job. Here, sit down an'
take your breakfast — it may be the last you'll get,
for I don't know where the next is goin' to come from.

Boyle. If I get this job we'll be all right.

Mrs. Boyle. Did ye see Jerry Devine ?

Boyle [*testily*]. No, I didn't see him.

Mrs. Boyle. No, but you seen Joxer. Well, he was here
lookin' for you.

Boyle. Well, let him look !

Mrs. Boyle. Oh, indeed, he may well look, for it ud be
hard for him to see you, an' you stuck in Ryan's snug.

Boyle. I wasn't in Ryan's snug — I don't go into Ryan's.

Mrs. Boyle. Oh, is there a mad dog there ? Well, if you weren't in Ryan's you were in Foley's.

Boyle. I'm telling you for the last three weeks I haven't tasted a dhrop of intoxicatin' liquor. I wasn't in ayther wan snug or dh'other — I could swear that on a prayer-book — I'm as innocent as the child unborn !

Mrs. Boyle. Well, if you'd been in for your breakfast you'd ha' seen him.

Boyle [*suspiciously*]. What does he want me for ?

Mrs. Boyle. He'll be back any minute an' then you'll soon know.

Boyle. I'll dhrop out an' see if I can meet him.

Mrs. Boyle. You'll sit down an' take your breakfast, an' let me go to me work, for I'm an hour late already waitin' for you.

Boyle. You needn't ha' waited, for I'll take no breakfast — I've a little spirit left in me still !

Mrs. Boyle. Are you goin' to have your breakfast — yes or no ?

Boyle [*too proud to yield*]. I'll have no breakfast — yous can keep your breakfast. [*Plaintively*] I'll knock out a bit somewhere, never fear.

Mrs. Boyle. Nobody's goin' to coax you — don't think that.

 [*She vigorously replaces the pan and the sausages in the press.*

Boyle. I've a little spirit left in me still.

 [*Jerry Devine enters hastily.*

Jerry. Oh, here you are at last ! I've been searchin' for you everywhere. The foreman in Foley's told me you hadn't left the snug with Joxer ten minutes before I went in.

Mrs. Boyle. An' he swearin' on the holy prayer-book that he wasn't in no snug !

Boyle [*to Jerry*]. What business is it o' yours whether I was in a snug or no ? What do you want to be gallopin' about afther me for ? Is a man not to be allowed to leave his house for a minute without havin' a pack o' spies, pimps an' informers cantherin' at his heels ?

Jerry. Oh, you're takin' a wrong view of it, Mr. Boyle ; I simply was anxious to do you a good turn. I have a message for you from Father Farrell : he says that if you go to the job that's on in Rathmines, an' ask for Foreman Managan, you'll get a start.

Boyle. That's all right, but I don't want the motions of me body to be watched the way an asthronomer ud watch a star. If you're folleyin' Mary aself, you've no pereeogative to be folleyin' me. [*Suddenly catching his thigh*] U-ugh, I'm afther gettin' a terrible twinge in me right leg !

Mrs. Boyle. Oh, it won't be very long now till it travels into your left wan. It's miraculous that whenever he scents a job in front of him, his legs begin to fail him ! Then, me bucko, if you lose this chance, you may go an' furrage for yourself !

Jerry. This job'll last for some time too, Captain, an' as soon as the foundations are in, it'll be cushy enough.

Boyle. Won't it be a climbin' job ? How d'ye expect me

to be able to go up a ladder with these legs ? An', if I get up aself, how am I goin' to get down agen ?

Mrs. Boyle [*viciously*]. Get wan o' the labourers to carry you down in a hod ! You can't climb a laddher, but you can skip like a goat into a snug !

Jerry. I wouldn't let myself be let down that easy, Mr. Boyle ; a little exercise, now, might do you all the good in the world.

Boyle. It's a docthor you should have been, Devine — maybe you know more about the pains in me legs than meself that has them ?

Jerry [*irritated*]. Oh, I know nothin' about the pains in your legs ; I've brought the message that Father Farrell gave me, an' that's all I can do.

Mrs. Boyle. Here, sit down an' take your breakfast, an' go an' get ready ; an' don't be actin' as if you couldn't pull a wing out of a dead bee.

Boyle. I want no breakfast, I tell you ; it ud choke me afther all that's been said. I've a little spirit left in me still.

Mrs. Boyle. Well, let's see your spirit, then, an' go in at wanst an' put on your moleskin trousers !

Boyle [*moving towards the door on left*]. It ud be betther for a man to be dead ! U-ugh ! There's another twinge in me other leg ! Nobody but meself knows the sufferin' I'm goin' through with the pains in these legs o' mine !

[*He goes into the room on left as Mary comes out with her hat in her hand.*

Mrs. Boyle. I'll have to push off now, for I'm terrible

late already, but I was determined to stay an' hunt
that Joxer this time.   [*She goes off.*

Jerry. Are you going out, Mary ?

Mary. It looks like it when I'm putting on my hat,
doesn't it ?

Jerry. The bitther word agen, Mary.

Mary. You won't allow me to be friendly with you ;
if I thry, you deliberately misundherstand it.

Jerry. I didn't always misundherstand it ; you were often
delighted to have the arms of Jerry around you.

Mary. If you go on talkin' like this, Jerry Devine, you'll
make me hate you !

Jerry. Well, let it be either a weddin' or a wake !
Listen, Mary, I'm standin' for the Secretaryship of our
Union. There's only one opposin' me ; I'm popular
with all the men, an' a good speaker — all are sayin'
that I'll get elected.

Mary. Well ?

Jerry. The job's worth three hundred an' fifty pounds a
year, Mary. You an' I could live nice an' cosily on
that ; it would lift you out o' this place an' . . .

Mary. I haven't time to listen to you now — I have to go.
        [*She is going out, when Jerry bars the way.*

Jerry [*appealingly*]. Mary, what's come over you with me
for the last few weeks ? You hardly speak to me, an'
then only a word with a face o' bittherness on it. Have
you forgotten, Mary, all the happy evenins that were
as sweet as the scented hawthorn that sheltered the
sides o' the road as we saunthered through the country ?

Mary. That's all over now. When you get your new job, Jerry, you won't be long findin' a girl far betther than I am for your sweetheart.

Jerry. Never, never, Mary ! No matther what happens, you'll always be the same to me.

Mary. I must be off ; please let me go, Jerry.

Jerry. I'll go a bit o' the way with you.

Mary. You needn't, thanks ; I want to be by meself.

Jerry [*catching her arm*]. You're goin' to meet another fella ; you've clicked with someone else, me lady !

Mary. That's no concern o' yours, Jerry Devine ; let me go !

Jerry. I saw yous comin' out o' the Cornflower Dance Class, an' you hangin' on his arm — a thin, lanky strip of a Micky Dazzler, with a walkin'-stick an' gloves !

Voice of Johnny [*loudly*]. What are you doin' there — pullin' about everything !

Voice of Boyle [*loudly and viciously*]. I'm puttin' on me moleskin trousers !

Mary. You're hurtin' me arm ! Let me go, or I'll scream, an' then you'll have the oul' fella out on top of us !

Jerry. Don't be so hard on a fella, Mary, don't be so hard.

Boyle [*appearing at the door*]. What's the meanin' of all this hillabaloo ?

Mary. Let me go, let me go !

Boyle. D'ye hear me — what's all this hillabaloo about ?

Jerry [*plaintively*]. Will you not give us one kind word, one kind word, Mary ?

Boyle. D'ye hear me talkin' to yous ?   What's all this hillabaloo for ?

Jerry. Let me kiss your hand, your little, tiny, white hand !

Boyle. Your little, tiny, white hand — are you takin' leave o' your senses, man ?
                              [*Mary breaks away and rushes out.*

Boyle. This is nice goins on in front of her father !

Jerry. Ah, dhry up, for God's sake !   [*He follows Mary.*

Boyle. Chiselurs don't care a damn now about their parents, they're bringin' their fathers' grey hairs down with sorra to the grave, an' laughin' at it, laughin' at it.   Ah, I suppose it's just the same everywhere — the whole worl's in a state o' chassis ! [*He sits by the fire*] Breakfast !   Well, they can keep their breakfast for me.   Not if they were down on their bended knees would I take it — I'll show them I've a little spirit left in me still ! [*He goes over to the press, takes out a plate and looks at it*] Sassige ! Well, let her keep her sassige. [*He returns to the fire, takes up the teapot and gives it a gentle shake*] The tea's wet right enough.
     [*A pause ; he rises, goes to the press, takes out the sausage, puts it on the pan, and puts both on the fire.   He attends the sausage with a fork.*

Boyle [*singing*] :

When the robins nest agen,
And the flowers are in bloom,
When the Springtime's sunny smile seems to banish all
    sorrow an' gloom ;
Then me bonny blue-ey'd lad, if me heart be true till then —
He's promised he'll come back to me,
When the robins nest agen !

> [*He lifts his head at the high note, and then drops his eyes
> to the pan.*

Boyle [*singing*] :

> When the . . .

> [*Steps are heard approaching ; he whips the pan off the fire
> and puts it under the bed, then sits down at the fire. The
> door opens and a bearded man looking in says :*

You don't happen to want a sewin' machine ?

Boyle [*furiously*]. No, I don't want e'er a sewin' machine !
> [*He returns the pan to the fire, and commences to sing again.*

Boyle [*singing*] :

> When the robins nest agen,
> And the flowers they are in bloom,
> He's . . .

> [*A thundering knock is heard at the street door.*

Boyle. There's a terrible tatheraraa — that's a stranger —
that's nobody belongin' to the house.

> [*Another loud knock.*

Joxer [*sticking his head in at the door*]. Did ye hear them
tatherarahs ?

Boyle. Well, Joxer, I'm not deaf.

Johnny [*appearing in his shirt and trousers at the door on* **left** ;

his face is anxious and his voice is tremulous]. Who's that at the door ; who's that at the door ? Who gave that knock — d'ye yous hear me — are yous deaf or dhrunk or what ?

Boyle [*to Johnny*]. How the hell do I know who 'tis ? Joxer, stick your head out o' the window an' see.

Joxer. An' mebbe get a bullet in the kisser ? Ah, none o' them thricks for Joxer ! It's betther to be a coward than a corpse !

Boyle [*looking cautiously out of the window*]. It's a fella in a thrench coat.

Johnny. Holy Mary, Mother o' God, I . . .

Boyle. He's goin' away — he must ha' got tired knockin'.
[*Johnny returns to the room on left.*

Boyle. Sit down an' have a cup o' tay, Joxer.

Joxer. I'm afraid the missus ud pop in on us agen before we'd know where we are. Somethin's tellin' me to go at wanst.

Boyle. Don't be superstitious, man ; we're Dublin men, an' not boyos that's only afther comin' up from the bog o' Allen — though if she did come in, right enough, we'd be caught like rats in a thrap.

Joxer. An' you know the sort she is — she wouldn't listen to reason — an' wanse bitten twice shy.

Boyle [*going over to the window at back*]. If the worst came to the worst, you could dart out here, Joxer ; it's only a dhrop of a few feet to the roof of the return room, an' the first minute she goes into dh'other room I'll give you the bend, an' you can slip in an' away.

Joxer [*yielding to the temptation*]. Ah, I won't stop very long anyhow. [*Picking up a book from the table*] Whose is the buk?

Boyle. Aw, one o' Mary's; she's always readin' lately — nothin' but thrash, too. There's one I was lookin' at dh'other day: three stories, The Doll's House, Ghosts, an' The Wild Duck — buks only fit for chiselurs!

Joxer. Didja ever rade *Elizabeth, or Th' Exile o' Sibayria*? . . . Ah, it's a darlin' story, a daarlin' story!

Boyle. You eat your sassige, an' never min' *Th' Exile o' Sibayria*.
  [*Both sit down; Boyle fills out tea, pours gravy on Joxer's plate, and keeps the sausage for himself.*

Joxer. What are you wearin' your moleskin trousers for?

Boyle. I have to go to a job, Joxer. Just afther you'd gone, Devine kem runnin' in to tell us that Father Farrell said if I went down to the job that's goin' on in Rathmines I'd get a start

Joxer. Be the holy, that's good news!

Boyle. How is it good news? I wondher if you were in my condition, would you call it good news?

Joxer. I thought . . .

Boyle. You thought! You think too sudden sometimes, Joxer. D'ye know, I'm hardly able to crawl with the pains in me legs!

Joxer. Yis, yis; I forgot the pains in your legs. I know you can do nothin' while they're at you.

Boyle. You forgot; I don't think any of yous realize the

state I'm in with the pains in me legs. What ud happen if I had to carry a bag o' cement?

Joxer. Ah, any man havin' the like of them pains id be down an' out, down an' out.

Boyle. I wouldn't mind if he had said it to meself; but, no, oh no, he rushes in an' shouts it out in front o' Juno, an' you know what Juno is, Joxer. We all know Devine knows a little more than the rest of us, but he doesn't act as if he did; he's a good boy, sober, able to talk an' all that, but still . . .

Joxer. Oh ay; able to argufy, but still . . .

Boyle. If he's runnin' afther Mary, aself, he's not goin' to be runnin' afther me. Captain Boyle's able to take care of himself. Afther all, I'm not gettin' brought up on Virol. I never heard him usin' a curse; I don't believe he was ever dhrunk in his life — sure he's not like a Christian at all!

Joxer. You're afther takin' the word out o' me mouth — afther all, a Christian's natural, but he's unnatural.

Boyle. His oul' fella was just the same — a Wicklow man.

Joxer. A Wicklow man! That explains the whole thing. I've met many a Wicklow man in me time, but I never met wan that was any good.

Boyle. " Father Farrell," says he, " sent me down to tell you." Father Farrell! . . . D'ye know, Joxer, I never like to be beholden to any o' the clergy.

Joxer. It's dangerous, right enough.

Boyle. If they do anything for you, they'd want you to be livin' in the Chapel. . . . I'm goin' to tell you

somethin', Joxer, that I wouldn't tell to anybody else
— the clergy always had too much power over the people
in this unfortunate country.

Joxer. You could sing that if you had an air to it!

Boyle [*becoming enthusiastic*]. Didn't they prevent the people
in " '47 " from seizin' the corn, an' they starvin';
didn't they down Parnell; didn't they say that hell
wasn't hot enough nor eternity long enough to punish
the Fenians? We don't forget, we don't forget them
things, Joxer. If they've taken everything else from
us, Joxer, they've left us our memory.

Joxer [*emotionally*]. For mem'ry's the only friend that
grief can call its own, that grief . . . can . . . call
. . . its own!

Boyle. Father Farrell's beginnin' to take a great intherest
in Captain Boyle; because of what Johnny did for his
country, says he to me wan day. It's a curious way to
reward Johnny be makin' his poor oul' father work.
But that's what the clergy want, Joxer— work, work,
work for me an' you; havin' us mulin' from mornin'
till night, so that they may be in betther fettle when
they come hoppin' round for their dues! Job! Well,
let him give his job to wan of his hymn-singin',
prayer-spoutin', craw-thumpin' Confraternity men!
[*The voice of a coal-block vendor is heard chanting in the
street.*

Voice of Coal Vendor. Blocks . . . coal-blocks! Blocks
. . . coal-blocks!

Joxer. God be with the young days when you were
steppin' the deck of a manly ship, with the win'
blowin' a hurricane through the masts, an' the only

sound you'd hear was, " Port your helm ! " an' the only answer, " Port it is, sir ! "

Boyle. Them was days, Joxer, them was days. Nothin' was too hot or too heavy for me then. Sailin' from the Gulf o' Mexico to the Antanartic Ocean. I seen things, I seen things, Joxer, that no mortal man should speak about that knows his Catechism. Ofen, an' ofen, when I was fixed to the wheel with a marlin-spike, an' the wins blowin' fierce an' the waves lashin' an' lashin', till you'd think every minute was goin' to be your last, an' it blowed, an' blowed — blew is the right word, Joxer, but blowed is what the sailors use. . . .

Joxer. Aw, it's a darlin' word, a daarlin' word.

Boyle. An', as it blowed an' blowed, I ofen looked up at the sky an' assed meself the question — what is the stars, what is the stars ?

Voice of Coal Vendor. Any blocks, coal-blocks ; blocks, coal-blocks !

Joxer. Ah, that's the question, that's the question — what is the stars ?

Boyle. An' then, I'd have another look, an' I'd ass meself — what is the moon ?

Joxer. Ah, that's the question — what is the moon, what is the moon ?

> [*Rapid steps are heard coming towards the door. Boyle makes desperate efforts to hide everything ; Joxer rushes to the window in a frantic effort to get out ; Boyle begins to innocently lilt " Oh, me darlin' Jennie, I will be thrue to thee ", when the door is opened, and the black face of the Coal Vendor appears.*

The Coal Vendor. D'yes want any blocks ?

Boyle [*with a roar*]. No, we don't want any blocks !

Joxer [*coming back with a sigh of relief*]. That's afther puttin'
the heart across me — I could ha' sworn it was Juno.
I'd betther be goin', Captain ; you couldn't tell the
minute Juno'd hop in on us.

Boyle. Let her hop in ; we may as well have it out first
as at last. I've made up me mind — I'm not goin' to
do only what she damn well likes.

Joxer. Them sentiments does you credit, Captain ; I
don't like to say anything as between man an' wife,
but I say as a butty, as a butty, Captain, that you've
stuck it too long, an' that it's about time you showed
a little spunk.

    How can a man die betther than facin' fearful odds,
    For th' ashes of his fathers an' the temples of his gods ?

Boyle. She has her rights — there's no one denyin' it,
but haven't I me rights too ?

Joxer. Of course you have — the sacred rights o' man !

Boyle. Today, Joxer, there's goin' to be issued a proclamation be me, establishin' an independent Republic,
an' Juno'll have to take an oath of allegiance.

Joxer. Be firm, be firm, Captain ; the first few minutes'll
be the worst : — if you gently touch a nettle it'll sting
you for your pains ; grasp it like a lad of mettle, an' as
soft as silk remains !

Voice of Juno outside. Can't stop, Mrs. Madigan — I
haven't a minute !

Joxer [*flying out of the window*]. Holy God, here she is !

Boyle [*packing the things away with a rush in the press*]. I knew that fella ud stop till she was in on top of us !

> [*He sits down by the fire.*
> [*Juno enters hastily ; she is flurried and excited.*

Juno. Oh, you're in — you must have been only afther comin' in ?

Boyle. No, I never went out.

Juno. It's curious, then, you never heard the knockin'.

> [*She puts her coat and hat on bed.*

Boyle. Knockin' ? Of course I heard the knockin'.

Juno. An' why didn't you open the door, then ? I suppose you were so busy with Joxer that you hadn't time.

Boyle. I haven't seen Joxer since I seen him before. Joxer ! What ud bring Joxer here ?

Juno. D'ye mean to tell me that the pair of yous wasn't collogin' together here when me back was turned ?

Boyle. What ud we be collogin' together about ? I have somethin' else to think of besides collogin' with Joxer. I can swear on all the holy prayer-books . . .

Mrs. Boyle. That you weren't in no snug ! Go on in at wanst now, an' take off that moleskin trousers o' yours, an' put on a collar an' tie to smarten yourself up a bit. There's a visitor comin' with Mary in a minute, an' he has great news for you.

Boyle. A job, I suppose ; let us get wan first before we start lookin' for another.

Mrs. Boyle. That's the thing that's able to put the win' up you. Well, it's no job, but news that'll give you the chance o' your life.

Boyle. What's all the mystery about ?

Mrs. Boyle. G'win an' take off the moleskin trousers when you're told !   [*Boyle goes into room on left.*
[*Mrs. Boyle tidies up the room, puts the shovel under the bed, and goes to the press.*

Mrs. Boyle. Oh, God bless us, looka the way everything's thrun about ! Oh, Joxer was here, Joxer was here !
[*Mary enters with Charlie Bentham ; he is a young man of twenty-five, tall, good-looking, with a very high opinion of himself generally. He is dressed in a brown coat, brown knee-breeches, grey stockings, a brown sweater, with a deep blue tie ; he carries gloves and a walking-stick.*

Mrs. Boyle [*fussing round*]. Come in, Mr. Bentham ; sit down, Mr. Bentham, in this chair ; it's more comfortabler than that, Mr. Bentham. Himself'll be here in a minute ; he's just takin' off his trousers.

Mary. Mother !

Bentham. Please don't put yourself to any trouble, Mrs. Boyle — I'm quite all right here, thank you.

Mrs. Boyle. An' to think of you knowin' Mary, an' she knowin' the news you had for us, an' wouldn't let on ; but it's all the more welcomer now, for we were on our last lap !

Voice of Johnny inside. What are you kickin' up all the racket for ?

Boyle [*roughly*]. I'm takin' off me moleskin trousers !

Johnny. Can't you do it, then, without lettin' th' whole

house know you're takin off your trousers? What
d'ye want puttin' them on an' takin' them off again?

Boyle. Will you let me alone, will you let me alone?
Am I never goin' to be done thryin' to please th' whole
o' yous?

Mrs Boyle [*to Bentham*]. You must excuse th' state o' th'
place, Mr. Bentham; th' minute I turn me back that
man o' mine always makes a litther o' th' place, a litther
o' th' place.

Bentham. Don't worry, Mrs. Boyle; it's all right, I
assure . . .

Boyle [*inside*]. Where's me braces; where in th' name o'
God did I leave me braces? . . . Ay, did you see where
I put me braces?

Johnny [*inside, calling out*]. Ma, will you come in here an'
take da away ou' o' this or he'll dhrive me mad.

Mrs. Boyle [*going towards the door*]. Dear, dear, dear, that
man'll be lookin' for somethin' on th' day o' Judgement. [*Looking into room and calling to Boyle*] Look at
your braces, man, hangin' round your neck!

Boyle [*inside*]. Aw, Holy God!

Mrs. Boyle [*calling*]. Johnny, Johnny, come out here for a
minute.

Johnny. Ah, leave Johnny alone, an' don't be annoyin'
him!

Mrs. Boyle. Come on, Johnny, till I inthroduce you to Mr.
Bentham. [*To Bentham*] My son, Mr. Bentham; he's
afther goin' through the mill. He was only a chiselur
of a Boy Scout in Easter Week, when he got hit in the

hip ; and his arm was blew off in the fight in O'Connell Street. [*Johnny comes in.*] Here he is, Mr. Bentham ; Mr. Bentham, Johnny. None can deny he done his bit for Irelan', if that's goin' to do him any good.

Johnny [*boastfully*]. I'd do it agen, ma, I'd do it agen ; for a principle's a principle.

Mrs. Boyle. Ah, you lost your best principle, me boy, when you lost your arm ; them's the only sort o' principles that's any good to a workin' man.

Johnny. Ireland only half free'll never be at peace while she has a son left to pull a trigger.

Mrs. Boyle. To be sure, to be sure — no bread's a lot betther than half a loaf. [*Calling loudly in to Boyle*] Will you hurry up there ?

[*Boyle enters in his best trousers, which aren't too good, and looks very uncomfortable in his collar and tie.*

Mrs. Boyle. This is me husband ; Mr. Boyle, Mr. Bentham.

Bentham. Ah, very glad to know you, Mr. Boyle. How are you ?

Boyle. Ah, I'm not too well at all ; I suffer terrible with pains in me legs. Juno can tell you there what . . .

Mrs. Boyle. You won't have many pains in your legs when you hear what Mr. Bentham has to tell you.

Bentham. Juno ! What an interesting name ! It reminds one of Homer's glorious story of ancient gods and heroes.

Boyle. Yis, doesn't it ? You see, Juno was born an' christened in June ; I met her in June ; we were

married in June, an' Johnny was born in June, so wan
day I says to her, " You should ha' been called Juno,"
an' the name stuck to her ever since.

Mrs. Boyle. Here, we can talk o' them things agen ; let
Mr. Bentham say what he has to say now.

Bentham. Well, Mr. Boyle, I suppose you'll remember a
Mr. Ellison of Santry — he's a relative of yours, I think.

Boyle [*viciously*]. Is it that prognosticator an' procrastinator ! Of course I remember him.

Bentham. Well, he's dead, Mr. Boyle . . .

Boyle. Sorra many'll go into mournin' for him.

Mrs. Boyle. Wait till you hear what Mr. Bentham has to
say, an' then, maybe, you'll change your opinion.

Bentham. A week before he died he sent for me to write
his will for him. He told me that there were two only
that he wished to leave his property to : his second
cousin, Michael Finnegan of Santry, and John Boyle, his
first cousin, of Dublin.

Boyle [*excitedly*]. Me, is it me, me ?

Bentham. You, Mr. Boyle ; I'll read a copy of the will
that I have here with me, which has been duly filed in
the Court of Probate.

[*He takes a paper from his pocket and reads :*

6th February 1922

This is the last Will and Testament of William Ellison,
of Santry, in the County of Dublin. I hereby order and
wish my property to be sold and divided as follows :—
    £20 to the St. Vincent de Paul Society.
    £60 for Masses for the repose of my soul (5s. for each
Mass).

The rest of my property to be divided between my first and second cousins.

I hereby appoint Timothy Buckly, of Santry, and Hugh Brierly, of Coolock, to be my Executors.

(*Signed*) WILLIAM ELLISON.
HUGH BRIERLY.
TIMOTHY BUCKLY.
CHARLES BENTHAM, N.T.

Boyle [*eagerly*]. An' how much'll be comin' out of it, Mr. Bentham ?

Bentham. The Executors told me that half of the property would be anything between £1500 and £2000.

Mary. A fortune, father, a fortune !

Johnny. We'll be able to get out o' this place now, an' go somewhere we're not known.

Mrs. Boyle. You won't have to trouble about a job for awhile, Jack.

Boyle [*fervently*]. I'll never doubt the goodness o' God agen.

Bentham. I congratulate you, Mr. Boyle.

[*They shake hands.*

Boyle. An' now, Mr. Bentham, you'll have to have a wet.

Bentham. A wet ?

Boyle. A wet — a jar — a boul !

Mrs. Boyle. Jack, you're speakin' to Mr. Bentham, an' not to Joxer.

Boyle [*solemnly*]. Juno . . . Mary . . . Johnny . . . we'll have to go into mournin' at wanst. . . . I never expected that poor Bill ud die so sudden. . . . Well,

we all have to die some day . . . you, Juno, to-day
. . . an' me, maybe, to-morrow. . . . It's sad, but
it can't be helped. . . . Requiescat in pace . . . or,
usin' our oul' tongue like St. Patrick or St. Bridget,
Guh sayeree jeea ayera !

Mary. Oh, father, that's not Rest in Peace ; that's God
save Ireland.

Boyle. U-u-ugh, it's all the same — isn't it a prayer ?
. . . Juno, I'm done with Joxer ; he's nothin' but a
prognosticator an' a . . .

*Joxer [climbing angrily through the window and bounding into
the room].* You're done with Joxer, are you ? Maybe
you thought I'd stop on the roof all the night for you !
Joxer out on the roof with the win' blowin' through
him was nothin' to you an' your friend with the collar
an' tie !

Mrs. Boyle. What in the name o' God brought you out
on the roof ; what were you doin' there ?

Joxer [ironically]. I was dhreamin' I was standin' on the
bridge of a ship, an' she sailin' the Antartic Ocean,
an' it blowed, an' blowed, an' I lookin' up at the sky
an' sayin', what is the stars, what is the stars ?

Mrs. Boyle [opening the door and standing at it]. Here, get ou'
o' this, Joxer Daly ; I was always thinkin' you had a
slate off.

Joxer [moving to the door]. I have to laugh every time I look
at the deep-sea sailor ; an' a row on a river ud make
him sea-sick !

Boyle. Get ou' o' this before I take the law into me own
hands !

Joxer [*going out*]. Say aw rewaeawr, but not good-bye. Lookin' for work, an' prayin' to God he won't get it ! [*He goes.*

Mrs. Boyle. I'm tired tellin' you what Joxer was ; maybe now you see yourself the kind he is.

Boyle. He'll never blow the froth off a pint o' mine agen, that's a sure thing.. Johnny . . . Mary . . . you're to keep yourselves to yourselves for the future. Juno, I'm done with Joxer. . . . I'm a new man from this out. . . .

[*Clasping Juno's hand, and singing emotionally :*

O, me darlin' Juno, I will be thrue to thee ;
Me own, me darlin' Juno, you're all the world to me.

CURTAIN

Act II

The same, but the furniture is more plentiful, and of a vulgar nature. A glaringly upholstered armchair and lounge ; cheap pictures and photos everywhere. Every available spot is ornamented with huge vases filled with artificial flowers. Crossed festoons of coloured paper chains stretch from end to end of ceiling. On the table is an old attaché case. It is about six in the evening, and two days after the First Act. Boyle, in his shirt-sleeves, is voluptuously stretched on the sofa ; he is smoking a clay pipe. He is half asleep. A lamp is lighting on the table. After a few moments' pause the voice of Joxer is heard singing softly outside at the door — "Me pipe I'll smoke, as I dhrive me moke — are you there, Mor . . . ee . . . ar . . . i . . . teee ! "

Boyle [*leaping up, takes a pen in his hand and busies himself with papers*]. Come along, Joxer, me son, come along.

Joxer [*putting his head in*]. Are you be yourself ?

Boyle. Come on, come on ; that doesn't matther ; I'm masther now, an' I'm goin' to remain masther.

> [*Joxer comes in.*

Joxer. How d'ye feel now, as a man o' money ?

Boyle [*solemnly*]. It's a responsibility, Joxer, a great responsibility.

Joxer. I suppose 'tis now, though you wouldn't think it.

Boyle. Joxer, han' me over that attackey case on the table there. [*Joxer hands the case.*] Ever since the Will was

36

passed I've run hundhreds o' dockyments through me hans — I tell you, you have to keep your wits about you.   [*He busies himself with papers.*

Joxer. Well, I won't disturb you ; I'll dhrop in when . . .

Boyle [*hastily*]. It's all right, Joxer, this is the last one to be signed to-day. [*He signs a paper, puts it into the case, which he shuts with a snap, and sits back pompously in the chair.*] Now, Joxer, you want to see me ; I'm at your service — what can I do for you, me man ?

Joxer. I've just dhropped in with the £3 : 5s. that Mrs. Madigan riz on the blankets an' table for you, an' she says you're to be in no hurry payin' it back.

Boyle. She won't be long without it ; I expect the first cheque for a couple o' hundhred any day. There's the five bob for yourself — go on, take it, man ; it'll not be the last you'll get from the Captain. Now an' agen we have our differ, but we're there together all the time.

Joxer. Me for you, an' you for me, like the two Musketeers.

Boyle. Father Farrell stopped me to-day an' tole me how glad he was I fell in for the money.

Joxer. He'll be stoppin' you ofen enough now ; I suppose it was " Mr." Boyle with him ?

Boyle. He shuk me be the han' . . .

Joxer [*ironically*]. I met with Napper Tandy, an' he shuk me be the han' !

Boyle. You're seldom asthray, Joxer, but you're wrong shipped this time. What you're sayin' of Father

Farrell is very near to blasfeemey. I don't like any
one to talk disrespectful of Father Farrell.

Joxer. You're takin' me up wrong, Captain ; I wouldn't
let a word be said agen Father Farrell — the heart o' the
rowl, that's what he is ; I always said he was a darlin'
man, a daarlin' man.

Boyle. Comin' up the stairs who did I meet but that
bummer, Nugent. "I seen you talkin' to Father
Farrell," says he, with a grin on him. "He'll be
folleyin' you," says he, "like a Guardian Angel from
this out" — all the time the oul' grin on him, Joxer.

Joxer. I never seen him yet but he had that oul' grin on
him !

Boyle. "Mr. Nugent," says I, "Father Farrell is a man
o' the people, an', as far as I know the History o' me
country, the priests was always in the van of the fight
for Irelan's freedom."

Joxer [*fervently*] :

> Who was it led the van, Soggart Aroon ?
> Since the fight first began, Soggart Aroon ?

Boyle. "Who are you tellin' ?" says he. "Didn't they
let down the Fenians, an' didn't they do in Parnell ?
An' now . . ." "You ought to be ashamed o' yourself," says I, interruptin' him, "not to know the
History o' your country." An' I left him gawkin'
where he was.

Joxer. Where ignorance 's bliss 'tis folly to be wise ; I
wondher did he ever read the Story o' Irelan'.

Boyle. Be J. L. Sullivan ? Don't you know he didn't.

Joxer. Ah, it's a darlin' buk, a daarlin' buk !

Boyle. You'd betther be goin', now, Joxer; his Majesty, Bentham, 'll be here any minute, now.

Joxer. Be the way things is lookin', it'll be a match between him an' Mary. She's thrun over Jerry altogether. Well, I hope it will, for he's a darlin' man.

Boyle. I'm glad you think so — I don't. [*Irritably*] What's darlin' about him ?

Joxer [*nonplussed*]. I only seen him twiced ; if you want to know me, come an' live with me.

Boyle. He's too dignified for me— to hear him talk you'd think he knew as much as a Boney's Oraculum. He's given up his job as teacher, an' is goin' to become a solicitor in Dublin — he's been studyin' law. I suppose he thinks I'll set him up, but he's wrong shipped. An' th' other fella — Jerry's as bad. The two o' them ud give you a pain in your face, listenin' to them ; Jerry believin' in nothin', an' Bentham believin' in everythin'. One that says all is God an' no man ; an' th' other that says all is man an' no God !

Joxer. Well, I'll be off now.

Boyle. Don't forget to dhrop down afther awhile ; we'll have a quiet jar, an' a song or two.

Joxer. Never fear.

Boyle. An' tell Mrs. Madigan that I hope we'll have the pleasure of her organization at our little enthertainment.

Joxer. Righto ; we'll come down together. [*He goes out.* [*Johnny comes from room on left, and sits down moodily at the fire. Boyle looks at him for a few moments, and shakes his head. He fills his pipe.*

Voice of Juno at the door. Open the door, Jack ; this thing has me nearly kilt with the weight.

> [*Boyle opens the door. Juno enters carrying the box of a gramophone, followed by Mary carrying the horn and some parcels. Juno leaves the box on the table and flops into a chair.*

Juno. Carryin' that from Henry Street was no joke.

Boyle. U-u-ugh, that's a grand-lookin' insthrument — how much was it ?

Juno. Pound down, an' five to be paid at two shillins a week.

Boyle. That's reasonable enough.

Juno. I'm afraid we're runnin' into too much debt ; first the furniture, an' now this.

Boyle. The whole lot won't be much out of £2000.

Mary. I don't know what you wanted a gramophone for — I know Charlie hates them ; he says they're destructive of real music.

Boyle. Desthructive of music — that fella ud give you a pain in your face. All a gramophone wants is to be properly played ; its thrue wondher is only felt when everythin's quiet — what a gramophone wants is dead silence !

Mary. But, father, Jerry says the same ; afther all, you can only appreciate music when your ear is properly trained.

Boyle. That's another fella ud give you a pain in your face. Properly thrained ! I suppose you couldn't appreciate football unless your fut was properly thrained.

Mrs. Boyle [*to Mary*]. Go on in ower that an' dress, or Charlie 'll be in on you, an' tea nor nothing 'll be ready.   [*Mary goes into room left.*

Mrs. Boyle [*arranging table for tea*]. You didn't look at our new gramophone, Johnny ?

Johnny. 'Tisn't gramophones I'm thinking of.

Mrs. Boyle. An' what is it you're thinkin' of, allanna ?

Johnny. Nothin', nothin', nothin'.

Mrs. Boyle. Sure, you must be thinkin' of somethin' ; it's yourself that has yourself the way y'are ; sleepin' wan night in me sisther's, an' the nex' in your father's brother's — you'll get no rest goin' on that way.

Johnny. I can rest nowhere, nowhere, nowhere.

Mrs. Boyle. Sure, you're not thryin' to rest anywhere.

Johnny. Let me alone, let me alone, let me alone, for God's sake.   [*A knock at street door.*

Mrs. Boyle [*in a flutter*]. Here he is ; here's Mr. Bentham !

Boyle. Well, there's room for him ; it's a pity there's not a brass band to play him in.

Mrs. Boyle. We'll han' the tea round, an' not be clusthered round the table, as if we never seen nothin'.
      [*Steps are heard approaching, and Juno, opening the door, allows Bentham to enter.*

Juno. Give your hat an' stick to Jack, there . . . sit down, Mr. Bentham . . . no, not there . . . in th' easy chair be the fire . . . there, that's betther. Mary'll be out to you in a minute.

Boyle [*solemnly*]. I seen be the paper this mornin' that Consols was down half per cent. That's serious, min' you, an' shows the whole counthry's in a state o' chassis.

Mrs. Boyle. What's Consols, Jack ?

Boyle. Consols ? Oh, Consols is — oh, there's no use tellin' women what Consols is — th' wouldn't undherstand.

Bentham. It's just as you were saying, Mr. Boyle . . .
                               [*Mary enters, charmingly dressed.*

Bentham. Oh, good evening, Mary ; how pretty you're looking !

Mary [*archly*]. Am I ?

Boyle. We were just talkin' when you kem in, Mary ; I was tellin' Mr. Bentham that the whole counthry's in a state o' chassis.

Mary [*to Bentham*]. Would you prefer the green or the blue ribbon round me hair, Charlie ?

Mrs. Boyle. Mary, your father's speakin'.

Boyle [*rapidly*]. I was jus' tellin' Mr. Bentham that the whole counthry's in a state o' chassis.

Mary. I'm sure you're frettin', da, whether it is or no.

Mrs. Boyle. With all our churches an' religions, the worl's not a bit the betther.

Boyle [*with a commanding gesture*]. Tay !
                          [*Mary and Mrs. Boyle dispense the tea.*

Mrs. Boyle. An' Irelan's takin' a leaf out o' the worl's buk ; when we got the makin' of our own laws I thought we'd never stop to look behind us, but instead of that we never stopped to look before us ! If the people ud folley up their religion betther there'd be a betther chance for us — what do you think, Mr. Bentham ?

Bentham. I'm afraid I can't venture to express an opinion on that point, Mrs. Boyle ; dogma has no attraction for me.

Mrs. Boyle. I forgot you didn't hold with us : what's this you said you were ?

Bentham. A Theosophist, Mrs. Boyle.

Mrs. Boyle. An' what in the name o' God's a Theo-sophist ?

Boyle. A Theosophist, Juno, 's a — tell her, Mr. Bentham, tell her.

Bentham. It's hard to explain in a few words : Theo-sophy's founded on The Vedas, the religious books of the East. Its central theme is the existence of an all-pervading Spirit — the Life-Breath. Nothing really exists but this one Universal Life-Breath. And what-ever even seems to exist separately from this Life-Breath, doesn't really exist at all. It is all vital force in man, in all animals, and in all vegetation. This Life-Breath is called the Prawna.

Mrs. Boyle. The Prawna ! What a comical name !

Boyle. Prawna ; yis, the Prawna. [*Blowing gently through his lips*] That's the Prawna !

Mrs. Boyle. Whist, whist, Jack.

Bentham. The happiness of man depends upon his sympathy with this Spirit. Men who have reached a high state of excellence are called Yogi. Some men become Yogi in a short time, it may take others millions of years.

Boyle. Yogi ! 1 seen hundhreds of them in the streets o' San Francisco.

Bentham. It is said by these Yogi that if we practise certain mental exercises that we would have powers denied to others — for instance, the faculty of seeing things that happen miles and miles away.

Mrs. Boyle. I wouldn't care to meddle with that sort o' belief ; it's a very curious religion, altogether.

Boyle. What's curious about it ? Isn't all religions curious ? — if they weren't, you wouldn't get any one to believe them. But religions is passin' away — they've had their day like everything else. Take the real Dublin people, f'rinstance : they know more about Charlie Chaplin an' Tommy Mix than they do about SS. Peter an' Paul !

Mrs. Boyle. You don't believe in ghosts, Mr. Bentham ?

Mary. Don't you know he doesn't, mother ?

Bentham. I don't know that, Mary. Scientists are beginning to think that what we call ghosts are sometimes seen by persons of a certain nature. They say that sensational actions, such as the killing of a person, demand great energy, and that that energy lingers in the place where the action occurred. People may live in the place and see nothing, when someone may come along whose personality has some peculiar connection with the energy of the place, and, in a flash, the person sees the whole affair.

Johnny [*rising swiftly, pale and affected*]. What sort o' talk is this to be goin' on with ? Is there nothin' betther to be talkin' about but the killin' o' people ? My God, isn't it bad enough for these things to happen without talkin' about them !

> [*He hurriedly goes into the room on left.*

Bentham. Oh, I'm very sorry, Mrs. Boyle ; I never thought . . .

Mrs. Boyle [*apologetically*]. Never mind, Mr. Bentham, he's very touchy.

> [*A frightened scream is heard from Johnny inside.*

Mrs. Boyle. Mother of God, what's that ?

> [*He rushes out again, his face pale, his lips twitching, his limbs trembling.*

Johnny. Shut the door, shut the door, quick, for God's sake ! Great God, have mercy on me ! Blessed Mother o' God, shelter me, shelther your son !

Mrs. Boyle [*catching him in her arms*]. What's wrong with you ? What ails you ? Sit down, sit down, here, on the bed . . . there now . . . there now.

Mary. Johnny, Johnny, what ails you ?

Johnny. I seen him, I seen him . . . kneelin' in front o' the statue . . . merciful Jesus, have pity on me !

Mrs. Boyle [*to Boyle*]. Get him a glass o' whisky . . . quick, man, an' don't stand gawkin'.

> [*Boyle gets the whisky.*

Johnny. Sit here, sit here, mother . . . between me an' the door.

Mrs. Boyle. I'll sit beside you as long as you like, only tell me what was it came across you at all ?

Johnny [*after taking some drink*]. I seen him. . . . I seen Robbie Tancred kneelin' down before the statue . . . an' the red light shinin' on him . . . an' when I went in . . . he turned an' looked at me . . . an' I seen the wouns bleedin' in his breast. . . . Oh, why did he look at me like that ? . . . it wasn't my fault that he was done in. . . . Mother o' God, keep him away from me !

Mrs. Boyle. There, there, child, you've imagined it all. There was nothin' there at all — it was the red light you seen, an' the talk we had put all the rest into your head. Here, dhrink more o' this — it'll do you good. . . . An', now, stretch yourself down on the bed for a little. [*To Boyle*] Go in, Jack, an' show him it was only in his own head it was.

Boyle [*making no move*]. E-e-e-e-eh ; it's all nonsense ; it was only a shadda he saw.

Mary. Mother o' God, he made me heart lep !

Bentham. It was simply due to an over-wrought imagination — we all get that way at times.

Mrs. Boyle. There, dear, lie down in the bed, an' I'll put the quilt across you . . . e-e-e-eh, that's it . . . you'll be as right as the mail in a few minutes.

Johnny. Mother; go into the room an' see if the light's lightin' before the statue.

Mrs. Boyle [*to Boyle*]. Jack, run in an' see if the light's lightin' before the statue.

Boyle [*to Mary*]. Mary, slip in an' see if the light's lightin' before the statue.   [*Mary hesitates to go in.*

Bentham. It's all right ; Mary, I'll go.

[*He goes into the room ; remains for a few moments, and returns.*

Bentham. Everything's just as it was — the light burning bravely before the statue.

Boyle. Of course ; I knew it was all nonsense.

[*A knock at the door.*

Boyle [*going to open the door*]. E-e-e-e-eh.

[*He opens it, and Joxer, followed by Mrs. Madigan, enters. Mrs. Madigan is a strong, dapper little woman of about forty-five ; her face is almost always a widespread smile of complacency. She is a woman who, in manner at least, can mourn with them that mourn, and rejoice with them that do rejoice. When she is feeling comfortable, she is inclined to be reminiscent ; when others say anything, or following a statement made by herself, she has a habit of putting her head a little to one side, and nodding it rapidly several times in succession, like a bird pecking at a hard berry. Indeed, she has a good deal of the bird in her, but the bird instinct is by no means a melodious one. She is ignorant, vulgar and forward, but her heart is generous withal. For instance, she would help a neighbour's sick child ; she would probably kill the child, but her intention would be to cure it ; she would be more at home helping a drayman to lift a fallen horse. She is dressed in a rather soiled grey dress and a vivid purple blouse ; in her hair is a huge comb, ornamented with huge coloured beads. She enters with a gliding step, beaming smile and nodding head. Boyle receives them effusively.*

Boyle. Come on in, Mrs. Madigan ; come on in ; I was

afraid you weren't comin'. . . . [*Slyly*] There's some people able to dhress, ay, Joxer ?

Joxer. Fair as the blossoms that bloom in the May, an' sweet as the scent of the new-mown hay. . . . Ah, well she may wear them.

Mrs. Madigan [*looking at Mary*]. I know some as are as sweet as the blossoms that bloom in the May — oh, no names, no pack dhrill !

Boyle. An' now I'll inthroduce the pair o' yous to Mary's intended : Mr. Bentham, this is Mrs. Madigan, an oul' back-parlour neighbour, that, if she could nelp it at all, ud never see a body shuk !

Bentham [*rising, and tentatively shaking the hand of Mrs. Madigan*]. I'm sure, it's a great pleasure to know you, Mrs. Madigan.

Mrs. Madigan. An' I'm goin' to tell you, Mr. Bentham, you're goin' to get as nice a bit o' skirt in Mary, there, as ever you seen in your puff. Not like some of the dhressed-up dolls that's knockin' about lookin' for men when it's a skelpin' they want. I remember, as well as I remember yestherday, the day she was born — of a Tuesday, the 25th o' June, in the year 1901, at thirty-three minutes past wan in the day be Foley's clock, the pub at the corner o' the street. A cowld day it was too, for the season o' the year, an' I remember sayin' to Joxer, there, who I met comin' up th' stairs, that the new arrival in Boyle's ud grow up a hardy chiselur if it lived, an' that she'd be somethin' one o' these days that nobody suspected, an' so signs on it, here she is to-day, goin' to be married to a young man lookin' as if he'd be fit to commensurate in any position in life it ud please God to call him !

Boyle [*effusively*]. Sit down, Mrs. Madigan, sit down, me oul' sport. [*To Bentham*] This is Joxer Daly, Past Chief Ranger of the Dear Little Shamrock Branch of the Irish National Foresters, an oul' front-top neighbour, that never despaired, even in the darkest days of Ireland's sorra.

Joxer. Nil desperandum, Captain, nil desperandum.

Boyle. Sit down, Joxer, sit down. The two of us was ofen in a tight corner.

Mrs. Boyle. Ay, in Foley's snug !

Joxer. An' we kem out of it flyin', we kem out of it flyin', Captain.

Boyle. An' now for a dhrink — I know yous won't refuse an oul' friend.

Mrs. Madigan [*to Juno*]. Is Johnny not well, Mrs. . . .

Mrs. Boyle [*warningly*]. S-s-s-sh.

Mrs. Madigan. Oh, the poor darlin'.

Boyle. Well, Mrs. Madigan, is it tea or what ?

Mrs. Madigan. Well, speakin' for meself, I jus' had me tea a minute ago, an' I'm afraid to dhrink any more — I'm never the same when I dhrink too much tay. Thanks, all the same, Mr. Boyle.

Boyle. Well, what about a bottle o' stout or a dhrop o' whisky ?

Mrs. Madigan. A bottle o' stout ud be a little too heavy for me stummock afther me tay. . . . A-a-ah, I'll thry the ball o' malt.   [*Boyle prepares the whisky.*

Mrs. Madigan. There's nothin' like a ball o' malt occasional like — too much of it isn't good. [*To Boyle, who
is adding water*] Ah, God, Johnny, don't put too much
wather on it ! [*She drinks.*] I suppose yous'll be lavin'
this place.

Boyle. I'm looking for a place near the sea ; I'd like the
place that you might say was me cradle, to be me
grave as well. The sea is always callin' me.

Joxer. She is callin', callin', callin', in the win' an' on the
sea.

Boyle. Another dhrop o' whisky, Mrs. Madigan ?

Mrs. Madigan. Well, now, it ut be hard to refuse seein'
the suspicious times that's in it.

Boyle [*with a commanding gesture*]. Song ! . . . Juno . . .
Mary . . . " Home to Our Mountains " !

Mrs. Madigan [*enthusiastically*]. Hear, hear !

Joxer. Oh, tha's a darlin' song, a daarlin' song !

Mary [*bashfully*]. Ah no, da ; I'm not in a singin' humour.

Mrs. Madigan. Gawn with you, child, an' you only goin'
to be marrid ; I remember as well as I remember
yestherday, — it was on a lovely August evenin', exactly,
according' to date, fifteen years ago, come the Tuesday
folleyin' the nex' that's comin' on, when me own man
— *the Lord be good to him* — an' me was sitting' shy together
in a doty little nook on a counthry road, adjacent to
The Stiles. " That'll scratch your lovely, little white
neck," says he, ketchin' hould of a danglin' bramble
branch, holdin' clusters of the loveliest flowers you
ever seen, an' breakin' it off, so that his arm fell,

accidental like, roun' me waist, an' as I felt it tightenin',
an' tightenin', an' tightenin ', I thought me buzzom
was every minute goin' to burst out into a roystherin'
song about

> The little green leaves that were shakin' on the threes,
> The gallivantin' buttherflies, an' buzzin' o' the bees ! "

Boyle. Ordher for the song !

Juno. Come on, Mary — we'll do our best.
    [*Juno and Mary stand up, and choosing a suitable position,
    sing simply " Home to Our Mountains ".*
    [*They bow to company, and return to their places.*

Boyle [*emotionally, at the end of song*]. Lull . . . me . . .
to . . . rest !

Joxer [*clapping his hands*]. Bravo, bravo ! Darlin' girulls,
darlin' girulls !

Mrs. Madigan. Juno, I never seen you in betther form.

Bentham. Very nicely rendered indeed.

Mrs. Madigan. A noble call, a noble call !

Mrs. Boyle. What about yourself, Mrs. Madigan ?
    [*After some coaxing, Mrs. Madigan rises, and in a
    quavering voice sings the following verse :*

> If I were a blackbird I'd whistle and sing ;
> I'd follow the ship that my thrue love was in ;
> An' on the top riggin', I'd there build me nest,
> An' at night I would sleep on me Willie's white breast !

    [*Becoming husky, amid applause, she sits down.*

Mrs. Madigan. Ah, me voice is too husky now, Juno ;
though I remember the time when Maisie Madigan

could sing like a nightingale at matin' time. I remember as well as I remember yesterday, at a party given to celebrate the comin' of the first chiselur to Annie an' Benny Jimeson — who was the barber, yous may remember, in Henrietta Street, that, afther Easter Week, hung out a green, white an' orange pole, an', then, when the Tans started their Jazz dancin', whipped it in agen, an' stuck out a red, white an' blue wan instead, givin' as an excuse that a barber's pole was strictly non-political — singin' " An' You'll Remember Me ", with the top notes quiverin' in a dead hush of pethrified attention, folleyed be a clappin' o' hans that shuk the tumblers on the table, an' capped by Jimeson, the barber, sayin' that it was the best rendherin' of " You'll Remember Me " he ever heard in his natural !

Boyle [*peremptorily*]. Ordher for Joxer's song !

Joxer. Ah no, I couldn't ; don't ass me, Captain.

Boyle. Joxer's song, Joxer's song— give us wan of your shut-eyed wans.

[*Joxer settles himself in his chair ; takes a drink ; clears his throat ; solemnly closes his eyes, and begins to sing in a very querulous voice :*

She is far from the lan' where her young hero sleeps,
An' lovers around her are sighing   [*He hesitates.*
An' lovers around her are sighin' . . . sighin' . . . sighin' . . .
[*A pause.*

Boyle [*imitating Joxer*] :

And lovers around her are sighing !

What's the use of you thryin' to sing the song if you don't know it ?

Mary. Thry another one, Mr. Daly — maybe you'd be more fortunate.

Mrs. Madigan. Gawn, Joxer ; thry another wan.

Joxer [*starting again*] :

I have heard the mavis singin' his love song to the morn ;
I have seen the dew-dhrop clingin' to the rose jus' newly
born ; but . . . but . . . [*frantically*] To the rose jus'
newly born . . . newly born . . . born.

Johnny. Mother, put on the gramophone, for God's sake, an' stop Joxer's bawlin'.

Boyle [*commandingly*]. Gramophone ! . . . I hate tb see fellas thryin' to do what they're not able to do.
[*Boyle arranges the gramophone, and is about to start it, when voices are heard of persons descending the stairs.*

Mrs. Boyle [*warningly*]. Whisht, Jack, don't put it on, don't put it on yet ; this must be poor Mrs. Tancred comin' down to go to the hospital — I forgot all about them bringin' the body to the church to-night. Open the door, Mary, an' give them a bit o' light.
[*Mary opens the door, and Mrs. Tancred — a very old woman, obviously shaken by the death of her son — appears, accompanied by several neighbours. The first few phrases are spoken before they appear.*

First Neighbour. It's a sad journey we're goin' on, but God's good, an' the Republicans won't be always down.

Mrs. Tancred. Ah, what good is that to me now ? Whether they're up or down — it won't bring me darlin' boy from the grave.

Mrs. Boyle. Come in an' have a hot cup o' tay, Mrs. Tancred, before you go.

Mrs. Tancred. Ah, I can take nothin' now, Mrs. Boyle —
I won't be long afther him.

First Neighbour. Still an' all, he died a noble death, an'
we'll bury him like a king.

Mrs. Tancred. An' I'll go on livin' like a pauper. Ah,
what's the pains I suffered bringin' him into the
world to carry him to his cradle, to the pains I'm
sufferin' now, carryin' him out o' the world to bring
him to his grave !

Mary. It would be better for you not to go at all, Mrs.
Tancred, but to stay at home beside the fire with some
o' the neighbours.

Mrs. Tancred. I seen the first of him, an' I'll see the last
of him.

Mrs. Boyle. You'd want a shawl, Mrs. Tancred ; it's a
cowld night, an' the win's blowin' sharp.

Mrs. Madigan [*rushing out*]. I've a shawl above.

Mrs. Tancred. Me home is gone now ; he was me only
child, an' to think that he was lyin' for a whole night
stretched out on the side of a lonely counthry lane,
with his head, his darlin' head, that I often kissed an'
fondled, half hidden in the wather of a runnin' brook.
An' I'm told he was the leadher of the ambush where
me nex' door neighbour, Mrs. Mannin', lost her Free
State soldier son. An' now here's the two of us oul'
women, standin' one on each side of a scales o' sorra,
balanced be the bodies of our two dead darlin' sons.
[*Mrs. Madigan returns, and wraps a shawl around her.*]
God bless you, Mrs. Madigan. . . . [*She moves slowly
towards the door*] Mother o' God, Mother o' God, have

pity on the pair of us ! . . . O Blessed Virgin, where
were you when me darlin' son was riddled with bullets,
when me darlin' son was riddled with bullets ! . . .
Sacred Heart of the Crucified Jesus, take away our
hearts o' stone . . . an' give us hearts o' flesh ! . . .
Take away this murdherin' hate . . . an' give us
Thine own eternal love !   [*They pass out of the room.*

Mrs. Boyle [*explanatorily to Bentham*]. That was Mrs.
Tancred of the two-pair back ; her son was found,
e'er yestherday, lyin' out beyant Finglas riddled with
bullets. A Die-hard he was, be all accounts. He was
a nice quiet boy, but lattherly he went to hell, with
his Republic first, an' Republic last an' Republic over
all. He ofen took tea with us here, in the oul' days,
an' Johnny, there, an' him used to be always together.

Johnny. Am I always to be havin' to tell you that he was
no friend o' mine ? I never cared for him, an' he could
never stick me. It's not because he was Commandant
of the Battalion that I was Quarther-Masther of, that
we were friends.

Mrs. Boyle. He's gone now — the Lord be good to him !
God help his poor oul' creature of a mother, for no
matther whose friend or enemy he was, he was her
poor son.

Bentham. The whole thing is terrible, Mrs. Boyle ; but
the only way to deal with a mad dog is to destroy him.

Mrs. Boyle. An' to think of me forgettin' about him
bein' brought to the church to-night, an' we singin' an'
all, but it was well we hadn't the gramophone goin',
anyhow.

Boyle. Even if we had aself. We've nothin' to do with

these things, one way or t'other. That's the Government's business, an' let them do what we're payin' them for doin'.

Mrs. Boyle. I'd like to know how a body's not to mind these things ; look at the way they're afther leavin' the people in this very house. Hasn't the whole house, nearly, been massacreed ? There's young Dougherty's husband with his leg off ; Mrs. Travers that had her son blew up be a mine in Inchegeela, in Co. Cork ; Mrs. Mannin' that lost wan of her sons in ambush a few weeks ago, an' now, poor Mrs. Tancred's only child gone west with his body made a collandher of. Sure, if it's not our business, I don't know whose business it is.

Boyle. Here, there, that's enough about them things ; they don't affect us, an' we needn't give a damn. If they want a wake, well, let them have a wake. When I was a sailor, I was always resigned to meet with a wathery grave ; an' if they want to be soldiers, well, there's no use o' them squealin' when they meet a soldier's fate.

Joxer. Let me like a soldier fall — me breast expandin' to th' ball !

Mrs. Boyle. In wan way, she deserves all she got ; for lately, she let th' Die-hards make an open house of th' place ; an' for th' last couple of months, either when th' sun was risin' or when th' sun was settin', you had C.I.D. men burstin' into your room, assin' you where were you born, where were you christened, where were you married, an' where would you be buried !

Johnny. For God's sake, let us have no more o' this talk.

Mrs. Madigan. What about Mr. Boyle's song before we start th' gramophone ?

Mary [*getting her hat, and putting it on*]. Mother, Charlie and I are goin' out for a little sthroll.

Mrs. Boyle. All right, darlin'.

Bentham [*going out with Mary*]. We won't be long away, Mrs. Boyle.

Mrs. Madigan. Gwan, Captain, gwan.

Boyle. E-e-e-e-eh, I'd want to have a few more jars in me, before I'd be in fettle for singin'.

Joxer. Give us that poem you writ t'other day. [*To the rest*] Aw, it's a darlin' poem, a daarlin' poem.

Mrs. Boyle. God bless us, is he startin' to write poetry !

Boyle [*rising to his feet*]. E-e-e-e-eh.
[*He recites in an emotional, consequential manner the following verses :*

Shawn an' I were friends, sir, to me he was all in all.
His work was very heavy and his wages were very small.
None betther on th' beach as Docker, I'll go bail,
'Tis now I'm feelin' lonely, for to-day he lies in jail.
He was not what some call pious — seldom at church or prayer ;
For the greatest scoundrels I know, sir, goes every Sunday there.
Fond of his pint — well, rather, but hated the Boss by creed
But never refused a copper to comfort a pal in need.

E-c-e e-eh.   [*He sits down.*

Mrs. Madigan. Grand, grand ; you should folly that up, you should folly that up.

Joxer. It's a daarlin' poem !

Boyle [*delightedly*]. E-e-e-e-eh.

Johnny. Are yous goin' to put on th' gramophone to night, or are yous not ?

Mrs. Boyle. Gwan, Jack, put on a record.

Mrs. Madigan. Gwan, Captain, gwan.

Boyle. Well, yous'll want to keep a dead silence.
   [*He sets a record, starts the machine, and it begins to play
   " If you're Irish, come into the Parlour ". As the tune
   is in full blare, the door is suddenly opened by a brisk,
   little bald-headed man, dressed circumspectly in a black
   suit ; he glares fiercely at all in the room ; he is " Needle
   Nugent ", a tailor. He carries his hat in his hand.*

Nugent [*loudly, above the noise of the gramophone*]. Are yous
   goin' to have that thing bawlin' an' the funeral of Mrs.
   Tancred's son passin' the house ? Have none of yous
   any respect for the Irish people's National regard for
   the dead ?   [*Boyle stops the gramophone.*

Mrs. Boyle. Maybe, Needle Nugent, it's nearly time we
   had a little less respect for the dead, an' a little more
   regard for the livin'.

Mrs. Madigan. We don't want you, Mr. Nugent, to
   teach us what we learned at our mother's knee. You
   don't look yourself as if you were dyin' of grief ; if
   y'ass Maisie Madigan anything, I'd call you a real
   thrue Die-hard an' live-soft Republican, attendin' Republican funerals in the day, an' stoppin' up half the
   night makin' suits for the Civic Guards !
   [*Persons are heard running down to the street, some saying,
   " Here it is, here it is." Nugent withdraws, and the*

rest, except Johnny, go to the window looking into the street, and look out. Sounds of a crowd coming nearer are heard ; portion are singing :

> To Jesus' Heart all burning
> With fervent love for men,
> My heart with fondest yearning
> Shall raise its joyful strain.
> While ages course along,
> Blest be with loudest song
> The Sacred Heart of Jesus
> By every heart and tongue.

Mrs. Boyle. Here's the hearse, here's the hearse !

Boyle. There's t'oul' mother walkin' behin' the coffin.

Mrs. Madigan. You can hardly see the coffin with the wreaths.

Joxer. Oh, it's a darlin' funeral, a daarlin' funeral !

Mrs. Madigan. W'd have a betther view from the street.

Boyle. Yes — this place ud give you a crick in your neck.

> [*They leave the room, and go down. Johnny sits moodily by the fire.*
> [*A young man enters ; he looks at Johnny for a moment.*

The Young Man. Quarther-Masther Boyle.

Johnny [*with a start*]. The Mobilizer !

The Young Man. You're not at the funeral ?

Johnny. I'm not well.

The Young Man. I'm glad I've found you ; you were stoppin' at your aunt's ; I called there but you'd gone. I've to give you an ordher to attend a Battalion Staff meetin' the night afther to-morrow.

Johnny. Where ?

The Young Man. I don't know ; you're to meet me at the Pillar at eight o'clock ; then we're to go to a place I'll be told of to-night ; there we'll meet a mothor that'll bring us to the meeting. They think you might be able to know somethin' about them that gave the bend where Commandant Tancred was shelterin'.

Johnny. I'm not goin', then. I know nothing about Tancred.

The Young Man [*at the door*]. You'd betther come for your own sake — remember your oath.

Johnny [*passionately*]. I won't go ! Haven't I done enough for Ireland ! I've lost me arm, an' me hip's desthroyed so that I'll never be able to walk right agen ! Good God, haven't I done enough for Ireland ?

The Young Man. Boyle, no man can do enough for Ireland !
[*He goes.*

[*Faintly in the distance the crowd is heard saying :*

Hail, Mary, full of grace, the Lord is with Thee ;
Blessed art Thou amongst women, and blessed, etc.

CURTAIN

ACT III

The same as Act II. It is about half-past six on a November evening ; a bright fire burns in the grate ; Mary, dressed to go out, is sitting on a chair by the fire, leaning forward, her hands under her chin, her elbows on her knees. A look of dejection, mingled with uncertain anxiety, is on her face. A lamp, turned low, is lighting on the table. The votive light under the picture of the Virgin gleams more redly than ever. Mrs. Boyle is putting on her hat and coat. It is two months later.

Mrs. Boyle. An' has Bentham never even written to you since — not one line for the past month ?

Mary [*tonelessly*]. Not even a line, mother.

Mrs. Boyle. That's very curious. . . . What came between the two of yous at all ? To leave you so sudden, an' yous so great together. . . . To go away t' England, an' not to even leave you his address. . . . The way he was always bringin' you to dances, I thought he was mad afther you. Are you sure you said nothin' to him ?

Mary. No, mother — at least nothing that could possibly explain his givin' me up.

Mrs. Boyle. You know you're a bit hasty at times, Mary, an' say things you shouldn't say.

Mary. I never said to him what I shouldn't say, I'm sure of that.

61

Mrs. Boyle. How are you sure of it?

Mary. Because I love him with all my heart and soul, mother. Why, I don't know; I often thought to myself that he wasn't the man poor Jerry was, but I couldn't help loving him, all the same.

Mrs. Boyle. But you shouldn't be frettin' the way you are; when a woman loses a man, she never knows what she's afther losin', to be sure, but, then, she never knows what she's afther gainin', either. You're not the one girl of a month ago — you look like one pinin' away. It's long ago I had a right to bring you to the doctor, instead of waitin' till to-night.

Mary. There's no necessity, really, mother, to go to the doctor; nothing serious is wrong with me — I'm run down and disappointed, that's all.

Mrs. Boyle. I'll not wait another minute; I don't like the look of you at all. . . . I'm afraid we made a mistake in throwin' over poor Jerry. . . . He'd have been betther for you than that Bentham.

Mary. Mother, the best man for a woman is the one for whom she has the most love, and Charlie had it all.

Mrs. Boyle. Well, there's one thing to be said for him — he couldn't have been thinkin' of the money, or he wouldn't ha' left you . . . it must ha' been somethin' else.

Mary [*wearily*]. I don't know . . . I don't know, mother . . . only I think . . .

Mrs. Boyle. What d'ye think?

Mary. I imagine . . . he thought . . . we weren't . . . good enough for him.

Mrs. Boyle. An' what was he himself, only a school
teacher ? Though I don't blame him for fightin' shy of
people like that Joxer fella an' that oul' Madigan
wan — nice sort o' people for your father to inthroduce
to a man like Mr. Bentham. You might have told
me all about this before now, Mary ; I don't know why
you like to hide everything from your mother ; you
knew Bentham, an' I'd ha' known nothin' about it if
it hadn't bin for the Will ; an' it was on'y to-day, afther
long coaxin', that you let out that he's left you.

Mary. It would have been useless to tell you — you
wouldn't understand.

Mrs. Boyle [*hurt*]. Maybe not. . . . Maybe I wouldn't
understand. . . . Well, we'll be off now.
     [*She goes over to door left, and speaks to Boyle inside.*

Mrs. Boyle. We're goin' now to the doctor's. Are you
goin' to get up this evenin' ?

Boyle [*from inside*]. The pains in me legs is terrible !
It's me should be poppin' off to the doctor instead o'
Mary, the way I feel.

Mrs. Boyle. Sorra mend you ! A nice way you were in
last night — carried in in a frog's march, dead to the
world. If that's the way you'll go on when you get
the money it'll be the grave for you, an asylum for me
and the Poorhouse for Johnny.

Boyle. I thought you were goin' ?

Mrs. Boyle. That's what has you as you are — you can't
bear to be spoken to. Knowin' the way we are, up
to our ears in debt, it's a wondher you wouldn't ha'
got up to go to th' solicitor's an' see if we could ha'
gotten a little o' the money even.

Boyle [*shouting*]. I can't be goin' up there night, noon an' mornin', can I? He can't give the money till he gets it, can he? I can't get blood out of a turnip, can I?

Mrs. Boyle. It's nearly two months since we heard of the Will, an' the money seems as far off as ever. . . . I suppose you know we owe twenty pouns to oul' Murphy?

Boyle. I've a faint recollection of you tellin' me that before.

Mrs. Boyle. Well, you'll go over to the shop yourself for the things in future — I'll face him no more.

Boyle. I thought you said you were goin'?

Mrs. Boyle. I'm goin' now; come on, Mary.

Boyle. Ey, Juno, ey!

Mrs. Boyle. Well, what d'ye want now?

Boyle. Is there e'er a bottle o' stout left?

Mrs. Boyle. There's two o' them here still.

Boyle. Show us in one o' them an' leave t'other there till I get up. An' throw us in the paper that's on the table, an' the bottle o' Sloan's Liniment that's in th' drawer.

Mrs. Boyle [*getting the liniment and the stout*]. What paper is it you want — the *Messenger*?

Boyle. Messenger! The *News o' the World*!
   [*Mrs. Boyle brings in the things asked for, and comes out again.*

Mrs. Boyle [*at door*]. Mind the candle, now, an' don't burn the house over our heads. I left t'other bottle o' stout on the table.

[*She puts bottle of stout on table. She goes out with Mary. A cork is heard popping inside.*

[*A pause ; then outside the door is heard the voice of Joxer lilting softly :* " *Me pipe I'll smoke, as I dhrive me moke . . . are you . . . there . . . Mor . . . ee . . . ar . . . i . . . teee !* " *A gentle knock is heard, and after a pause the door opens, and Joxer, followed by Nugent, enters.*

Joxer. Be God, they must be all out ; I was thinkin' there was somethin' up when he didn't answer the signal. We seen Juno an' Mary goin', but I didn't see him, an' it's very seldom he escapes me.

Nugent. He's not goin' to escape me — he's not goin' to be let go to the fair altogether.

Joxer. Sure, the house couldn't hould them lately ; an' he goin' about like a mastherpiece of the Free State counthry ; forgettin' their friends ; forgettin' God — wouldn't even lift his hat passin' a chapel ! Sure they were bound to get a dhrop ! An' you really think there's no money comin' to him afther all ?

Nugent. Not as much as a red rex, man ; I've been a bit anxious this long time over me money, an' I went up to the solicitor's to find out all I could — ah, man, they were goin' to throw me down the stairs. They toul' me that the oul' cock himself had the stairs worn away comin' up afther it, an' they black in the face tellin' him he'd get nothin'. Some way or another that the Will is writ he won't be entitled to get as much as a make !

Joxer. Ah, I thought there was somethin' curious about the whole thing ; I've bin havin' sthrange dhreams for the last couple o' weeks. An' I notice that that Bentham fella doesn't be comin' here now — there must be somethin' on the mat there too. Anyhow, who, in the name o' God, ud leave anythin' to that oul' bummer ? Sure it ud be unnatural. An' the way Juno an' him's been throwin' their weight about for the last few months ! Ah, him that goes a borrowin' goes a sorrowin' !

Nugent. Well, he's not goin' to throw his weight about in the suit I made for him much longer. I'm tellin' you seven pouns aren't to be found growin' on the bushes these days.

Joxer. An' there isn't hardly a neighbour in the whole street that hasn't lent him money on the strength of what he was goin' to get, but they're after backing the wrong horse. Wasn't it a mercy o' God that I'd nothin' to give him ! The softy I am, you know, I'd ha' lent him me last juice ! I must have had some-body's good prayers. Ah, afther all, an honest man's the noblest work o' God !   [*Boyle coughs inside.*

Joxer. Whisht, damn it, he must be inside in bed.

Nugent. Inside o' bed or outside of it, he's goin' to pay me for that suit, or give it back — he'll not climb up my back as easily as he thinks.

Joxer. Gwan in at wanst, man, an' get it off him, an' don't be a fool.

Nugent [*going to door left, opening it and looking in*]. Ah, don't disturb yourself, Mr. Boyle ; I hope you're not sick ?

Boyle. Th' oul' legs, Mr. Nugent, the oul' legs.

Nugent. I just called over to see if you could let me have anything off the suit ?

Boyle. E-e-e-eh, how much is this it is ?

Nugent. It's the same as it was at the start — seven pouns.

Boyle. I'm glad you kem, M. Nugent ; I want a good heavy top-coat — Irish frieze, if you have it. How much would a top-coat like that be, now ?

Nugent. About six pouns.

Boyle. Six pouns — six an' seven, six an' seven is thirteen — that'll be thirteen pouns I'll owe you.
     [*Joxer slips the bottle of stout that is on the table into his pocket. Nugent rushes into the room, and returns with suit on his arm ; he pauses at the door.*

Nugent. You'll owe me no thirteen pouns. Maybe you think you're betther able to owe it than pay it !

Boyle [*frantically*]. Here, come back to hell ower that — where're you goin' with them clothes o' mine ?

Nugent. Where am I goin' with them clothes o' yours ? Well, I like your damn cheek !

Boyle. Here, what am I goin' to dhress meself in when I'm goin' out ?

Nugent. What do I care what you dhress yourself in ! You can put yourself in a bolsther cover, if you like.
     [*He goes towards the other door, followed by Joxer.*

Joxer. What'll he dhress himself in ! Gentleman Jack an' his frieze coat !   [*They go out.*

Boyle [*inside*]. Ey, Nugent ; ey, Mr. Nugent, Mr. Nugent !

> [*After a pause Boyle enters hastily, buttoning the braces of his moleskin trousers ; his coat and vest are on his arm ; he throws these on a chair and hurries to the door on right.*

Boyle. Ey, Mr. Nugent, Mr. Nugent !

Joxer [*meeting him at the door*]. What's up, what's wrong, Captain ?

Boyle. Nugent's been here an' took away me suit — the only things I had to go out in !

Joxer. Tuk your suit — for God's sake ! An' what were you doin' while he was takin' them ?

Boyle. I was in bed, when he stole in like a thief in the night, an' before I knew even what he was thinkin' of, he whipped them from the chair an' was off like a redshank !

Joxer. An' what, in the name o' God, did he do that for ?

Boyle. What did he do it for ? How the hell do I know what he done it for ? — jealousy an' spite, I suppose.

Joxer. Did he not say what he done it for ?

Boyle. Amn't I afther tellin' you that he had them whipped up an' was gone before I could open me mouth ?

Joxer. That was a very sudden thing to do ; there mus' be somethin' behin' it. Did he hear anythin', I wondher ?

Boyle. Did he hear anythin' ? — you talk very queer, Joxer — what could he hear ?

Joxer. About you not gettin' the money, in some way or t'other ?

Boyle. An' what ud prevent me from gettin' th' money ?

Joxer. That's jus' what I was thinkin' — what ud prevent you from gettin' the money — nothin', as far as I can see.

Boyle [*looking round for bottle of stout, with an exclamation*]. Aw, holy God !

Joxer. What's up, Jack ?

Boyle. He must have afther lifted the bottle o' stout that Juno left on the table !

Joxer [*horrified*]. Ah no, ah no ; he wouldn't be afther doin' that now.

Boyle. An' who done it then ? Juno left a bottle o' stout here, an' it's gone — it didn't walk, did it ?

Joxer. Oh, that's shockin' ; ah, man's inhumanity to man makes countless thousands mourn !

Mrs. Madigan [*appearing at the door*]. I hope I'm not disturbin' you in any discussion on your forthcomin' legacy — if I may use the word — an' that you'll let me have a barny for a minute or two with you, Mr. Boyle.

Boyle [*uneasily*]. To be sure, Mrs. Madigan — an oul' friend's always welcome.

Joxer. Come in the evenin', come in th' mornin' ; come when you're assed, or come without warnin', Mrs. Madigan.

Boyle. Sit down, Mrs. Madigan.

Mrs. Madigan [*ominously*]. Th' few words I have to say can be said standin'. Puttin' aside all formularies, I suppose you remember me lendin' you some time ago three pouns that I raised on blankets an' furniture in me uncle's ?

Boyle. I remember it well.   I have it recorded in me book — three pouns five shillins from Maisie Madigan, raised on articles pawned ; an', item : fourpence, given to make up the price of a pint, on th' principle that no bird ever flew on wan wing ; all to be repaid at par, when the ship comes home.

Mrs. Madigan. Well, ever since I shoved in the blankets I've been perishing with th' cowld, an' I've decided, if I'll be too hot in th' nex' world aself, I'm not goin' to be too cowld in this wan ; an' consequently, I want me three pouns, if you please.

Boyle. This is a very sudden demand, Mrs. Madigan, an' can't be met ; but I'm willin' to give you a receipt in full, in full.

Mrs. Madigan. Come on, out with th' money, an' don't be jack-actin'.

Boyle. You can't get blood out of a turnip, can you ?

Mrs. Madigan [*rushing over and shaking him*]. Gimme me money, y'oul' reprobate, or I'll shake the worth of it out of you !

Boyle. Ey, houl' on, there ; houl' on, there !   You'll wait for your money now, me lassie !

Mrs. Madigan [*looking around the room and seeing the gramophone*]. I'll wait for it, will I ?   Well, I'll not wait long ;

if I can't get th' cash, I'll get th' worth of it.

[*She catches up the gramophone.*

Boyle. Ey, ey, there, wher'r you goin' with that ?

Mrs. Madigan. I'm goin' to th' pawn to get me three quid five shillins ; I'll brin' you th' ticket, an' then you can do what you like, me bucko.

Boyle. You can't touch that, you can't touch that ! It's not my property, an' it's not ped for yet !

Mrs. Madigan. So much th' betther. It'll be an ayse to me conscience, for I'm takin' what doesn't belong to you. You're not goin' to be swankin' it like a paycock with Maisie Madigan's money — I'll pull some o' th' gorgeous feathers out o' your tail !

[*She goes off with the gramophone.*

Boyle. What's th' world comin' to at all ? I ass you, Joxer Daly, is there any morality left anywhere ?

Joxer. I wouldn't ha' believed it, only I seen it with me own two eyes. I didn't think Maisie Madigan was that sort of woman ; she has either a sup taken, or she's heard somethin'.

Boyle. Heard somethin' — about what, if it's not any harm to ass you ?

Joxer. She must ha' heard some rumour or other that you weren't goin' to get th' money'

Boyle. Who says I'm not goin' to get th' money ?

Joxer. Sure, I don't know — I was only sayin'.

Boyle. Only sayin' what ?

Joxer. Nothin'.

Boyle. You were goin' to say somethin' — don't be a twisther.

Joxer [*angrily*]. Who's a twisther?

Boyle. Why don't you speak your mind, then?

Joxer. You never twisted yourself — no, you wouldn't know how!

Boyle. Did you ever know me to twist; did you ever know me to twist?

Joxer [*fiercely*]. Did you ever do anythin' else! Sure, you can't believe a word that comes out o' your mouth.

Boyle. Here, get out, ower o' this; I always knew you were a prognosticator an' a procrastinator!

Joxer [*going out as Johnny comes in*]. The anchor's weighed, farewell, ree . . . mem . . . ber . . . me. Jacky Boyle, Esquire, infernal rogue an' damned liar.

Johnny. Joxer an' you at it agen? — when are you goin' to have a little respect for yourself, an' not be always makin' a show of us all?

Boyle. Are you goin' to lecture me now?

Johnny. Is mother back from the doctor yet, with Mary?
 [*Mrs. Boyle enters; it is apparent from the serious look on her face that something has happened. She takes off her hat and coat without a word and puts them by. She then sits down near the fire, and there is a few moments' pause.*

Boyle. Well, what did the doctor say about Mary?

Mrs. Boyle [*in an earnest manner and with suppressed agitation*].

Sit down here, Jack; I've something to say to you
. . . about Mary.

Boyle [*awed by her manner*]. About . . . Mary?

Mrs. Boyle. Close that door there and sit down here.

Boyle [*closing the door*]. More throuble in our native land,
is it? [*He sits down.*] Well, what is it?

Mrs. Boyle. It's about Mary.

Boyle. Well, what about Mary — there's nothin' wrong
with her, is there?

Mrs. Boyle. I'm sorry to say there's a gradle wrong with
her.

Boyle. A gradle wrong with her! [*Peevishly*] First
Johnny an' now Mary; is the whole house goin' to
become an hospital! It's not consumption, is it?

Mrs. Boyle. No . . . it's not consumption . . . it's
worse.

Johnny. Worse! Well, we'll have to get her into some
place ower this, there's no one here to mind her.

Mrs. Boyle. We'll all have to mind her now. You might
as well know now, Johnny, as another time. [*To
Boyle*] D'ye know what the doctor said to me about her,
Jack?

Boyle. How ud I know — I wasn't there, was I?

Mrs. Boyle. He told me to get her married at wanst.

Boyle. Married at wanst! An' why did he say the like
o' that?

Mrs. Boyle. Because Mary's goin' to have a baby in a short
time.

Boyle. Goin' to have a baby ! — my God, what'll Bentham say when he hears that ?

Mrs. Boyle. Are you blind, man, that you can't see that it was Bentham that has done this wrong to her ?

Boyle [*passionately*]. Then he'll marry her, he'll have to marry her !

Mrs. Boyle. You know he's gone to England, an' God knows where he is now.

Boyle. I'll folly him, I'll folly him, an' bring him back, an' make him do her justice. The scoundrel, I might ha' known what he was, with his yogees an' his prawna !

Mrs. Boyle. We'll have to keep it quiet till we see what we can do.

Boyle. Oh, isn't this a nice thing to come on top o' me, an' the state I'm in ! A pretty show I'll be to Joxer an' to that oul' wan, Madigan ! Amn't I afther goin' through enough without havin' to go through this !

Mrs. Boyle. What you an' I'll have to go through'll be nothin' to what poor Mary'll have to go through ; for you an' me is middlin' old, an' most of our years is spent ; but Mary'll have maybe forty years to face an' handle, an' every wan of them'll be tainted with a bitther memory.

Boyle. Where is she ? Where is she till I tell her off ? I'm tellin' you when I'm done with her she'll be a sorry girl !

Mrs. Boyle. I left her in me sister's till I came to speak to you. You'll say nothin' to her, Jack ; ever since she left school she's earned her livin', an' your fatherly care never throubled the poor girl.

Boyle. Gwan, take her part agen her father ! But I'll let you see whether I'll say nothin' to her or no ! Her an' her readin' ! That's more o' th' blasted nonsense that has the house fallin' down on top of us ! What did th' likes of her, born in a tenement house, want with readin' ? Her readin's afther bringin' her to a nice pass — oh, it's madnin', madnin', madnin' !

Mrs. Boyle. When she comes back say nothin' to her, Jack, or she'll leave this place.

Boyle. Leave this place ! Ay, she'll leave this place, an' quick too !

Mrs. Boyle. If Mary goes, I'll go with her.

Boyle. Well, go with her ! Well, go, th' pair o' yous ! I lived before I seen yous, an' I can live when yous are gone. Isn't this a nice thing to come rollin' in on top o' me afther all your prayin' to St. Anthony an' The Little Flower ! An' she's a Child o' Mary, too — I wonder what'll the nuns think of her now ? An' it'll be bellows'd all over th' disthrict before you could say Jack Robinson ; an' whenever I'm seen they'll whisper, " That's th' father of Mary Boyle that had th' kid be th' swank she used to go with ; d'ye know, d'ye know ? " To be sure they'll know — more about it than I will meself !

Johnny. She should be dhriven out o' th' house she's brought disgrace on !

Mrs. Boyle. Hush, you, Johnny. We needn't let it be bellows'd all over the place ; all we've got to do is to leave this place quietly an' go somewhere where we're not known, an' nobody'll be th' wiser.

Boyle. You're talkin' like a two-year-oul', woman. Where'll we get a place ou' o' this? — places aren't that easily got.

Mrs. Boyle. But, Jack, when we get the money . . .

Boyle. Money — what money?

Mrs. Boyle. Why, oul' Ellison's money, of course.

Boyle. There's no money comin' from oul' Ellison, or any one else. Since you've heard of wan throuble, you might as well hear of another. There's no money comin' to us at all — the Will's a wash-out!

Mrs. Boyle. What are you sayin', man — no money?

Johnny. How could it be a wash-out?

Boyle. The boyo that's afther doin' it to Mary done it to me as well. The thick made out the Will wrong; he said in th' Will, only first cousin an' second cousin, instead of mentionin' our names, an' now any one that thinks he's a first cousin or second cousin t'oul' Ellison can claim the money as well as me, an' they're springin' up in hundreds, an' comin' from America an' Australia, thinkin' to get their whack out of it, while all the time the lawyers is gobblin' it up, till there's not as much as ud buy a stockin' for your lovely daughter's baby!

Mrs. Boyle. I don't believe it, I don't believe it, I don't believe it!

Johnny. Why did you say nothin' about this before?

Mrs. Boyle. You're not serious, Jack; you're not serious!

Boyle. I'm tellin' you the scholar, Bentham, made a banjax o' th' Will; instead o' sayin', " th' rest o' me property to be divided between me first cousin, Jack Boyle, an' me second cousin, Mick Finnegan, o' Santhry ", he writ down only, " me first an' second cousins ", an' the world an' his wife are afther th' property now.

Mrs. Boyle. Now I know why Bentham left poor Mary in th' lurch ; I can see it all now — oh, is there not even a middlin' honest man left in th' world ?

Johnny [*to Boyle*]. An' you let us run into debt, an' you borreyed money from everybody to fill yourself with beer ! An' now you tell us the whole thing's a wash-out ! Oh, if it's thrue, I'm done with you, for you're worse than me sisther Mary !

Boyle. You hole your tongue, d'ye hear ? I'll not take any lip from you. Go an' get Bentham if you want satisfaction for all that's afther happenin' us.

Johnny. I won't hole me tongue, I won't hole me tongue ! I'll tell you what I think of you, father an' all as you are . . . you . . .

Mrs. Boyle. Johnny, Johnny, Johnny, for God's sake, be quiet !

Johnny. I'll not be quiet, I'll not be quiet ; he's a nice father, isn't he ? Is it any wondher Mary went asthray, when . . .

Mrs. Boyle. Johnny, Johnny, for my sake be quiet — for your mother's sake !

Boyle. I'm goin' out now to have a few dhrinks with th' last few makes I have, an' tell that lassie o' yours not to be here when I come back ; for if I lay me eyes on her, I'll lay me hans on her, an' if I lay me hans on her, I won't be accountable for me actions !

Johnny. Take care somebody doesn't lay his hands on you — y'oul' . . .

Mrs. Boyle. Johnny, Johnny !

Boyle [*at door, about to go out*]. Oh, a nice son, an' a nicer daughter, I have. [*Calling loudly upstairs*] Joxer, Joxer, are you there ?

Joxer [*from a distance*]. I'm here, More . . . ee . . . aar . . . i . . . tee !

Boyle. I'm goin' down to Foley's — are you comin' ?

Joxer. Come with you ? With that sweet call me heart is stirred ; I'm only waiting for the word, an' I'll be with you, like a bird !

> [*Boyle and Joxer pass the door going out.*

Johnny [*throwing himself on the bed*]. I've a nice sisther, an' a nice father, there's no bettin' on it. I wish to God a bullet or a bomb had whipped me ou' o' this long ago ! Not one o' yous, not one o' yous, have any thought for me !

Mrs. Boyle [*with passionate remonstrance*]. If you don't whisht, Johnny, you'll drive me mad. Who has kep' th' home together for the past few years — only me ? An' who'll have to bear th' biggest part o' this throuble but me ? — but whinin' an' whingin' isn't goin' to do any good.

Johnny. You're to blame yourself for a gradle of it — givin' him his own way in everything, an' never assin' to check him, no matther what he done. Why didn't you look afther th' money ? why . . .

> [*There is a knock at the door ; Mrs. Boyle opens it ; Johnny rises on his elbow to look and listen ; two men enter.*

First Man. We've been sent up be th' Manager of the Hibernian Furnishing Co., Mrs. Boyle, to take back the furniture that was got a while ago.

Mrs. Boyle. Yous'll touch nothin' here — how do I know who yous are ?

First Man [*showing a paper*]. There's the ordher, ma'am. [*Reading*] A chest o' drawers, a table, wan easy an' two ordinary chairs ; wan mirror ; wan chestherfield divan, an' a wardrobe an' two vases. [*To his comrade*] Come on, Bill, it's afther knockin'-off time already.

Johnny. For God's sake, mother, run down to Foley's an' bring father back, or we'll be left without a stick.

> [*The men carry out the table.*

Mrs. Boyle. What good would it be ? — you heard what he said before he went out.

Johnny. Can't you thry ? He ought to be here, an' the like of this goin' on.

> [*Mrs. Boyle puts a shawl around her, as Mary enters.*

Mary. What's up, mother ? I met men carryin' away the table, an' everybody's talking about us not gettin' the money after all.

Mrs. Boyle. Everythin's gone wrong, Mary, everythin'. We're not gettin' a penny out o' the Will, not a penny — I'll tell you all when I come back ; I'm goin' for your father.   [*She runs out.*

Johnny [*to Mary, who has sat down by the fire*]. It's a wondher you're not ashamed to show your face here, afther what has happened.

> [*Jerry enters slowly ; there is a look of earnest hope on his face. He looks at Mary for a few moments.*

Jerry [*softly*]. Mary !   [*Mary does not answer.*

Jerry. Mary, I want to speak to you for a few moments, may I ?

[*Mary remains silent ; Johnny goes slowly into room on left.*

Jerry. Your mother has told me everything, Mary, and I have come to you. . . . I have come to tell you, Mary, that my love for you is greater and deeper than ever. . . .

Mary [*with a sob*]. Oh, Jerry, Jerry, say no more ; all that is over now ; anything like that is impossible now !

Jerry. Impossible ? Why do you talk like that, Mary ?

Mary. After all that has happened.

Jerry. What does it matter what has happened ? We are young enough to be able to forget all those things. [*He catches her hand*] Mary, Mary, I am pleading for your love. With Labour, Mary, humanity is above everything ; we are the Leaders in the fight for a new life. I want to forget Bentham, I want to forget that you left me — even for a while.

Mary. Oh, Jerry, Jerry, you haven't the bitter word of scorn for me after all.

Jerry [*passionately*]. Scorn ! I love you, love you, Mary !

Mary [*rising, and looking him in the eyes*]. Even though . . .

Jerry. Even though you threw me over for another man ; even though you gave me many a bitter word !

Mary. Yes, yes, I know ; but you love me, even though . . . even though . . . I'm . . . goin' . . . goin'

. . . [*He looks at her questioningly, and fear gathers in his eyes.*] Ah, I was thinkin' so. . . . You don't know everything !

Jerry [*poignantly*]. Surely to God, Mary, you don't mean that . . . that . . . that . . .

Mary. Now you know all, Jerry ; now you know all !

Jerry. My God, Mary, have you fallen as low as that ?

Mary. Yes, Jerry, as you say, I have fallen as low as that.

Jerry. I didn't mean it that way, Mary . . . it came on me so sudden, that I didn't mind what I was sayin'. . . . I never expected this — your mother never told me. . . . I'm sorry . . . God knows, I'm sorry for you, Mary.

Mary. Let us say no more, Jerry ; I don't blame you for thinkin' it's terrible. . . . I suppose it is. . . . Everybody'll think the same . . . it's only as I expected — your humanity is just as narrow as the humanity of the others.

Jerry. I'm sorry, all the same. . . . I shouldn't have troubled you. . . . I wouldn't if I'd known. . . . If I can do anything for you . . . Mary . . . I will.
                    [*He turns to go, and halts at the door.*

Mary. Do you remember, Jerry, the verses you read when you gave the lecture in the Socialist Rooms some time ago, on Humanity's Strife with Nature ?

Jerry. The verses — no ; I don't remember them.

Mary. I do. They're runnin' in me head now —

An' we felt the power that fashion'd
All the lovely things we saw,
That created all the murmur
Of an everlasting law,
Was a hand of force an' beauty,
With an eagle's tearin' claw.

Then we saw our globe of beauty
Was an ugly thing as well,
A hymn divine whose chorus
Was an agonizin' yell ;
Like the story of a demon,
That an angel had to tell ;

Like a glowin' picture by a
Hand unsteady, brought to ruin ;
Like her craters, if their deadness
Could give life unto the moon ;
Like the agonizing horror
Of a violin out of tune.

[*There is a pause, and Devine goes slowly out.*

Johnny [*returning*]. Is he gone ?

Mary. Yes.   [*The two men re-enter.*

First Man. We can't wait any longer for t'oul' fella —
sorry, Miss, but we have to live as well as th' nex'
man.   [*They carry out some things.*

Johnny. Oh, isn't this terrible ! . . . I suppose you
told him everything . . . couldn't you have waited
for a few days ? . . . he'd have stopped th' takin' of
the things, if you'd kep' your mouth shut. Are you
burnin' to tell every one of the shame you've brought
on us ?

Mary [*snatching up her hat and coat*]. Oh, this is unbearable !
                              [*She rushes out.*

First Man [*re-entering*]. We'll take the chest o' drawers
next — it's the heaviest.

> [*The votive light flickers for a moment, and goes out.*

Johnny [*in a cry of fear*]. Mother o' God, the light's afther
goin' out !

First Man. You put the win' up me the way you bawled
that time.   The oil's all gone, that's all.

Johnny [*with an agonizing cry*]. Mother o' God, there's a
shot I'm afther gettin' !

First Man. What's wrong with you, man ?   Is it a fit
you're takin' ?

Johnny. I'm afther feelin' a pain in me breast, like the
tearin' by of a bullet !

First Man. He's goin' mad — it's a wondher they'd leave
a chap like that here by himself.

> [*Two Irregulars enter swiftly ;   they carry revolvers ;   one
> goes over to Johnny ;   the other covers the two furniture
> men.*

First Irregular [*to the men, quietly and incisively*]. Who are
you ? — what are yous doin' here ? — quick !

First Man. Removin' furniture that's not paid for.

Irregular. Get over to the other end of the room an'
turn your faces to the wall — quick !

> [*The two men turn their faces to the wall, with their hands
> up.*

Second Irregular [*to Johnny*]. Come on, Sean Boyle, you're
wanted ;   some of us have a word to say to you.

Johnny. I'm sick, I can't — what do you want with me ?

Second Irregular. Come on, come on ; we've a distance to go, an' haven't much time — come on.

Johnny. I'm an oul' comrade — yous wouldn't shoot an oul' comrade.

Second Irregular. Poor Tancred was an oul' comrade o' yours, but you didn't think o' that when you gave him away to the gang that sent him to his grave. But we've no time to waste ; come on — here, Dermot, ketch his arm. [*To Johnny*] Have you your beads ?

Johnny. Me beads ! Why do you ass me that, why do you ass me that ?

Second Irregular. Go on, go on, march !

Johnny. Are yous goin' to do in a comrade ? — look at me arm, I lost it for Ireland.

Second Irregular. Commandant Tancred lost his life for Ireland.

Johnny. Sacred Heart of Jesus, have mercy on me ! Mother o' God, pray for me — be with me now in the agonies o' death ! . . . Hail, Mary, full o' grace . . . the Lord is . . . with Thee.

[*They drag out Johnny Boyle, and the curtain falls. When it rises again the most of the furniture is gone. Mary and Mrs. Boyle, one on each side, are sitting in a darkened room, by the fire ; it is an hour later.*]

Mrs. Boyle. I'll not wait much longer . . . what did they bring him away in the mothor for ? Nugent says he thinks they had guns . . . is me throubles never goin' to be over ? . . . If anything ud happen to poor Johnny, I think I'd lose me mind. . . . I'll go to the

Police Station, surely they ought to be able to do somethin'.   [*Below is heard the sound of voices.*

Mrs. Boyle. Whisht, is that something? Maybe, it's your father, though when I left him in Foley's he was hardly able to lift his head. Whisht!
[*A knock at the door, and the voice of Mrs. Madigan, speaking very softly*]: Mrs. Boyle, Mrs. Boyle.
[*Mrs. Boyle opens the door.*

Mrs. Madigan. Oh, Mrs. Boyle, God an' His Blessed Mother be with you this night!

Mrs. Boyle [*calmly*]. What is it, Mrs. Madigan? It's Johnny — something about Johnny.

Mrs. Madigan. God send it's not, God send it's not Johnny!

Mrs. Boyle. Don't keep me waitin', Mrs. Madigan; I've gone through so much lately that I feel able for anything.

Mrs. Madigan. Two polismen below wantin' you.

Mrs. Boyle. Wantin' me; an' why do they want me?

Mrs. Madigan. Some poor fella's been found, an' they think it's, it's . . .

Mrs. Boyle. Johnny, Johnny!

Mary [*with her arms round her mother*]. Oh, mother, mother, me poor, darlin' mother.

Mrs. Boyle. Hush, hush, darlin'; you'll shortly have your own throuble to bear. [*To Mrs. Madigan*] An' why do the polis think it's Johnny, Mrs. Madigan?

Mrs. Madigan. Because one o' the doctors knew him when he was attendin' with his poor arm.

Mrs. Boyle. Oh, it's thrue, then ; it's Johnny, it's me son, me own son !

Mary. Oh, it's thrue, it's thrue what Jerry Devine says — there isn't a God, there isn't a God ; if there was He wouldn't let these things happen !

Mrs. Boyle. Mary, Mary, you musn't say them things. We'll want all the help we can get from God an' His Blessed Mother now ! These things have nothin' to do with the Will o' God. Ah, what can God do agen the stupidity o' men !

Mrs. Madigan. The polis want you to go with them to the hospital to see the poor body — they're waitin' below.

Mrs. Boyle. We'll go. Come, Mary, an' we'll never come back here agen. Let your father furrage for himself now ; I've done all I could an' it was all no use — he'll be hopeless till the end of his days. I've got a little room in me sisther's where we'll stop till your throuble is over, an' then we'll work together for the sake of the baby.

Mary. My poor little child that'll have no father !

Mrs. Boyle. It'll have what's far betther — it'll have two mothers.

A Rough Voice shouting from below. Are yous goin' to keep us waitin' for yous all night ?

Mrs. Madigan [*going to the door, and shouting down*]. Take your hour, there, take your hour ! If yous are in such a hurry, skip off, then, for nobody wants you here —

if they did yous wouldn't be found. For you're the
same as yous were undher the British Government —
never where yous are wanted ! As far as I can see, the
Polis as Polis, in this city, is Null an' Void !

Mrs. Boyle. We'll go, Mary, we'll go ; you to see your
poor dead brother, an' me to see me poor dead son !

Mary. I dhread it, mother, I dhread it !

Mrs. Boyle. I forgot, Mary, I forgot ; your poor oul'
selfish mother was only thinkin' of herself. No, no,
you mustn't come — it wouldn't be good for you. You
go on to me sisther's an' I'll face th' ordeal meself.
Maybe I didn't feel sorry enough for Mrs. Tancred
when her poor son was found as Johnny's been found
now — because he was a Die-hard ! Ah, why didn't I
remember that then he wasn't a Diehard or a Stater,
but only a poor dead son ! It's well I remember all
that she said — an' it's my turn to say it now : What
was the pain I suffered, Johnny, bringin' you into the
world to carry you to your cradle, to the pains I'll
suffer carryin' you out o' the world to bring you to
your grave ! Mother o' God, Mother o' God, have
pity on us all ! Blessed Virgin, where were you when
me darlin' son was riddled with bullets, when me
darlin' son was riddled with bullets ? Sacred Heart
o' Jesus, take away our hearts o' stone, and give us
hearts o' flesh ! Take away this murdherin' hate, an'
give us Thine own eternal love !

[*They all go slowly out.*

[*There is a pause; then a sound of shuffling steps on the
stairs outside. The door opens and Boyle and Joxer, both
of them very drunk, enter.*

Boyle. I'm able to go no farther. . . . Two polis, ey

. . . what were they doin' here, I wondher? . . . Up
to no good, anyhow . . . an' Juno an' that lovely
daughter o' mine with them. [*Taking a sixpence from
his pocket and looking at it*] Wan single, solitary tanner
left out of all I borreyed. . . . [*He lets it fall.*] The
last o' the Mohicans. . . . The blinds is down, Joxer,
the blinds is down !

Joxer [*walking unsteadily across the room, and anchoring at the
bed*]. Put all . . . your throubles . . . in your oul'
kit-bag . . . an' smile . . . smile . . . smile !

Boyle. The counthry'll have to steady itself . . . it's
goin' . . . to hell. . . . Where'r all . . . the chairs
. . . gone to . . . steady itself, Joxer. . . . Chairs'll
. . . have to . . . steady themselves. . . . No matther . . . what any one may . . . say. . . . Irelan'
sober . . . is Irelan' . . . free.

Joxer [*stretching himself on the bed*]. Chains . . . an' . . .
slaveree . . . that's a darlin' motto . . . a daaarlin'
. . . motto !

Boyle. If th' worst comes . . . to th' worse . . . I can
join a . . . flyin' . . . column. . . . I done . . . me
bit . . . in Easther Week . . . had no business . . .
to . . . be . . . there . . . but Captain Boyle's
Captain Boyle !

Joxer. Breathes there a man with soul . . . so . . .
de . . . ad . . . this . . . me . . . o . . . wn, me
nat . . . ive l . . . an' !

Boyle [*subsiding into a sitting posture on the floor*]. Commandant Kelly died . . . in them . . . arms . . .
Joxer. . . . Tell me Volunteer Butties . . . says he
. . . that . . . I died for . . . Irelan' !

Joxer. D'jever rade Willie . . . Reilly . . . an' his own
. . . Colleen . . . Bawn? It's a darlin' story, a daarlin'
story!

Boyle. I'm telling you . . . Joxer . . . th' whole worl's
. . . in a terr . . . ible state o' . . . chassis!

CURTAIN

THE SHADOW OF A GUNMAN

A Tragedy in Two Acts

CHARACTERS IN THE PLAY

DONAL DAVOREN
SEUMAS SHIELDS, *a pedlar*
TOMMY OWENS ⎫ *Residents in*
ADOLPHUS GRIGSON ⎬ *the Tenement*
MRS. GRIGSON
MINNIE POWELL ⎭
MR. MULLIGAN, *the landlord*
MR. MAGUIRE, *soldier of the I.R.A.*
MRS. HENDERSON ⎱ *Residents of an*
MR. GALLOGHER ⎰ *adjoining Tenement*
AN AUXILIARY

SCENE

A room in a tenement in Hilljoy Square, Dublin.
Some hours elapse between the two acts.   The period of
the Play is May 1920.

ACT I

A Return Room in a tenement house in Hilljoy Square. At the back two large windows looking out into the yard; they occupy practically the whole of the back wall space. Between the windows is a cupboard, on the top of which is a pile of books. The doors are open, and on these are hanging a number of collars and ties. Running parallel with the windows is a stretcher bed; another runs at right angles along the wall at right. At the head of this bed is a door leading to the rest of the house. The wall on the left runs diagonally, so that the fireplace — which is in the centre — is plainly visible. On the mantelshelf to the right is a statue of the Virgin, to the left a statue of the Sacred Heart, and in the centre a crucifix. Around the fireplace are a few common cooking utensils. In the centre of the room is a table, on which are a typewriter, a candle and candlestick, a bunch of wild flowers in a vase, writing materials and a number of books. There are two chairs, one near the fireplace and one at the table. The aspect of the place is one of absolute untidiness, engendered on the one hand by the congenital slovenliness of Seumas Shields, and on the other by the temperament of Donal Davoren, making it appear impossible to effect an improvement in such a place.

Davoren is sitting at the table typing. He is about thirty. There is in his face an expression that seems to indicate an eternal war between weakness and strength; there is in the lines of the brow and chin an indication of a desire for activity, while in his eyes there is visible an unquenchable tendency towards rest. His struggle through life has been a hard one, and his efforts have been handicapped by an inherited and self-developed devotion to " the might of design, the mystery of colour, and the belief in the redemption of all things by beauty everlasting". His life

*would drive him mad were it not for the fact that he never knew
any other. He bears upon his body the marks of the struggle for
existence and the efforts towards self-expression.*

*Seumas Shields, who is in the bed next the wall to the right,
is a heavily built man of thirty-five ; he is dark-haired and
sallow-complexioned. In him is frequently manifested the super-
stition, the fear and the malignity of primitive man.*

Davoren [*lilting an air as he composes*] :

> Or when sweet Summer's ardent arms outspread,
> Entwined with flowers,
> Enfold us, like two lovers newly wed,
> Thro' ravish'd hours —
> Then sorrow, woe and pain lose all their powers,
> For each is dead, and life is only ours.

> [*A woman's figure appears at the window and taps loudly
> on one of the panes ; at the same moment there is loud
> knocking at the door.*

Voice of Woman at Window. Are you awake, Mr. Shields
— Mr. Shields, are you awake ? Are you goin' to get
up to-day at all, at all ?

Voice at the Door. Mr. Shields, is there any use of callin'
you at all ? This is a nice nine o'clock : do you know
what time it is, Mr. Shields ?

Seumas [*loudly*]. Yus !

Voice at the Door. Why don't you get up, then, an' not
have the house turned into a bedlam tryin' to waken
you ?

Seumas [*shouting*]. All right, all right, all right ! The
way these oul' ones bawl at a body ! Upon my soul !
I'm beginnin' to believe that the Irish People are still

in the stone age.   If they could they'd throw a bomb
at you.

Davoren. A land mine exploding under the bed is the
only thing that would lift you out of it.

Seumas [stretching himself]. Oh-h-h.   I was fast in the
arms of Morpheus — he was one of the infernal deities,
son of Somnus, wasn't he ?

Davoren. I think so.

Seumas. The poppy was his emblem, wasn't it ?

Davoren. Ah, I don't know.

Seumas. It's a bit cold this morning, I think, isn't it ?

Davoren. It's quite plain I'm not going to get much
quietness in this house.

Seumas [after a pause]. I wonder what time is it ?

Davoren. The Angelus went some time ago.

Seumas [sitting up in bed suddenly]. The Angelus !   It
couldn't be that late, could it ?   I asked them to call
me at nine so that I could get Mass before I went on
my rounds.   Why didn't you give us a rap ?

Davoren. Give you a rap !   Why, man, they've been
thundering at the door and hammering at the window
for the past two hours, till the house shook to its very
foundations, but you took less notice of the infernal din
than I would take of the strumming of a grasshopper.

Seumas. There's no fear of you thinking of any one else
when you're at your poetry.   The land of Saints
and Scholars 'ill shortly be a land of bloody poets.
[Anxiously] I suppose Maguire has come and gone ?

Davoren. Maguire ? No, he hasn't been here — why, did you expect him ?

Seumas [*in a burst of indignation*]. He said he'd be here at nine. " Before the last chime has struck," says he, " I'll be coming in on the door," and it must be — what time is it now ?

Davoren. Oh, it must be half-past twelve.

Seumas. Did anybody ever see the like of the Irish People ? Is there any use of tryin' to do anything in this country ? Have everything packed and ready, have everything packed and ready, have . . .

Davoren. And have you everything packed and ready ?

Seumas. What's the use of having anything packed and ready when he didn't come ? [*He rises and dresses himself.*] No wonder this unfortunate country is as it is, for you can't depend upon the word of a single individual in it. I suppose he was too damn lazy to get up ; he wanted the streets to be well aired first. —Oh, Kathleen ni Houlihan, your way's a thorny way.

Davoren. Ah me ! alas, pain, pain ever, for ever !

Seumas. That's from Shelley's *Prometheus Unbound.* I could never agree with Shelley, not that there's anything to be said against him as a poet — as a poet — but . . .

Davoren. He flung a few stones through stained-glass windows.

Seumas. He wasn't the first nor he won't be the last to do that, but the stained-glass windows — more than ever of them — are here still, and Shelley is doing a jazz dance down below.

[*He gives a snarling laugh of pleasure.*

Davoren [*shocked*]. And you actually rejoice and are exceedingly glad that, as you believe, Shelley, the sensitive, high-minded,' noble-hearted Shelley, is suffering the tortures of the damned.

Seumas. I rejoice in the vindication of the Church and Truth.

Davoren. Bah. You know as little about truth as anybody else, and you care as little about the Church as the least of those that profess her faith ; your religion is simply the state of being afraid that God will torture your soul in the next world as you are afraid the Black and Tans will torture your body in this.

Seumas. Go on, me boy ; I'll have a right laugh at you when both of us are dead.

Davoren. You're welcome to laugh as much as you like at me when both of us are dead.

Seumas [*as he is about to put on his collar and tie*]. I don't think I need to wash meself this morning ; do I look all right ?

Davoren. Oh, you're all right ; it's too late now to start washing yourself. Didn't you wash yourself yesterday morning ?

Seumas. I gave meself a great rub yesterday. [*He proceeds to pack various articles into an attaché case — spoons, forks, laces, thread, etc.*] I think I'll bring out a few of the braces too ; damn it, they're well worth sixpence each ; there's great stuff in them — did you see them ?

Davoren. Yes, you showed them to me before.

Seumas. They're great value; I only hope I'll be able to get enough o' them. I'm wearing a pair of them meself — they'd do Cuchullian, they're so strong. [*Counting the spoons*] There's a dozen in each of these parcels — three, six, nine — damn it, there's only eleven in this one. I better try another. Three, six, nine — my God, there's only eleven in this one too, and one of them bent! Now I suppose I'll have to go through the whole bloody lot of them, for I'd never be easy in me mind thinkin' there'd be more than a dozen in some o' them. And still we're looking for freedom — ye gods, it's a glorious country! [*He lets one fall, which he stoops to pick up.*] Oh, my God, there's the braces after breakin'.

Davoren. That doesn't look as if they were strong enough for Cuchullian.

Seumas. I put a heavy strain on them too sudden. There's that fellow Maguire never turned up, either; he's almost too lazy to wash himself. [*As he is struggling with the braces the door is hastily shoved in and Maguire rushes in with a handbag.*] This is a nice nine o'clock. What's the use of you coming at this hour o' the day? Do you think we're going to work be moonlight? If you weren't goin' to come at nine couldn't you say you weren't. . . .

Maguire. Keep your hair on; I just blew in to tell you that I couldn't go to-day at all. I have to go to Knocksedan.

Seumas. Knocksedan! An' what, in the name o' God, is bringin' you to Knocksedan?

Maguire. Business, business.   I'm going out to catch butterflies.

Seumas. If you want to make a cod of anybody, make a cod of somebody else, an' don't be tryin' to make a cod o' me.   Here I've had everything packed an' ready for hours ; you were to be here at nine, an' you wait till just one o'clock to come rushin' in like a mad bull to say you've got to go to Knocksedan !   Can't you leave Knocksedan till to-morrow ?

Maguire. Can't be did, can't be did, Seumas ; if I waited till to-morrow all the butterflies might be dead. I'll leave this bag here till this evening.   [*He puts the bag in a corner of the room.*]   Good-bye . . . ee.
                    [*He is gone before Seumas is aware of it.*

Seumas [*with a gesture of despair*]. Oh, this is a hopeless country !   There's a fellow that thinks that the four cardinal virtues are not to be found outside an Irish Republic.   I don't want to boast about myself — I don't want to boast about myself, and I suppose I could call meself as good a Gael as some of those that are knocking about now — knocking about now — as good a Gael as some that are knocking about now, — but I remember the time when I taught Irish six nights a week, when in the Irish Republican Brotherhood I paid me rifle levy like a man, an' when the Church refused to have anything to do with James Stephens, I tarred a prayer for the repose of his soul on the steps of the Pro-Cathedral.   Now, after all me work for Dark Rosaleen, the only answer you can get from a roarin' Republican to a simple question is " good-bye . . . ee ".   What, in the name o' God, can be bringin' him to Knocksedan ?

Davoren. Hadn't you better run out and ask him?

Seumas. That's right, that's right — make a joke about it! That's the Irish People all over — they treat a joke as a serious thing and a serious thing as a joke. Upon me soul, I'm beginning to believe that the Irish People aren't, never were, an' never will be fit for self-government. They've made Balor of the Evil Eye King of Ireland, an' so signs on it there's neither conscience nor honesty from one end of the country to the other. Well, I hope he'll have a happy day in Knocksedan. [*A knock at the door.*] Who's that?
                                                    [*Another knock.*

Seumas [*irritably*]. Who's that; who's there?

Davoren [*more irritably*]. Halt and give the countersign — damn it, man, can't you go and see?
     [*Seumas goes over and opens the door. A man of about sixty is revealed, dressed in a faded blue serge suit; a half tall hat is on his head. It is evident that he has no love for Seumas, who denies him the deference he believes is due from a tenant to a landlord. He carries some papers in his hand.*

The Landlord [*ironically*]. Good-day, Mr. Shields; it's meself that hopes you're feelin' well — you're lookin' well, anyhow — though you can't always go be looks nowadays.

Seumas. It doesn't matter whether I'm lookin' well or feelin' well; I'm all right, thanks be to God.

The Landlord. I'm very glad to hear it.

Seumas. It doesn't matter whether you're glad to hear it or not, Mr. Mulligan.

The Landlord. You're not inclined to be very civil, Mr. Shields.

Seumas. Look here, Mr. Mulligan, if you come here to raise an argument, I've something to do — let me tell you that.

The Landlord. I don't come here to raise no argument ; a person ud have small gains argufyin' with you — let me tell you that.

Seumas. I've no time to be standin' here gostherin' with you — let me shut the door, Mr. Mulligan.

The Landlord. You'll not shut no door till you've heard what I've got to say.

Seumas. Well, say it then, an' go about your business.

The Landlord. You're very high an' mighty, but take care you're not goin' to get a drop. What a baby you are not to know what brings me here ! Maybe you thought I was goin' to ask you to come to tea.

Davoren. Ah me ! alas, pain, pain ever, for ever !

Seumas. Are you goin' to let me shut the door, Mr. Mulligan ?

The Landlord. I'm here for me rent ; you don't like the idea of bein' asked to pay your just an' lawful debts.

Seumas. You'll get your rent when you learn to keep your rent-book in a proper way.

The Landlord. I'm not goin' to take any lessons from you, anyhow.

Seumas. I want to have no more talk with you, Mr. Mulligan.

The Landlord. Talk or no talk, you owe me eleven weeks' rent, an' it's marked down again' you in black an' white.

Seumas. I don't care a damn if it was marked down in green, white, an' yellow.

The Landlord. You're a terribly independent fellow, an' it ud be fitter for you to be less funny an' stop tryin' to be billickin' honest an' respectable people.

Seumas. Just you be careful what you're sayin', Mr. Mulligan. There's law in the land still.

The Landlord. Be me sowl there is, an' you're goin' to get a little of it now. [*He offers the papers to Seumas*] Them's for you.

Seumas [*hesitating to take them*]. I want to have nothing to do with you, Mr. Mulligan.

The Landlord [*throwing the papers in the centre of the room*]. What am I better? It was the sorry day I ever let you come into this house. Maybe them notices to quit will stop your writin' letters to the papers about me an' me house.

Davoren. For goodness' sake, bring the man in, and don't be discussing the situation like a pair of primitive troglodytes.

Seumas [*taking no notice*]. Writing letters to the papers is my business, an' I'll write as often as I like, when I like, an' how I like.

The Landlord. You'll not write about this house at all events. You can blow about the state of the yard, but you took care to say nothin' about payin' rent :

oh no, that's not in your line. But since you're not satisfied with the house, you can pack up an' go to another.

Seumas. I'll go, Mr. Mulligan, when I think fit, an' no sooner.

The Landlord. Not content with keeping the rent, you're startin' to bring in lodgers — [*to Davoren*] not that I'm sayin' anythin' again' you, sir. Bringin' in lodgers without as much as be your leave — what's the world comin' to at all that a man's house isn't his own? But I'll soon put a stop to your gallop, for on the twenty-eight of the next month out you go, an' there'll be few sorry to see your back.

Seumas. I'll go when I like.

The Landlord. I'll let you see whether you own the house or no.

Seumas. I'll go when I like !

The Landlord. We'll see about that.

Seumas. We'll see.

The Landlord. Ay, we'll see.
            [*The Landlord goes out and Seumas shuts the door.*

The Landlord [*outside*]. Mind you, I'm in earnest ; you'll not stop in this house a minute longer than the twenty-eight.

Seumas [*with a roar*]. Ah, go to hell !

Davoren [*pacing the room as far as the space will permit*]. What in the name of God persuaded me to come to such a house as this ?

Seumas. It's nothing when you're used to it ; you're too

thin-skinned altogether.   The oul' sod's got the wind
up about you, that's all.

Davoren. Got the wind up about me !

Seumas. He thinks you're on the run. He's afraid of a
raid, and that his lovely property'll be destroyed.

Davoren. But why, in the name of all that's sensible,
should he think that I'm on the run ?

Seumas. Sure they all think you're on the run.   Mrs.
Henderson thinks it, Tommy Owens thinks it, Mrs.
an' Mr. Grigson think it, an' Minnie Powell thinks it
too.   [*Picking up his attaché case*] I'd better be off if I'm
goin' to do anything to-day.

Davoren. What are we going to do with these notices to
quit ?

Seumas. Oh, shove them up on the mantelpiece behind
one of the statues.

Davoren. Oh, I mean what action shall we take ?

Seumas. I haven't time to stop now.   We'll talk about
them when I come back. . . . I'll get me own back
on that oul' Mulligan yet.   I wish to God they would
come an' smash his rookery to pieces, for it's all he
thinks of, and, mind you, oul' Mulligan would call
himself a descendant of the true Gaels of Banba — [*as
he goes out*] :

> Oh, proud were the chieftains of famed Inisfail.
> Is truagh gan oidher 'na Vfarradh.
> The stars of our sky an' the salt of our soil —

Oh, Kathleen ni Houlihan, your way's a thorny way !
[*He goes out.*

Davoren [*returning to the table and sitting down at the type-writer*]. Oh, Donal Og O'Davoren, your way's a thorny way. Your last state is worse than your first. Ah me, alas! Pain, pain ever, for ever. Like thee, Prometheus, no change, no pause, no hope. Ah, life, life, life! [*There is a gentle knock at the door.*] Another Fury come to plague me now! [*Another knock, a little louder.*

Davoren. You can knock till you're tired.

[*The door opens and Minnie Powell enters with an easy confidence one would not expect her to possess from her gentle way of knocking. She is a girl of twenty-three, but the fact of being forced to earn her living, and to take care of herself, on account of her parents' early death, has given her a force and an assurance beyond her years. She has lost the sense of fear (she does not know this), and, consequently, she is at ease in all places and before all persons, even those of a superior education, so long as she meets them in the atmosphere that surrounds the members of her own class. Her hair is brown, neither light nor dark, but partaking of both tints according to the light or shade she may happen to be in. Her well-shaped figure — a rare thing in a city girl — is charmingly dressed in a brown tailor-made costume, her stockings and shoes are a darker brown tint than the costume, and all are crowned by a silk tam-o'-shanter of a rich blue tint.*

Minnie. Are you in, Mr. Shields?

Davoren [*rapidly*]. No, he's not, Minnie; he's just gone out — if you run out quickly you're sure to catch him.

Minnie. Oh, it's all right, Mr. Davoren, you'll do just

as well ; I just come in for a drop o' milk for a cup o' tea ; I shouldn't be troublin' you this way, but I'm sure you don't mind.

Davoren [*dubiously*]. No trouble in the world ; delighted, I'm sure. [*Giving her the milk*] There, will you have enough ?

Minnie. Plenty, lashins, thanks. Do you be all alone all the day, Mr. Davoren ?

Davoren. No, indeed ; I wish to God I was.

Minnie. It's not good for you then. I don't know how you like to be by yourself — I couldn't stick it long.

Davoren [*wearily*]. No ?

Minnie. No, indeed ; [*with rapture*] there's nothin' I'm more fond of than a Hooley. I was at one last Sunday — I danced rings round me ! Tommy Owens was there — you know Tommy Owens, don't you ?

Davoren. I can't say I do.

Minnie. D'ye not ? The little fellow that lives with his mother in the two-pair back — [*ecstatically*] he's a gorgeous melodeon player !

Davoren. A gifted son of Orpheus, eh ?

Minnie [*who never heard of Orpheus*]. You've said it, Mr. Davoren : the son of poor oul' Battie Owens, a weeshy, dawny, bit of a man that was never sober an' was always talkin' politics. Poor man, it killed him in the long run.

Davoren. A man should always be drunk, Minnie, when he talks politics — it's the only way in which to make them important.

Minnie. Tommy takes after the oul' fellow, too ; he'd talk from morning till night when he has a few jars in him. [*Suddenly ; for like all of her class, Minnie is not able to converse very long on the one subject, and her thoughts spring from one thing to another*] Poetry is a grand thing, Mr. Davoren, I'd love to be able to write a poem — a lovely poem on Ireland an' the men o' '98.

Davoren. Oh, we've had enough of poems, Minnie, about '98, and of Ireland, too.

Minnie. Oh, there's a thing for a Republican to say ! But I know what you mean : it's time to give up the writing an' take to the gun. [*Her roving eye catches sight of the flowers in the vase*] What's Mr. Shields doin' with the oul' weeds ?

Davoren. Those aren't Shields', they're mine. Wild flowers is a kindlier name for them, Minnie, than weeds. These are wild violets, this is an *Arum maculatum*, or Wake Robin, and these are Celandines, a very beautiful flower related to the buttercups. [*He quotes*] :

> One day, when Morn's half-open'd eyes
> Were bright with Spring sunshine —
> My hand was clasp'd in yours, dear love,
> And yours was clasp'd in mine —
> We bow'd as worshippers before
> The Golden Celandine.

Minnie. Oh, aren't they lovely, an' isn't the poem lovely, too ! I wonder, now, who she was.

Davoren [*puzzled*]. She, who ?

Minnie. Why, the . . . [*roguishly*] Oh, be the way you don't know.

Davoren. Know ? I'm sure I don't know.

Minnie. It doesn't matter, anyhow — that's your own business ; I suppose I don't know her.

Davoren. Know her — know whom ?

Minnie [*shyly*]. Her whose hand was clasped in yours, an' yours was clasped in hers.

Davoren. Oh, that — that was simply a poem I quoted about the Celandine, that might apply to any girl — to you, for instance.

Minnie [*greatly relieved, coming over and sitting beside Davoren*]. But you have a sweetheart, all the same, Mr. Davoren, haven't you ?

Davoren. I ? No, not one, Minnie.

Minnie. Oh, now, you can tell that to some one else ; aren't you a poet an' aren't all the girls fond o' poets ?

Davoren. That may be, but all the poets aren't fond of girls.

Minnie. They are in the story-books, ay, and fond of more than one, too. [*With a questioning look*] Are you fond of them, Mr. Davoren ?

Davoren. Of course I like girls, Minnie, especially girls who can add to their charms by the way in which they dress, like you, for instance.

Minnie. Oh, now, you're on for coddin' me, Mr. Davoren.

Davoren. No, really, Minnie, I'm not ; you are a very charming little girl indeed.

Minnie. Then if I'm a charmin' little girl, you ought to be able to write a poem about me.

Davoren [*who has become susceptible to the attractiveness of Minnie, catching her hand*]. And so I will, so I will, Minnie ; I have written them about girls not half so pretty as yourself.

Minnie. Ah, I knew you had one, I knew you had one now.

Davoren. Nonsense. Every girl a poet writes about isn't his sweetheart ; Annie Laurie wasn't the sweetheart of Bobbie Burns.

Minnie. You needn't tell me she wasn't ; " An' for bonnie Annie Laurie I'd lay me down an' die ". No man ud lay down an' die for any but a sweetheart, not even for a wife.

Davoren. No man, Minnie, willingly dies for anything.

Minnie. Except for his country, like Robert Emmet.

Davoren. Even he would have lived on if he could ; he died not to deliver Ireland. The British Government killed him to save the British nation.

Minnie. You're only jokin' now ; you'd die for your country.

Davoren. I don't know so much about that.

Minnie. You would, you would, you would — I know what you are.

Davoren. What am I ?

Minnie [*in a whisper*]. A gunman on the run !

Davoren [*too pleased to deny it*]. Maybe I am, and maybe I'm not.

Minnie. Oh, I know, I know, I know. Do you never be afraid ?

Davoren. Afraid ! Afraid of what ?

Minnie. Why, the ambushes of course ; *I'm* all of a tremble when I hear a shot go off, an' what must it be in the middle of the firin' ?

Davoren [*delighted at Minnie's obvious admiration ; leaning back in his chair, and lighting a cigarette with placid affectation*]. I'll admit one does be a little nervous at first, but a fellow gets used to it after a bit, till, at last, a gunman throws a bomb as carelessly as a schoolboy throws a snowball.

Minnie [*fervently*]. I wish it was all over, all the same. [*Suddenly, with a tremor in her voice*] You'll take care of yourself, won't you, won't you, Donal — I mean, Mr. Davoren ?

Davoren [*earnestly*]. Call me Donal, Minnie ; we're friends, great friends now — [*putting his arm around her*] go on, Minnie, call me Donal, let me hear you say Donal.

Minnie. The place badly needs a tidyin' up . . . Donal — there now, are you satisfied ? [*Rapidly, half afraid of Davoren's excited emotions*] But it really does, it's in an awful state. To-morrow's a half-day, an' I'll run in an' straighten it up a bit.

Davoren [*frightened at the suggestion*]. No, no, Minnie, you're too pretty for that sort of work ; besides, the people of the house would be sure to start talking about you.

Minnie. An' do you think Minnie Powell cares whether

they'll talk or no? She's had to push her way through life up to this without help from any one, an' she's not goin' to ask their leave, now, to do what she wants to do.

Davoren [*forgetting his timidity in the honest joy of appreciating the independent courage of Minnie*]. My soul within art thou, Minnie! A pioneer in action as I am a pioneer in thought. The two powers that shall " grasp this sorry scheme of things entire, and mould life nearer to the heart's desire ". Lovely little Minnie, and brave as well; brave little Minnie, and lovely as well!

[*His disengaged hand lifts up her bent head, and he looks earnestly at her; he is stooping to kiss her, when Tommy Owens appears at the door, which Minnie has left partially open. Tommy is about twenty-five years of age. He is small and thin; his words are uttered in a nasal drawl; his voice is husky, due to frequent drinks and perpetual cigarette-smoking. He tries to get rid of the huskiness by an occasional cough. Tommy is a hero-worshipper, and, like many others, he is anxious to be on familiar terms with those who he thinks are braver than he is himself, and whose approbation he tries to win by an assumption equal to their own. He talks in a staccato manner. He has a few drinks taken — it is too early to be drunk — that make him talkative. He is dressed in a suit of dungarees, and gives a gentle cough to draw attention to his presence.*]

Tommy. I seen nothin' — honest — thought you was learnin' to typewrite — Mr. Davoren teachin' you. I seen nothin' else — s'help me God!

Minnie. We'd be hard put to it if we minded what you seen, Tommy Owens.

Tommy. Right, Minnie, Tommy Owens has a heart —
Evenin', Mr. Davoren — don't mind me comin' in —
I'm Tommy Owens — live up in the two-pair back,
workin' in Ross an' Walpole's — Mr. Shields knows
me well ; you needn't be afraid o' me, Mr. Davoren.

Davoren. Why should I be afraid of you, Mr. Owens, or
of anybody else ?

Tommy. Why should you, indeed ? We're all friends
here — Mr. Shields knows me well — all you've got
to say is, "Do you know Tommy Owens ?" an'
he'll tell you the sort of a man Tommy Owens is.
There's no flies on Tommy — got me ?

Minnie. For goodness' sake, Tommy, leave Mr. Davoren
alone — he's got enough burgeons on him already.

Tommy. Not a word, Minnie, not a word — Mr.
Davoren understands me well, as man to man. It's
" Up the Republic " all the time — eh, Mr. Davoren ?

Davoren. I know nothing about the Republic ; I have
no connection with the politics of the day, and I don't
want to have any connection.

Tommy. You needn't say no more — a nod's as good as
a wink to a blind horse — you've no meddlin' or
makin' with it, good, bad, or indifferent, pro nor con ;
I know it an' Minnie knows it — give me your hand.
[*He catches Davoren's hand*] Two firm hands clasped
together will all the power outbrave of the heartless
English tyrant, the Saxon coward an' knave. That's
Tommy Owens' hand, Mr. Davoren, the hand of a
man, a man — Mr. Shields knows me well.

[*He breaks into song.*

High upon the gallows tree stood the noble-hearted three,
By the vengeful tyrant stricken in their bloom ;
But they met him face to face with the spirit of their race,
And they went with souls undaunted to their doom !

Minnie [*in an effort to quell his fervour*]. Tommy Owens, for
goodness' sake . . .

Tommy [*overwhelming her with a shout*] :

God save Ireland ses the hayros, God save Ireland ses we all,
Whether on the scaffold high or the battle-field we die,
Oh, what matter when for Ayryinn dear we fall !

[*Tearfully*] Mr. Davoren, I'd die for Ireland !

Davoren. I know you would, I know you would, Tommy.

Tommy. I never got a chance — they never gave me a
chance — but all the same I'd be there if I was called
on — Mr. Shields knows that — ask Mr. Shields, Mr.
Davoren.

Davoren. There's no necessity, Tommy ; I know you're
the right stuff if you got the chance, but remember that
" he also serves who only stands and waits ".

Tommy [*fiercely*]. I'm bloody well tired o' waitin' — we're
all tired o' waitin'. Why isn't every man in Ireland
out with the I.R.A. ? Up with the barricades, up
with the barricades ; it's now or never, now an' for
ever, as Sarsfield said at the battle o' Vinegar Hill.
Up with the barricades — that's Tommy Owens —
an' a penny buys a whistle. Let them as thinks
different say different — what do you say, Mr.
Davoren ?

Davoren. I say, Tommy, you ought to go up and get your

dinner, for if you wait much longer it won't be worth eating.

Tommy. Oh, damn the dinner ; who'd think o' dinner an' Ireland fightin' to be free ? — not Tommy Owens, anyhow. It's only the Englishman who's always thinkin' of his belly.

Minnie. Tommy Owens !

Tommy. Excuse me, Miss Powell, in the ardure ov me anger I disremembered there was a lady present.

> [*Voices are heard outside, and presently Mrs. Henderson comes into the room, followed by Mr. Gallogher, who, however, lingers at the door, too timid to come any farther. Mrs. Henderson is a massive woman in every way ; massive head, arms, and body ; massive voice, and a massive amount of self-confidence. She is a mountain of good nature, and during the interview she behaves towards Davoren with deferential self-assurance. She dominates the room, and seems to occupy the whole of it. She is dressed poorly but tidily, wearing a white apron and a large shawl. Mr. Gallogher, on the other hand, is a spare little man with a spare little grey beard and a thin, nervous voice. He is dressed as well as a faded suit of blue will allow him to be. He is obviously ill at ease during his interview with Davoren. He carries a hard hat, much the worse for wear, under his left arm, and a letter in his right hand.*

Mrs. Henderson [*entering the room*]. Come along in, Mr. Gallicker, Mr. Davoren won't mind ; it's him as can put you in the way o' havin' your wrongs righted ; come on in, man, an' don't be so shy — Mr. Davoren is wan ov ourselves that stands for govermint ov the people with the people by the people. You'll find you'll be as welcome as the flowers in May.   Good evenin', Mr. Davoren, an' God an' His holy angels be between you an' all harm.

Tommy [*effusively*]. Come on, Mr. Gallicker, an' don't be a stranger — we're all friends here — anything special to be done or particular advice asked, here's your man here.

Davoren [*subconsciously pleased, but a little timid of the belief that he is connected with the gunmen*]. I'm very busy just now, Mrs. Henderson, and really . . .

Mrs. Henderson [*mistaking the reason of his embarrassment*]. Don't be put out, Mr. Davoren, we won't keep you more nor a few minutes.   It's not in me or in Mr. Gallicker to spoil sport.   Him an' me was young once, an' knows what it is to be strolling at night in the pale moonlight, with arms round one another.   An' I wouldn't take much an' say there's game in Mr. Gallicker still, for I seen, sometimes, a dangerous cock in his eye.   But we won't keep you an' Minnie long asunder ; he's the letter an' all written.   You must know, Mr. Davoren — excuse me for not introducin' him sooner — this is Mr. Gallicker, that lives in the front drawin'-room ov number fifty-five, as decent an' honest an' quiet a man as you'd meet in a day's walk. An' so signs on it, it's them as 'ill be imposed upon — read the letter, Mr. Gallicker.

Tommy. Read away, Mr. Gallicker, it will be attended to, never fear ; we know our own know, eh, Mr. Davoren ?

Minnie. Hurry up, Mr. Gallicker, an' don't be keeping Mr. Davoren.

Mrs. Henderson. Give him time, Minnie Powell. Give him time. You must know in all fairity, Mr. Davoren, that the family livin' in the next room to Mr. Gallicker — the back drawin'-room, to be particular — am I right or am I wrong, Mr. Gallicker?

Mr. Gallogher. You're right, Mrs. Henderson, perfectly right, indeed — that's the very identical room.

Mrs. Henderson. Well, Mr. Davoren, the people in the back drawin'-room, or, to be more particular, the residents — that's the word that's writ in the letter — am I right or am I wrong, Mr. Gallicker?

Mr. Gallogher. You're right, Mrs. Henderson, perfectly accurate — that's the very identical word.

Mrs. Henderson. Well, Mr. Davoren, the residents in the back drawin'-room, as I aforesaid, is nothin' but a gang o' tramps that oughtn't to be allowed to associate with honest, decent, quiet, respectable people. Mr. Gallicker has tried to reason with them, and make them behave themselves — which in my opinion they never will — however, that's only an opinion, an' not legal — ever since they have made Mr. Gallicker's life a HELL! Mr. Gallicker, am I right or am I wrong?

Mr. Gallogher. I'm sorry to say you're right, Mrs. Henderson, perfectly right — not a word of exaggeration.

Mrs. Henderson. Well, now, Mr. Gallicker, seein' as I have given Mr. Davoren a fair account ov how you're situated, an' ov these tramps' cleverality, I'll ask you to read the letter, which I'll say, not because you're there, or that you're a friend o' mine, is as good a letter as was decomposed by a scholar. Now, Mr. Gallicker, an' don't forget the top sayin'.

[*Mr. Gallogher prepares to read ; Minnie leans forward to listen ; Tommy takes out a well-worn note-book and a pencil stump, and assumes a very important attitude.*

Tommy. One second. Mr. Gallicker, is this the twenty-first or twenty-second ?

Mr. Gallogher. The twenty-first, sir.

Tommy. Thanks ; proceed, Mr. Gallicker.

Mr. Gallogher [*with a few preliminary tremors, reads the letter. Reading*] :

"To All to Whom These Presents Come, Greeting

"Gentlemen of the Irish Republican Army . . ."

Mrs. Henderson. There's a beginnin' for you, Mr. Davoren.

Minnie. That's some swank.

Tommy. There's a lot in that sayin', mind you ; it's a hard wallop at the British Empire.

Mrs. Henderson [*proudly*]. Go on, Mr. Gallicker.

Mr. Gallogher [*reading*] :

"I wish to call your attention to the persecution me and my family has to put up with in respect of and appertaining to the residents of the back drawing-room of the house known as fifty-five, Saint Teresa Street, situate in the Parish of St. Thomas, in the Borough and City of Dublin. This persecution started eighteen months ago — or to be precise — on the tenth day of the sixth month, in the year nineteen hundred and twenty."

Mrs. Henderson. That's the word I was trying to think ov — precise — it cuts the ground from under their feet — so to speak.

Mr. Gallogher [*reading*] :

"We, the complainants, resident on the ground floor, deeming it disrespectable . . ."

Mrs. Henderson [*with an emphatic nod*]. Which it was.

Mr. Gallogher [*reading*] :

"Deeming it disrespectable to have an open hall door, and to have the hall turned into a playground, made a solemn protest, and, in consequence, we the complainants aforesaid has had no peace ever since. Owing to the persecution, as aforesaid specified, we had to take out a summons again them some time ago as there was no Republican Courts then ; but we did not proceed again them as me and my wife — to wit, James and Winifred Gallogher — has a strong objection to foreign Courts as such. We had peace for some time after that, but now things have gone from bad to worse. The name calling and the language is something abominable . . ."

Mrs. Henderson [*holding out her hand as a constable would extend his to stop a car that another may pass*]. Excuse me, Mr. Gallicker, but I think the word " shockin' " should be put in there after abominable ; for the language used be these tramps has two ways o' bein' looked at — for it's abominable to the childer an' shockin' to your wife — am I right or am I wrong, Mr. Davoren ?

Tommy [*judicially*]. Shockin' is a right good word, with a great deal o' meanin', an' . . .

Mrs. Henderson [*with a deprecating gesture that extinguishes Tommy*]. Tommy, let Mr. Davoren speak ; whatever Mr. Davoren ses, Julia Henderson'll abide be.

Davoren [*afraid to say anything else*]. I think the word might certainly be introduced with advantage.

Mrs. Henderson. Go over there, Mr. Gallicker, an' put in the word shockin', as aforesaid.

[*Gallogher goes over to the table, and with a great deal of difficulty enters the word.*

Tommy [*to Mr. Gallogher as he writes*]. Ey, there's two k's in shockin' !

Mr. Gallogher [*reading*] :

" The language is something abominable and shocking. My wife has often to lock the door of the room to keep them from assaulting her. If you would be so kind as to send some of your army or police down to see for themselves we would give them full particulars. I have to be always from home all day, as I work with Mr. Hennessy, the harness maker of the Coombe, who will furnish all particulars as to my unvarnished respectability, also my neighbours. The name of the resident-tenant who is giving all this trouble and who, pursuant to the facts of the case aforesaid, mentioned, will be the defendant, is Dwyer. The husband of the aforesaid Mrs. Dwyer, or the aforesaid defendant, as the case may be, is a seaman, who is coming home shortly, and we beg The Irish Republican Army to note that the said Mrs. Dwyer says he will settle us when he comes home. While leaving it entirely in the hands of the gentlemen of The Republican Army, the defendant, that is to say, James Gallogher of fifty-five St. Teresa Street, ventures to say that he thinks he has made out a Primmy Fashy Case against Mrs. Dwyer and all her heirs, male and female as aforesaid mentioned in the above written schedule.

" *N.B.* — If you send up any of your men, please tell them to bring their guns. I beg to remain the humble servant and devoted admirer of the Gentlemen of the Irish Republican Army.

" Witness my hand this tenth day of the fifth month of the year nineteen hundred and twenty.

" JAMES GALLOGHER."

Mr. Gallogher [*with a modest cough*]. Ahem.

Mrs. Henderson. There's a letter for you, Mr. Davoren !

Tommy. It's the most powerfullest letter I ever heard read.

Minnie. It wasn't you, really, that writ it, Mr. Gallicker ?

Mrs. Henderson. Sinn Fein Amhain : him an' him only, Minnie. I seen him with me own two eyes when me an' Winnie — Mrs. Gallicker, Mr. Davoren, aforesaid as appears in the letter — was havin' a chat be the fire.

Minnie. You'd never think it was in him to do it.

Mrs. Henderson. An' to think that the likes ov such a man is to have the sowl-case worried out ov him by a gang o' tramps ; but it's in good hands now, an' instead ov them settlin' yous, Mr. Gallicker, it's yous 'ill settle them. Give the letter to Mr. Davoren, an' we'll be goin'.

[*Gallogher gives the letter to Davoren.*

Mrs. Henderson [*moving towards the door*]. I hope you an' Mr. Shields is gettin' on all right together, Mr. Davoren.

Davoren. Fairly well, thanks, Mrs. Henderson. We don't see much of each other. He's out during the day, and I'm usually out during the evening.

Mrs. Henderson. I'm afraid he'll never make a fortune out ov what he's sellin'. He'll talk above an hour over a pennorth o' pins. Every time he comes to our place I buy a package o' hairpins from him to give him a little encouragement. I 'clare to God I have as many pins now as üd make a wire mattress for a double bed. All the young divils about the place are beginnin' to make a jeer ov him, too ; I gave one ov them a mallavogin' the other day for callin' him oul' hairpins !

Mr. Gallogher [*venturing an opinion*]. Mr. Shields is a man of exceptional mental capacity, and is worthy of a more dignified position.

Mrs. Henderson. Them words is true, Mr. Gallicker, and they aren't. For to be wise is to be a fool, an' to be a fool is to be wise.

Mr. Gallogher [*with deprecating tolerance*]. Oh, Mrs. Henderson, that's a parrotox.

Mrs. Henderson. It may be what a parrot talks, or a blackbird, or, for the matter of that, a lark — but it's what Julia Henderson thinks, any . . . whisht, is that a *Stop Press* ?
  [*Outside is heard the shriek of a newsboy calling " Stop Press ".*

Mrs. Henderson. Run out, Tommy, an' get it till we see what it is.

Tommy. I haven't got a make.

Mrs. Henderson. I never seen you any other way, an' you'll be always the same if you keep follyin' your Spearmints, an' your Bumble Bees an' your Night Patrols. [*Shouting to someone outside*] Is that a *Stop Press*, Mrs. Grigson ?

Voice outside. Yis ; an ambush out near Knocksedan.

Mrs. Henderson. That's the stuff to give them. [*Loudly*] Was there anybody hurted ?

Voice outside. One poor man killed — some chap named Maguire, the paper says.

Davoren [*agitated*]. What name did she say ?

Minnie. Maguire ; did you know him, Mr. Davoren ?

Davoren. Yes — no, no ; I didn't know him, no, I didn't know him, Minnie.

Minnie. I wonder is it the Maguire that does be with Mr. Shields ?

Davoren. Oh no, not at all, it couldn't be.

Mrs. Henderson. Knocksedan ? That's in the County Sligo, now, or I'm greatly mistaken — am I right, Mr. Gallicker, or am I wrong ?

Mr. Gallogher [*who knows perfectly well that it is in the County Dublin, but dare not correct Mrs. Henderson*]. That's where it is — Knocksedan, that's the very identical county.

Mrs. Henderson. Well, I think we better be makin' a move, Mr. Gallicker ; we've kep' Mr. Davoren long enough, an' you'll find the letter'll be in good hans.
    [*Mr. Gallogher and Mrs. Henderson move towards the door, which when he reaches it Mr. Gallogher grips, hesitates, buttons his coat, and turns to Davoren.*

Mr. Gallogher. Mr. Davoren, sir, on behalf ov meself, James Gallicker, an' Winifred, Mrs. Gallicker, wife ov the said James, I beg to offer, extend an' furnish our humble an' hearty thanks for your benevolent goodness in interferin' in the matter specified, particularated an' expanded upon in the letter, mandamus or schedule, as the case may be. An' let me interpretate to you on behalf ov meself an' Winifred Gallicker, that when-

ever you visit us you will be supernally positive ov a
hundred thousand welcomes — ahem.

Mrs. Henderson [*beaming with pride for the genius of her friend*].
There's a man for you, Mr. Davoren! You forgot
to mention Biddy and Shaun, Mr. Gallicker — [*to
Davoren*] his two children — it's himself has them
trained well. It ud make your heart thrill like an
alarm clock to hear them singin' " Faith ov Our
Fathers " an' " Wrap the Green Flag Roun' Me ".

Mr. Gallogher [*half apologetically and half proudly*]. Faith an'
Fatherland, Mrs. Henderson, Faith and Fatherland.

Mrs. Henderson. Well, good-day, Mr. Davoren, an' God
keep you an' strengthen all the men that are fightin' for
Ireland's freedom.   [*She and Gallogher go out.*

Tommy. I must be off too ; so-long, Mr. Davoren, an'
remember that Tommy Owens only waits the call.
    [*He goes out too.*

Davoren. Well, Minnie, we're by ourselves once more.

Minnie. Wouldn't that Tommy Owens give you the
sick — only waitin' to hear the call ! Ah, then it'll
take all the brass bands in the country to blow the call
before Tommy Owens ud hear it. [*She looks at her
wristlet watch.*] Sacred Heart, I've only ten minutes
to get back to work ! I'll have to fly ! Quick, Mr.
Davoren, write me name in typewritin' before I go —
just " Minnie ".   [*Davoren types the name.*

Minnie [*shyly but determinedly*]. Now yours underneath —
just " Donal ". [*Davoren does so.*] Minnie, Donal ;
Donal, Minnie ; good-bye now.

Davoren. Here, what about your milk?

Minnie. I haven't time to take it now. [*Slyly*] I'll come for it this evening.   [*They both go towards the door.*

Davoren. Minnie, the kiss I didn't get.

Minnie. What kiss?

Davoren. When we were interrupted; you know, you little rogue, come, just one.

Minnie. Quick, then.
  [*Davoren kisses her and she runs out. Davoren returns thoughtfully to the table.*

Davoren. Minnie, Donal; Donal, Minnie. Very pretty, but very ignorant. A gunman on the run! Be careful, be careful, Donal Davoren. But Minnie is attracted to the idea, and I am attracted to Minnie. And what danger can there be in being the shadow of a gunman?

CURTAIN

ACT II

The same as in Act I. But it is now night. Seumas is in the bed that runs along the wall at back. Davoren is seated near the fire, to which he has drawn the table. He has a fountain-pen in his hand, and is attracted in thought towards the moon, which is shining in through the windows. An open writing-pad is on the table at Davoren's elbow. The bag left by Maguire is still in the same place.

Davoren :

> The cold chaste moon, the Queen of Heaven's bright isles,
> Who makes all beautiful on which she smiles ;
> That wandering shrine of soft yet icy flame,
> Which ever is transformed yet still the same.

Ah, Shelley, Shelley, you yourself were a lovely human orb shining through clouds of whirling human dust. " She makes all beautiful on which she smiles." Ah, Shelley, she couldn't make this thrice accursed room beautiful. Her beams of beauty only make its horrors more full of horrors still. There is an ugliness that can be made beautiful, and there is an ugliness that can only be destroyed, and this is part of that ugliness. Donal, Donal, I fear your last state is worse than your first.

[He lilts a verse, which he writes on the pad before him.

> When night advances through the sky with slow
>   And solemn tread,
> The queenly moon looks down on life below,
>   As if she read
> Man's soul, and in her scornful silence said :
>   All beautiful and happiest things are dead.

125

Seumas [*sleepily*]. Donal, Donal, are you awake ? [*A pause.*] Donal, Donal, are you asleep ?

Davoren. I'm neither awake nor asleep : I'm thinking.

Seumas. I was just thinkin', too — I was just thinkin', too, that Maguire is sorry now that he didn't come with me instead of going to Knocksedan. He caught something besides butterflies — two of them he got, one through each lung.

Davoren. The Irish people are very fond of turning a serious thing into a joke ; that was a serious affair — for poor Maguire.

Seumas [*defensively*]. Why didn't he do what he arranged to do ? Did he think of me when he was goin' to Knocksedan ? How can he expect me to have any sympathy with him now ?

Davoren. He can hardly expect that now that he's dead.

Seumas. The Republicans 'll do a lot for him, now. How am I goin' to get back the things he has belongin' to me, either ? There's some of them in that bag over there, but that's not quarter of what he had ; an' I don't know where he was stoppin', for he left his old digs a week or so ago — I suppose there's nothing to be said about my loss ; I'm to sing dumb.

Davoren. I hope there's nothing else in the bag, besides thread and hairpins.

Seumas. What else ud be in it ? . . . I can't sleep properly ever since they put on this damned curfew. A minute ago I thought I heard some of the oul' ones standin' at the door ; they won't be satisfied till they bring a raid on the house ; an' they never begin to stand at the door till after curfew. . . . Are you gone to bed, Donal ?

Davoren. No ; I'm trying to finish this poem.

Seumas [*sitting up in bed*]. If I was you I'd give that game up ; it doesn't pay a working-man to write poetry. I don't profess to know much about poetry — I don't profess to know much about poetry — about poetry — I don't know much about the pearly glint of the morning dew, or the damask sweetness of the rare wild rose, or the subtle greenness of the serpent's eye — but I think a poet's claim to greatness depends upon his power to put passion in the common people.

Davoren. Ay, passion to howl for his destruction. The People ! Damn the people ! They live in the abyss, the poet lives on the mountain-top ; to the people there is no mystery of colour : it is simply the scarlet coat of the soldier ; the purple vestments of a priest ; the green banner of a party ; the brown or blue overalls of industry. To them the might of design is a three-roomed house or a capacious bed. To them beauty is for sale in a butcher's shop. To the people the end of life is the life created for them ; to the poet the end of life is the life that he creates for himself ; life has a stifling grip upon the people's throat — it is the poet's musician. The poet ever strives to save the people ; the people ever strive to destroy the poet. The people view life through creeds, through customs, and through necessities ; the poet views creeds, customs, and necessities through life. The people . . .

Seumas [*suddenly, and with a note of anxiety in his voice*]. Whisht ! What's that ? Is that the tappin' again ?

Davoren. Tappin'. What tappin' ?

Seumas [*in an awed whisper*]. This is the second night I heard that tappin' ! I believe it bodes no good to me. There, do you hear it again — a quiet, steady, mysterious tappin' on the wall.

Davoren. I hear no tappin'.

Seumas. It ud be better for me if you did. It's a sure sign of death when nobody hears it but meself.

Davoren. Death ! What the devil are you talking about, man ?

Seumas. I don't like it at all ; there's always something like that heard when one of our family dies.

Davoren. I don't know about that ; but I know there's a hell of a lot of things heard when one of your family lives.

Seumas. God between us an' all harm ! Thank God I'm where I ought to be — in bed. . . . It's always best to be in your proper place when such things happen — Sacred Heart ! There it is again ; do you not hear it now ?

Davoren. Ah, for God's sake go asleep.

Seumas. Do you believe in nothing ?

Davoren. I don't believe in tappin'.

Seumas. Whisht, it's stopped again ; I'll try to go asleep for fear it ud begin again.

Davoren. Ay, do ; and if it starts again I'll be sure to waken you up. [*A pause.*

Seumas. It's very cold to-night. Do you feel cold?

Davoren. I thought you were goin' asleep?

Seumas. The bloody cold won't let me. . . . You'd want a pair of pyjamas on you. [*A pause.*] Did you ever wear pyjamas, Donal?

Davoren. No, no, no.

Seumas. What kind of stuff is in them?

Davoren [*angrily*]. Oh, it depends on the climate; in India, silk; in Italy, satin; and the Eskimo wears them made from the skin of the Polar bear.

Seumas [*emphatically*]. If you take my advice you'll get into bed — that poem is beginnin' to get on your nerves.

Davoren [*extinguishing the candle with a vicious blow*]. Right; I'm going to bed now, so you can shut up.

[*Visibility is still maintained from the light of the moon.*

Seumas. I was goin' to say something when you put out the light — what's this it was? — um, um, oh, ay: when I was comin' in this evenin' I saw Minnie Powell goin' out. If I was you I wouldn't have that one comin' in here.

Davoren. She comes in; I don't bring her in, do I?

Seumas. The oul' ones'll be talkin', an' once they start you don't know how it'll end. Surely a man that has read Shelley couldn't be interested in an ignorant little bitch that thinks of nothin' but jazz dances, fox-trots, picture theatres an' dress.

Davoren. Right glad I am that she thinks of dress, for she thinks of it in the right way, and makes herself a pleasant picture to the eye. Education has been wasted on many persons, teaching them to talk only, but leaving them with all their primitive instincts. Had poor Minnie received an education she would have been an artist. She is certainly a pretty girl. I'm sure she is a good girl, and I believe she is a brave girl.

Seumas. A Helen of Troy come to live in a tenement ! You think a lot about her simply because she thinks a lot about you, an' she thinks a lot about you because she looks upon you as a hero — a kind o' Paris . . . she'd give the world an' all to be gaddin' about with a gunman. An' what ecstasy it ud give her if after a bit you were shot or hanged ; she'd be able to go about then — like a good many more — singin', " I do not mourn me darlin' lost, for he fell in his Jacket Green ". An' then, for a year an' a day, all round her hat she'd wear the Tri-coloured Ribbon O, till she'd pick up an' marry someone else — possibly a British Tommy with a Mons Star. An' as for bein' brave, it's easy to be that when you've no cause for cowardice ; I wouldn't care to have me life dependin' on brave little Minnie Powell — she wouldn't sacrifice a jazz dance to save it.

Davoren [*sitting on the bed and taking off his coat and vest, preparatory to going to bed*]. There ; that's enough about Minnie Powell. I'm afraid I'll soon have to be on the run out of this house, too ; it is becoming painfully obvious that there is no peace to be found here.

Seumas. Oh, this house is all right ; barrin' the children, it does be quiet enough. Wasn't there children in the last place you were in too ?

Davoren. Ay, ten ; [*viciously*] and they were all over forty.
[*A pause as Davoren is removing his collar and tie.*

Seumas. Everything is very quiet now ; I wonder what time is it ?

Davoren. The village cock hath thrice done salutation to the morn.

Seumas. Shakespeare, Richard the III, Act Five, Scene III. It was Ratcliffe said that to Richard just before the battle of Bosworth. . . . How peaceful the heavens look now with the moon in the middle ; you'd never think there were men prowlin' about tryin' to shoot each other. I don't know how a man who has shot any one can sleep in peace at night.

Davoren. There's plenty of men can't sleep in peace at night now unless they know that they have shot somebody.

Seumas. I wish to God it was all over. The country is gone mad. Instead of counting their beads now they're countin' bullets ; their Hail Marys and paternosters are burstin' bombs — burstin' bombs, an' the rattle of machine-guns ; petrol is their holy water ; their Mass is a burnin' buildin' ; their De Profundis is " The Soldiers' Song ", an' their creed is, I believe in the gun almighty, maker of heaven an' earth — an' it's all for " the glory o' God an' the honour o' Ireland ".

Davoren. I remember the time when you yourself believed in nothing but the gun.

Seumas. Ay, when there wasn't a gun in the country ; I've a different opinion now when there's nothin' but guns in the country. . . . An' you daren't open your mouth, for Kathleen ni Houlihan is very different now to the woman who used to play the harp an' sing

E*

" Weep on, weep on, your hour is past ", for she's a ragin' divil now, an' if you only look crooked at her you're sure of a punch in th' eye. But this is the way I look at it — I look at it this way : You're not goin' — you're not goin' to beat the British Empire — the British Empire, by shootin' an occasional Tommy at the corner of an occasional street. Besides, when the Tommies have the wind up — when the Tommies have the wind up they let bang at everything they see — they don't give a God's curse who they plug.

Davoren. Maybe they ought to get down off the lorry and run to the Records Office to find out a man's pedigree before they plug him.

Seumas. It's the civilians that suffer ; when there's an ambush they don't know where to run. Shot in the back to save the British Empire, an' shot in the breast to save the soul of Ireland. I'm a Nationalist meself, right enough — a Nationalist right enough, but all the same — I'm a Nationalist right enough ; I believe in the freedom of Ireland, an' that England has no right to be here, but I draw the line when I hear the gunmen blowin' about dyin' for the people, when it's the people that are dyin for the gunmen ! With all due respect to the gunmen, I don't want them to die for me.

Davoren. Not likely ; you object to any one of them deliberately dying for you for fear that one of these days you might accidentally die for one of them.

Seumas. You're one of the brave fellows that doesn't fear death.

Davoren. Why should I be afraid of it ? It's all the same

to me how it comes, where it comes, or when it comes. I leave fear of death to the people that are always praying for eternal life ; " Death is here and death is there, death is busy everywhere ".

Seumas. Ay, in Ireland. Thanks be to God I'm a daily communicant. There's a great comfort in religion ; it makes a man strong in time of trouble an' brave in time of danger. No man need be afraid with a crowd of angels round him ; thanks to God for His Holy religion !

Davoren. You're welcome to your angels ; philosophy is mine ; philosophy that makes the coward brave ; the sufferer defiant ; the weak strong ; the . . .
  [*A volley of shots is heard in a lane that runs parallel with the wall of the back-yard. Religion and philosophy are forgotten in the violent fear of a nervous equality.*

Seumas. Jesus, Mary, an' Joseph, what's that ?

Davoren. My God, that's very close.

Seumas. Is there no Christianity at all left in the country ?

Davoren. Are we ever again going to know what peace and security are ?

Seumas. If this continues much longer I'll be nothing but a galvanic battery o' shocks.

Davoren. It's dangerous to be in and it's equally dangerous to be out.

Seumas. This is a dangerous spot to be in with them windows ; you couldn't tell the minute a bullet ud come in through one of them — through one of them, an' hit the — hit the — an' hit the . . .

Davoren [*irritably*]. Hit the what, man ?

Seumas. The wall.

Davoren. Couldn't you say that at first without making a song about it ?

Seumas [*suddenly*]. I don't believe there's horses in the stable at all.

Davoren. Stable ! What stable are you talking about ?

Seumas. There's a stable at the back of the house with an entrance from the yard ; it's used as a carpenter's shop. Didn't you often hear the peculiar noises at night ? They give out that it's the horses shakin' their chains.

Davoren. And what is it ?

Seumas. Oh, there I'll leave you !

Davoren. Surely you don't mean . . .

Seumas. But I do mean it.

Davoren. You do mean what ?

Seumas. I wouldn't — I wouldn't be surprised — wouldn't be surprised — surprised . . .

Davoren. Yes, yes, surprised — go on.

Seumas. I wouldn't be surprised if they were manufacturin' bombs there.

Davoren. My God, that's a pleasant contemplation ! The sooner I'm on the run out of this house the better. How is it you never said anything about this before ?

Seumas. Well — well, I didn't want — I didn't want to — to . . .

Davoren. You didn't want to what?

Seumas. I didn't want to frighten you.

Davoren [*sarcastically*]. You're bloody kind!
[*A knock at the door ; the voice of Mrs. Grigson heard.*

Mrs. Grigson. Are you asleep, Mr. Shields?

Seumas. What the devil can she want at this hour of the night? [*To Mrs. Grigson*] No, Mrs. Grigson, what is it?

Mrs. Grigson [*opening the door and standing at the threshold. She is a woman about forty, but looks much older. She is one of the cave-dwellers of Dublin, living as she does in a tenement kitchen, to which only an occasional sickly beam of sunlight filters through a grating in the yard ; the consequent general dimness of her abode has given her a habit of peering through half-closed eyes. She is slovenly dressed in an old skirt and bodice ; her face is grimy, not because her habits are dirty — for, although she is untidy, she is a clean woman — but because of the smoky atmosphere of her room. Her hair is constantly falling over her face, which she is as frequently removing by rapid movements of her right hand*]. He hasn't turned up yet, an' I'm stiff with the cold waitin' for him.

Seumas. Mr. Grigson, is it?

Mrs. Grigson. Adolphus, Mr. Shields, after takin' his tea at six o'clock — no, I'm tellin' a lie — it was before six, for I remember the Angelus was ringin' out an' we sittin' at the table — after takin' his tea he went out for a breath o' fresh air, an' I haven't seen sign or light of him since. 'Clare to God me heart is up in me mouth, thinkin' he might be shot be the Black an' Tans.

Seumas. Aw, he'll be all right, Mrs. Grigson. You ought to go to bed an' rest yourself ; it's always the worst that comes into a body's mind ; go to bed, Mrs. Grigson, or you'll catch your death of cold.

Mrs. Grigson. I'm afraid to go to bed, Mr. Shields, for I'm always in dread that some night or another, when he has a sup taken, he'll fall down the kitchen stairs an' break his neck. Not that I'd be any the worse if anything did happen to him, for you know the sort he is, Mr. Shields ; sure he has me heart broke.

Seumas. Don't be downhearted, Mrs. Grigson ; he may take a thought one of these days an' turn over a new leaf.

Mrs. Grigson. Sorra leaf Adolphus 'll ever turn over, he's too far gone in the horns for that now. Sure no one ud mind him takin' a pint or two, if he'd stop at that, but he won't ; nothin' could fill him with beer, an' no matter how much he may have taken, when he's taken more he'll always say, " Here's the first to-day ".

Davoren [*to Seumas*]. Christ ! Is she going to stop talking there all the night ?

Seumas. 'Sh, she'll hear you ; right enough, the man has the poor woman's heart broke.

Davoren. And because he has her heart broken, she's to have the privilege of breaking everybody else's.

Mrs. Grigson. Mr. Shields.

Seumas. Yes ?

Mrs. Grigson. Do the insurance companies pay if a man is shot after curfew ?

Seumas. Well, now, that's a thing I couldn't say, Mrs. Grigson.

Mrs. Grigson [plaintively]. Isn't he a terrible man to be takin' such risks, an' not knowin' what'll happen to him. He knows them Societies only want an excuse to do people out of their money — is it after one, now, Mr. Shields ?

Seumas. Aw, it must be after one, Mrs. Grigson.

Mrs. Grigson [emphatically]. Ah, then, if I was a young girl again I'd think twice before gettin' married. Whisht ! There's somebody now — it's him, I know be the way he's fumblin'.
    [*She goes out a little way. Stumbling steps are heard in the hall.*

Mrs. Grigson [outside]. Is that you, Dolphie, dear ?
    [*After a few moments Adolphus, with Mrs. Grigson holding his arm, stumbles into the room.*

Mrs. Grigson. Dolphie, dear, mind yourself.

Adolphus [he is a man of forty-five, but looks, relatively, much younger than Mrs. Grigson. His occupation is that of a solicitor's clerk. He has all the appearance of being well fed ; and, in fact, he gets most of the nourishment, Mrs. Grigson getting just enough to give her strength to do the necessary work of the household. On account of living most of his life out of the kitchen, his complexion is fresh, and his movements, even when sober, are livelier than those of his wife. He is comfortably dressed ; heavy top-coat, soft trilby hat, a fancy coloured scarf about his neck, and he carries an umbrella]. I'm all right ; do you see anything wrong with me ?

Mrs. Grigson. Of course you're all right, dear ; there's no one mindin' you.

Adolphus Grigson. Mindin' me, is it, mindin' me ? He'd want to be a good thing that ud mind me. There's a man here — a man, mind you, afraid av nothin' — not in this bloody house anyway.

Mrs. Grigson [*imploringly*]. Come on downstairs, Dolphie, dear ; sure there's not one in the house ud say a word to you.

Adolphus Grigson. Say a word to me, is it ? He'd want to be a good thing that ud say anything to Dolphus Grigson. [*Loudly*] Is there anyone wants to say anything to Dolphus Grigson ? If there is, he's here — a man, too — there's no blottin' it out — a man.

Mrs. Grigson. You'll wake everybody in the house ; can't you speak quiet.

Adolphus Grigson [*more loudly still*]. What do I care for anybody in the house ? Are they keepin' me ; are they givin' me anything ? When they're keepin' Grigson it'll be time enough for them to talk. [*With a shout*] I can tell them Adolphus Grigson wasn't born in a bottle !

Mrs. Grigson [*tearfully*]. Why do you talk like that, dear ? We all know you weren't born in a bottle.

Adolphus Grigson. There's some of them in this house think that Grigson was born in a bottle.

Davoren [*to Seumas*]. A most appropriate place for him to be born in.

Mrs. Grigson. Come on down to bed, now, an' you can talk about them in the mornin'.

Grigson. I'll talk about them, now ; do you think I'm
afraid of them ? Dolphus Grigson's afraid av nothin',
creepin' or walkin', — if there's any one in the house
thinks he's fit to take a fall out av Adolphus Grigson,
he's here — a man ; they'll find that Grigson's no
soft thing.

Davoren. Ah me, alas ! Pain, pain ever, for ever.

Mrs. Grigson. Dolphie, dear, poor Mr. Davoren wants to
go to bed.

Davoren. Oh, she's terribly anxious about poor Mr.
Davoren, all of a sudden.

Grigson [*stumbling towards Davoren, and holding out his hand*].
Davoren ! He's a man. Leave it there, mate. You
needn't be afraid av Dolphus Grigson ; there never
was a drop av informer's blood in the whole family av
Grigson. I don't know what you are or what you
think, but you're a man, an' not like some of the
goughers in this house, that ud hang you. Not re-
ferrin' to you, Mr. Shields.

Mrs. Grigson. Oh, you're not deludin' to Mr. Shields.

Seumas. I know that, Mr. Grigson ; go on down, now,
with Mrs. Grigson, an' have a sleep.

Grigson. I tie meself to no woman's apron strings, Mr.
Shields ; I know how to keep Mrs. Grigson in her
place ; I have the authority of the Bible for that. I
know the Bible from cover to cover, Mr. Davoren, an'
that's more than some in this house could say. And
what does the Holy Scripture say about woman ? It
says, " The woman shall be subject to her husband",
an' I'll see that Mrs. Grigson keeps the teachin' av the

Holy Book in the letter an' in the spirit. If you're ever in trouble, Mr. Davoren, an' Grigson can help — I'm your man — have you me?

Davoren. I have you, Mr. Grigson, I have you.

Grigson. Right; I'm an Orangeman, an' I'm not ashamed av it, an' I'm not afraid av it, but I can feel for a true man, all the same — have *you* got me, Mr. Shields?

Seumas. Oh, we know you well, Mr. Grigson; many a true Irishman was a Protestant — Tone, Emmet an' Parnell.

Grigson. Mind you, I'm not sayin' as I agree with them you've mentioned, Mr. Shields, for the Bible forbids it, an' Adolphus Grigson 'll always abide be the Bible. Fear God an' honour the King — that's written in Holy Scripture, an' there's no blottin' it out. [*Pulling a bottle out of his pocket*] But here, Mr. Davoren, have a drink, just to show there's no coolness.

Davoren. No, no, Mr. Grigson, it's too late now to take anything. Go on down with Mrs. Grigson, and we can have a chat in the morning.

Grigson. Sure you won't have a drink?

Davoren. Quite sure — thanks all the same.

Grigson [*drinking*]. Here's the first to-day! To all true men, even if they were born in a bottle. Here's to King William, to the battle av the Boyne; to the Hobah Black Chapter — that's my Lodge, Mr. Davoren; an' to The Orange Lily O.

[*Singing in a loud shout:*

An' dud ya go to see the show, each rose an' pinkadilly O,
To feast your eyes an' view the prize won be the Orange
     Lily O.
The Vic'roy there, so debonair, just like a daffadilly O,
With Lady Clarke, blithe as a lark, approached the Orange
     Lily O.
          Heigh Ho the Lily O,
          The Royal, Loyal Lily O,
Beneath the sky what flower can vie with Erin's Orange
     Lily O !

Davoren. Holy God, isn't this terrible !

Grigson [*singing*] :

The elated Muse, to hear the news, jumped like a Connaught
     filly O,
As gossip Fame did loud proclaim the triumph av the
     Lily O.
The Lowland field may roses yield, gay heaths the High-
     lands hilly O ;
But high or low no flower can show like Erin's Orange
     Lily O.
          Heigh Ho the Lily O,
          The Royal, Loyal Lily O,
Beneath the sky what flower can vie with Erin's Or . . .

[*While Grigson has been singing, the sound of a rapidly
moving motor is heard, faintly at first, but growing
rapidly louder, till it apparently stops suddenly somewhere very near the house, bringing Grigson's song to an
abrupt conclusion. They are all startled, and listen
attentively to the throbbing of the engines, which can be
plainly heard. Grigson is considerably sobered, and
anxiously keeps his eyes on the door. Seumas sits up in
bed and listens anxiously. Davoren, with a shaking
hand, lights the candle, and begins to search hurriedly
among the books and papers on the table.*

Grigson [*with a tremor in his voice*]. There's no need to be afraid, they couldn't be comin' here.

Mrs. Grigson. God forbid ! It ud be terrible if they came at this hour ov the night.

Seumas. You never know now, Mrs. Grigson ; they'd rush in on you when you'd be least expectin' them. What, in the name o' God, is goin' to come out of it all ? Nobody now cares a traneen about the orders of the Ten Commandments ; the only order that anybody minds now is, " Put your hands up ". Oh, it's a hopeless country.

Grigson. Whisht ; do you hear them talking outside at the door ? You're sure of your life nowhere now ; it's just as safe to go everywhere as it is to anywhere. An' they don't give a damn whether you're a loyal man or not. If you're a Republican they make you sing " God save the King ", an' if you're loyal they'll make you sing the " Soldiers' Song ". The singin' ud be all right if they didn't make you dance afterwards.

Mrs. Grigson. They'd hardly come here unless they heard something about Mr. Davoren.

Davoren. About me ! What could they hear about me ?

Grigson. You'll never get some people to keep their mouths shut. I was in the Blue Lion this evening, an' who do you think was there, blowin' out av him, but that little blower, Tommy Owens ; there he was tellin' everybody that *he* knew where there was bombs ; that *he* had a friend that was a General in the I.R.A. ; that *he* could tell them what the Staff was thinkin' av doin' ; that *he* could lay his hand on tons av revolvers ; that they wasn't a mile from where he was livin', but that *he* knew his own know, an' would keep it to himself.

Seumas. Well, God blast the little blower, anyway ; it's the like ov him that deserves to be plugged ! [*To Davoren*] What are you lookin' for among the books, Donal ?

Davoren. A letter that I got to-day from Mr. Gallogher and Mrs. Henderson ; I'm blessed if I know where I put it.

Seumas [*peevishly*]. Can't you look for it in the mornin' ?

Davoren. It's addressed to the Irish Republican Army, and, considering the possibility of a raid, it would be safer to get rid of it.

[*Shots again heard out in the lane, followed by loud shouts of Halt, halt, halt !*

Grigson. I think we had better be gettin' to bed, Debby ; it's not right to be keepin' Mr. Davoren an' Mr. Shields awake.

Seumas. An' what made them give you such a letter as that ; don't they know the state the country is in ? An' you were worse to take it. Have you got it ?

Davoren. I can't find it anywhere ; isn't this terrible !

Grigson. Good-night, Mr. Davoren ; good-night, Mr. Shields.

Mrs. Grigson. Good-night, Mr. Shields ; good-night, Mr. Davoren.

[*They go out. Seumas and Davoren are too much concerned about the letter to respond to their good-nights.*

Seumas. What were you thinkin' of when you took such a

letter as that ? Ye gods, has nobody any brains at all, at all ? Oh, this is a hopeless country. Did you try in your pockets ?

Davoren [*searching in his pockets*]. Oh, thanks be to God, here it is.

Seumas. Burn it now, an', for God's sake, don't take any letters like that again. . . . There's the motor goin' away ; we can sleep in peace now for the rest of the night. Just to make sure of everything now, have a look in that bag o' Maguire's : not that there can be anything in it.

Davoren. If there's nothing in it, what's the good of looking ?

Seumas. It won't kill you to look, will it ?

[*Davoren goes over to the bag, puts it on the table, opens it, and jumps back, his face pale and his limbs trembling.*

Davoren. My God, it's full of bombs, Mills bombs !

Seumas. Holy Mother of God, you're jokin' !

Davoren. If the Tans come you'll find whether I'm jokin' or no.

Seumas. Isn't this a nice pickle to be in ? St. Anthony, look down on us !

Davoren. There's no use of blaming St. Anthony ; why did you let Maguire leave the bag here ?

Seumas. Why did I let him leave the bag here ; why did I let him leave the bag here ! How did I know what was in it ? Didn't I think there was nothin' in it but spoons an' hairpins ? What'll we do now ; what'll we do now ? Mother o' God, grant there'll be no raid to-night. I knew things ud go wrong when I missed Mass this mornin'.

Davoren. Give over your praying and let us try to think of what is best to be done. There's one thing certain : as soon as morning comes I'm on the run out of this house.

Seumas. Thinkin' of yourself, like the rest of them. Leavin' me to bear the brunt of it.

Davoren. And why shouldn't you bear the brunt of it ? Maguire was no friend of mine ; besides, it's your fault ; you knew the sort of a man he was, and you should have been on your guard.

Seumas. Did I know he was a gunman ; did I know he was a gunman ; did I know he was a gunman ? Did . . .

Davoren. Do you mean to tell me that . . .

Seumas. Just a moment . . .

Davoren. You didn't know . . .

Seumas. Just a moment . . .

Davoren. That Maguire was connected with . . .

Seumas [*loudly*]. Just a moment ; can't . . .

Davoren. The Republican Movement ? What's the use of trying to tell damn lies !

[*Minnie Powell rushes into the room. She is only partly dressed, and has thrown a shawl over her shoulders. She is in a state of intense excitement.*

Minnie. Mr. Davoren, Donal, they're all round the house ; they must be goin' to raid the place ; I was

lookin' out of the window an' I seen them; I do be
on the watch every night; have you anything? If you
have . . .

> [*There is heard at street door a violent and continuous
> knocking, followed by the crash of glass and the beating of
> the door with rifle butts.*

Minnie. There they are, there they are, there they **are** !

> [*Davoren reclines almost fainting on the bed; Seumas sits
> up in an attitude of agonized prayerfulness; Minnie alone
> retains her presence of mind. When she sees their panic
> she becomes calm, though her words are rapidly spoken,
> and her actions are performed with decisive celerity.*

Minnie. What is it; what have you got; where are
they ?

Davoren. Bombs, bombs, bombs; my God! in the bag
on the table there; we're done, we're done !

Seumas. Hail, Mary, full of grace — pray for us miserable
sinners — Holy St. Anthony, do you hear them
batterin' at the door — now an' at the hour of our
death — say an act of contrition, Donal — there's the
glass gone !

Minnie. I'll take them to my room; maybe they won't
search it; if they do aself, they won't harm a girl.
Good-bye . . . Donal.

> [*She glances lovingly at Donal — who is only semi-
> conscious — as she rushes out with the bag.*

Seumas. If we come through this I'll never miss a Mass
again ! If it's the Tommies it won't be so bad, but if
it's the Tans, we're goin' to have a terrible time.

> [*The street door is broken open and heavy steps are heard
> in the hall, punctuated with shouts of " 'Old the light*

> *'ere "*, *" Put 'em up "*, *etc. An Auxiliary opens the*
> *door of the room and enters, revolver in one hand and*
> *electric torch in the other.   His uniform is black, and he*
> *wears a black beret.*

The Auxiliary. 'Oo's 'ere ?

Seumas [as if he didn't know]. Who — who's that ?

The Auxiliary [peremptorily]. 'Oo's 'ere ?

Seumas. Only two men, mister ; me an' me mate in
t'other bed.

The Auxiliary. Why didn't you open the door ?

Seumas. We didn't hear you knockin', sir.

The Auxiliary. You must be a little awd of 'earing, ay ?

Seumas. I had rheumatic fever a few years ago, an' ever
since I do be a — I do be a little deaf sometimes.

The Auxiliary [to Davoren]. 'Ow is it you're not in bed ?

Davoren. I was in bed ; when I heard the knockin' I got
up to open the door.

The Auxiliary. You're a koind blowke, you are.   De-
loighted, like, to have a visit from us, ay ?   Ay ?
[Threatening to strike him] Why down't you answer ?

Davoren. Yes, sir.

The Auxiliary. What's your name ?

Davoren. Davoren, Dan Davoren, sir.

The Auxiliary. You're not an Irishman, are you ?

Davoren. I-I-I was born in Ireland.

The Auxiliary. Ow, you were, were you ; Irish han'
proud of it, ay ? *[To Seumas]* What's *your* name ?

Seumas. Seuma . . . Oh no ; Jimmie Shields, sir.

The Auxiliary. Ow, you're a selt [*he means a Celt*], one of the seltic race that speaks a lingo of its ahn, and that's going to overthrow the British Empire — I don't think ! 'Ere, where's your gun ?

Seumas. I never had a gun in me hand in me life.

The Auxiliary. Now ; you wouldn't know what a gun is if you sawr one, I suppowse. [*Displaying his revolver in a careless way*] 'Ere, what's that ?

Seumas. Oh, be careful, please, be careful.

The Auxiliary. Why, what 'ave I got to be careful abaht ?

Seumas. The gun ; it-it-it might go off.

The Auxiliary. An' what prawse if it did ; it can easily be relowded. Any ammunition 'ere ? What's in that press ?   [*He searches and scatters contents of press.*

Seumas. Only a little bit o' grub ; you'll get nothin' here, sir ; no one in the house has any connection with politics.

The Auxiliary. Now ? I've never met a man yet that didn't say that, but we're a little bit too ikey now to be kidded with that sort of talk.

Seumas. May I go an' get a drink o' water ?

The Auxiliary. You'll want a barrel of watah before you're done with us. [*The Auxiliary goes about the room examining places*] 'Ello, what's 'ere ? A statue o' Christ ! An' a Crucifix ! You'd think you was in a bloomin' monastery.
    [*Mrs. Grigson enters, dressed disorderly and her hair awry.*

Mrs. Grigson. They're turning the place upside-down. Upstairs an' downstairs they're makin' a litter of everything ! I declare to God, it's awful what law-abidin' people have to put up with. An' they found a pint bottle of whisky under Dolphie's pillow, an' they're drinkin' every drop of it — an' Dolphie 'll be like a devil in the mornin' when he finds he has no curer.

The Auxiliary [*all attention when he hears the word whisky*]. A bottle of whisky, ay ? 'Ere, where do you live — quick, where do you live ?

Mrs. Grigson. Down in the kitchen — an' when you go down will you ask them not to drink — oh, he's gone without listenin' to me.
      [*While Mrs. Grigson is speaking the Auxiliary rushes out.*

Seumas [*anxiously to Mrs. Grigson*]. Are they searchin' the whole house, Mrs. Grigson ?

Mrs. Grigson. They didn't leave a thing in the kitchen that they didn't flitter about the floor ; the things in the cupboard, all the little odds an' ends that I keep in the big box, an . . .

Seumas. Oh, they're a terrible gang of blaguards — did they go upstairs ? — they'd hardly search Minnie Powell's room — do you think would they, Mrs. Grigson ?

Mrs. Grigson. Just to show them the sort of a man he was, before they come in, Dolphie put the big Bible on the table, open at the First Gospel of St. Peter, second chapter, an' marked the thirteenth to the seventeenth verse in red ink — you know the passages, Mr. Shields — [*quoting*] :

"Submit yourselves to every ordinance of man for the Lord's sake : whether it be to the king, as supreme ; or unto governors, as unto them that are sent by him for the punishment of evildoers, an' for the praise of them that do well. . . . Love the brotherhood. Fear God. Honour the King."

An' what do you think they did, Mr. Shields ? They caught a hold of the Bible an' flung it on the floor — imagine that, Mr. Shields — flingin' the Bible on the floor ! Then one of them says to another — " Jack," says he, " have you seen the light ; is your soul saved ? " An' then they grabbed hold of poor Dolphie, callin' him Mr. Moody an' Mr. Sankey, an' wanted him to offer up a prayer for the Irish Republic ! An' when they were puttin' me out, there they had the poor man sittin' up in bed, his hands crossed on his breast, his eyes lookin' up at the ceilin', an' he singin' a hymn — " We shall meet in the Sweet Bye an' Bye " — an' all the time, Mr. Shields, there they were drinkin' his whisky ; there's torture for you, an' they all laughin' at poor Dolphie's terrible sufferins.

Davoren. In the name of all that's sensible, what did he want to bring whisky home with him for ? They're bad enough sober, what'll they be like when they're drunk ?

Mrs. Grigson [*plaintively*]. He always brings a drop home with him — he calls it his medicine.

Seumas [*still anxious*]. They'll hardly search all the house ; do you think they will, Mrs. Grigson ?

Mrs. Grigson. An' we have a picture over the mantelpiece of King William crossing the Boyne, an' do you know what they wanted to make out, Mr. Shields, that it was Robert Emmet, an' the picture of a sacret society !

Seumas. She's not listenin' to a word I'm sayin'! Oh, the country is hopeless an' the people is hopeless.

Davoren. For God's sake tell her to go to hell out of this — she's worse than the Auxsie.

Seumas [*thoughtfully*]. Let her stay where she is; it's safer to have a woman in the room. If they come across the bombs I hope to God Minnie 'll say nothin'.

Davoren. We're a pair of pitiable cowards to let poor Minnie suffer when we know that we and not she are to blame.

Seumas. What else can we do, man? Do you want us to be done in? If you're anxious to be riddled, I'm not. Besides, they won't harm her, she's only a girl, an' so long as she keeps her mouth shut it'll be all right.

Davoren. I wish I could be sure of that.

Seumas. D'ye think are they goin', Mrs. Grigson? What are they doin' now?

Mrs. Grigson [*who is standing at the door, looking out into the hall*]. There's not a bit of me that's not shakin' like a jelly!

Seumas. Are they gone upstairs, Mrs. Grigson? Do you think, Mrs. Grigson, will they soon be goin'?

Mrs. Grigson. When they were makin' poor Dolphie sit up in the bed, I 'clare to God I thought every minute I'd hear their guns goin' off, an' see poor Dolphie stretched out dead in the bed— whisht, God bless us, I think I hear him moanin'!

Seumas. You might as well be talking to a stone ! They're all hopeless, hopeless, hopeless ! She thinks she hears him moanin' ! It's bloody near time somebody made him moan !

Davoren [*with a sickly attempt at humour*]. He's moaning for the loss of his whisky.

[*During the foregoing dialogue the various sounds of a raid — orders, the tramping of heavy feet, the pulling about of furniture, etc., are heard. Now a more definite and sustained commotion is apparent. Loud and angry commands of " Go on ", " Get out and get into the lorry ", are heard, mingled with a girl's voice — it is Minnie's — shouting bravely, but a little hysterically, " Up the Republic ".*]

Mrs. Grigson [*from the door*]. God save us, they're takin' Minnie, they're takin' Minnie Powell ! [*Running out*] What in the name of God can have happened ?

Seumas. Holy Saint Anthony grant that she'll keep her mouth shut.

Davoren [*sitting down on the bed and covering his face with his hands*]. We'll never again be able to lift up our heads if anything happens to Minnie.

Seumas. For God's sake keep quiet or somebody'll hear you ; nothin'll happen to her, nothin' at all — it'll be all right if she only keeps her mouth shut.

Mrs. Grigson [*running in*]. They're after gettin' a whole lot of stuff in Minnie's room ! Enough to blow up the whole street, a Tan says ! God to-night, who'd have ever thought that of Minnie Powell !

Seumas. Did she say anything, is she sayin' anything, what's she sayin', Mrs. Grigson ?

Mrs. Grigson. She's shoutin' " Up the Republic " at the top of her voice. An' big Mrs. Henderson is fightin' with the soldiers — she's after nearly knockin' one of them down, an' they're puttin' her into the lorry too.

Seumas. God blast her ! Can she not mind her own business ? What does she want here — didn't she know there was a raid on ? Is the whole damn country goin' mad ? They'll open fire in a minute an' innocent people'll be shot !

Davoren. What way are they using Minnie, Mrs. Grigson ; are they rough with her ?

Mrs. Grigson. They couldn't be half rough enough ; the little hussy, to be so deceitful ; she might as well have had the house blew up ! God to-night, who'd think it was in Minnie Powell !

Seumas. Oh, grant she won't say anything !

Mrs. Grigson. There they're goin' away now ; ah, then I hope they'll give that Minnie Powell a coolin'.

Seumas. God grant she won't say anything ! Are they gone, Mrs. Grigson ?

Mrs. Grigson. With her fancy stockins, an' her pom-poms, an' her crêpe de chine blouses ! I knew she'd come to no good !

Seumas. God grant she'll keep her mouth shut! Are they gone, Mrs. Grigson ?

Mrs. Grigson. They're gone, Mr. Shields, an' here's poor Dolphie an' not a feather astray on him. Oh, Dolphie, dear, you're all right, thanks to God; I thought you'd never see the mornin'.

Grigson [*entering without coat or vest*]. Of course I'm all right; what ud put a bother on Dolphie Grigson? — not the Tans anyway!

Mrs. Grigson. When I seen you stretched out on the bed, an' you . . . singin' a hymn . . .

Grigson [*fearful of possible humiliation*]. Who was singin' a hymn? D'ye hear me talkin' to you — where did you hear me singin' a hymn?

Mrs. Grigson. I was only jokin', Dolphie, dear; I . . .

Grigson. Your place is below, an' not gosterin' here to men; down with you quick!

[*Mrs. Grigson hurriedly leaves the room.*

Grigson [*nonchalantly taking out his pipe, filling it, lighting it, and beginning to smoke*]. Excitin' few moments, Mr. Davoren; Mrs. G. lost her head completely — panic-stricken. But that's only natural, all women is very nervous. The only thing to do is to show them that they can't put the wind up you; show the least sign of fright an' they'd walk on you, simply walk on you. Two of them come down — "Put them up", revolvers under your nose — you know, the usual way. "What's all the bother about?" says I, quite calm. "No bother at all," says one of them, "only this gun might go off an' hit somebody — have you me?" says he. "What if it does," says I, "a man can only die once, an' you'll find Grigson won't squeal." "God, you're a cool one," says the other, "there's no blottin' it out."

Seumas. That's the best way to take them ; it only makes things worse to show that you've got the wind up. " Any ammunition here ? " says the fellow that come in here. " I don't think so," says I, " but you better have a look." " No back talk," says he, " or you might get plugged." " I don't know of any clause," says I, " in the British Constitution that makes it a crime for a man to speak in his own room," — with that, he just had a look round, an' off he went.

Grigson. If a man keeps a stiff upper front — Merciful God, there's an ambush !

[*Explosions of two bursting bombs are heard on the street outside the house, followed by fierce and rapid revolver and rifle fire. People are heard rushing into the hall, and there is general clamour and confusion. Seumas and Davoren cower down in the room ; Grigson, after a few moments' hesitation, frankly rushes out of the room to what he conceives to be the safer asylum of the kitchen. A lull follows, punctuated by an odd rifle-shot ; then comes a peculiar and ominous stillness, broken in a few moments by the sounds of voices and movement. Questions are heard being asked : " Who was it was killed ? " " Where was she shot ?" which are answered by: "Minnie Powell " ; " She went to jump off the lorry an' she was shot"; " She's not dead, is she ? " ; " They say she's dead — shot through the buzzom ! "*

Davoren [*in a tone of horror-stricken doubt*]. D'ye hear what they're sayin', Shields, d'ye hear what they're sayin' ? — Minnie Powell is shot.

Seumas. For God's sake speak easy, an' don't bring them in here on top of us again.

Davoren. Is that all you're thinking of? Do you realize that she has been shot to save us?

Seumas. Is it my fault; am I to blame?

Davoren. It is your fault and mine, both; oh, we're a pair of dastardly cowards to have let her do what she did.

Seumas. She did it off her own bat — we didn't ask her to do it.

[*Mrs. Grigson enters. She is excited and semi-hysterical, and sincerely affected by the tragic occurrence.*

Mrs. Grigson [*falling down in a sitting posture on one of the beds*]. What's goin' to happen next.! Oh, Mr. Davoren, isn't it terrible, isn't it terrible! Minnie Powell, poor little Minnie Powell's been shot dead! They were raidin' a house a few doors down, an' had just got up in their lorries to go away, when they was ambushed. You never heard such shootin'! An' in the thick of it, poor Minnie went to jump off the lorry she was on, an' she was shot through the buzzom. Oh, it was horrible to see the blood pourin' out, an' Minnie moanin'. They found some paper in her breast, with " Minnie " written on it, an' some other name they couldn't make out with the blood; the officer kep' it. The ambulance is bringin' her to the hospital, but what good's that when she's dead! Poor little Minnie, poor little Minnie Powell, to think of you full of life a few minutes ago, an' now she's dead!

Davoren. Ah me, alas! Pain, pain, pain ever, for ever! It's terrible to think that little Minnie is dead, but it's still more terrible to think that Davoren and Shields are alive! Oh, Donal Davoren, shame is your

portion now till the silver cord is loosened and the
golden bowl be broken.   Oh, Davoren, Donal Davoren,
poet and poltroon, poltroon and poet !

Seumas [*solemnly*]. I knew something ud come of the
tappin' on the wall !

CURTAIN

THE PLOUGH AND THE STARS

A Tragedy in Four Acts

TO THE GAY LAUGH OF MY MOTHER
AT THE GATE OF THE GRAVE

CHARACTERS IN THE PLAY

JACK CLITHEROE (*a bricklayer*), *Commandant in the Irish Citizen Army*
NORA CLITHEROE, *his wife*
PETER FLYNN (*a labourer*), *Nora's uncle*
THE YOUNG COVEY (*a fitter*), *Clitheroe's cousin*
BESSIE BURGESS (*a street fruit-vendor*)
MRS. GOGAN (*a charwoman*)
MOLLSER, *her consumptive child*
FLUTHER GOOD (*a carpenter*)

} *Residents in the Tenement*

LIEUT. LANGON (*a Civil Servant*), *of the Irish Volunteers*
CAPT. BRENNAN (*a chicken butcher*), *of the Irish Citizen Army*
CORPORAL STODDART, *of the Wiltshires*
SERGEANT TINLEY, *of the Wiltshires*
ROSIE REDMOND, *a daughter of " the Digs "*
A BAR-TENDER
A WOMAN
THE FIGURE IN THE WINDOW

———

ACT   I.—The living-room of the Clitheroe flat in a Dublin tenement.
ACT. II.—A public-house, outside of which a meeting is being held.
ACT III.—The street outside the Clitheroe tenement.
ACT IV.—The room of Bessie Burgess.

———

TIME.—Acts I and II, November 1915 ; Acts III and IV, Easter Week, 1916. A few days elapse between Acts III and IV.

ACT I

The home of the Clitheroes. It consists of the front and back drawing-rooms in a fine old Georgian house, struggling for its life against the assaults of time, and the more savage assaults of the tenants. The room shown is the back drawing-room, wide, spacious, and lofty. At back is the entrance to the front drawing-room. The space, originally occupied by folding doors, is now draped with casement cloth of a dark purple, decorated with a design in reddish-purple and cream. One of the curtains is pulled aside, giving a glimpse of front drawing-room, at the end of which can be seen the wide, lofty windows looking out into the street. The room directly in front of the audience is furnished in a way that suggests an attempt towards a finer expression of domestic life. The large fireplace on right is of wood, painted to look like marble (the original has been taken away by the landlord). On the mantelshelf are two candlesticks of dark carved wood. Between them is a small clock. Over the clock is hanging a calendar which displays a picture of " The Sleeping Venus". In the centre of the breast of the chimney hangs a picture of Robert Emmet. On the right of the entrance to the front drawing-room is a copy of " The Gleaners", on the opposite side a copy of " The Angelus". Underneath " The Gleaners" is a chest of drawers on which stands a green bowl filled with scarlet dahlias and white chrysanthemums. Near to the fireplace is a settee which at night forms a double bed for Clitheroe and Nora. Underneath " The Angelus" are a number of shelves containing saucepans and a frying-pan. Under these is a table on which are various articles of delf ware. Near the end of the room, opposite to the fireplace is a gate-legged table, covered with a cloth. On top of the table a huge cavalry sword is lying. To the right is a door which leads to a lobby

*from which the staircase leads to the hall. The floor is covered
with a dark green linoleum. The room is dim except where it is
illuminated from the glow of the fire. Through the window of
the room at back can be seen the flaring of the flame of a gasolene
lamp giving light to workmen repairing the street. Occasionally
can be heard the clang of crowbars striking the setts. Fluther
Good is repairing the lock of door, Right. A claw-hammer is
on a chair beside him, and he has a screw-driver in his hand. He
is a man of forty years of age, rarely surrendering to thoughts
of anxiety, fond of his " oil " but determined to conquer the
habit before he dies. He is square-jawed and harshly featured ;
under the left eye is a scar, and his nose is bent from a smashing
blow received in a fistic battle long ago. He is bald, save for a
few peeping tufts of reddish hair around his ears ; and his upper
lip is hidden by a scrubby red moustache, embroidered here and
there with a grey hair. He is dressed in a seedy black suit, cotton
shirt with a soft collar, and wears a very respectable little black
bow. On his head is a faded jerry hat, which, when he is excited,
he has a habit of knocking farther back on his head, in a series
of taps. In an argument he usually fills with sound and fury
generally signifying a row. He is in his shirt-sleeves at present,
and wears a soiled white apron, from a pocket in which sticks a
carpenter's two-foot rule. He has just finished the job of putting
on a new lock, and, filled with satisfaction, he is opening and
shutting the door, enjoying the completion of a work well done.
Sitting at the fire, airing a white shirt, is Peter Flynn. He is a
little, thin bit of a man, with a face shaped like a lozenge ; on
his cheeks and under his chin is a straggling wiry beard of a dirty-
white and lemon hue. His face invariably wears a look of
animated anguish, mixed with irritated defiance, as if everybody
was at war with him, and he at war with everybody. He is
cocking his head in a way that suggests resentment at the presence
of Fluther, who pays no attention to him, apparently, but is
really furtively watching him. Peter is clad in a singlet, white*

whipcord knee-breeches, and is in his stocking-feet.

A voice is heard speaking outside of door, Left [it is that of Mrs. Gogan].

Mrs. Gogan [*outside*]. Who are you lookin' for, sir ? Who ?
   Mrs. Clitheroe ? . . . Oh, excuse me. Oh ay, up
   this way. She's out, I think : I seen her goin'. Oh,
   you've somethin' for her ; oh, excuse me. You're
   from Arnott's. . . . I see. . . . You've a parcel for
   her. . . . Righto. . . . I'll take it. . . . I'll give it
   to her the minute she comes in. . . . It'll be quite
   safe. . . . Oh, sign that. . . . Excuse me. . . .
   Where ? . . . Here ? . . . No, there ; righto. Am
   I to put Maggie or Mrs. ? What is it ? You dunno ?
   Oh, excuse me.

   [*Mrs. Gogan opens the door and comes in. She is a doleful-
   looking little woman of forty, insinuating manner and
   sallow complexion. She is fidgety and nervous, terribly
   talkative, has a habit of taking up things that may be
   near her and fiddling with them while she is speaking. Her
   heart is aflame with curiosity, and a fly could not come
   into nor go out of the house without her knowing. She
   has a draper's parcel in her hand, the knot of the twine
   tying it is untied. Peter, more resentful of this intrusion
   than of Fluther's presence, gets up from the chair, and
   without looking around, his head carried at an angry
   cock, marches into the room at back.*

Mrs. Gogan [*removing the paper and opening the cardboard box
   it contains*]. I wondher what's that now ? A hat ! [*She
   takes out a hat, black, with decorations in red and gold.*] God,
   she's goin' to th' divil lately for style ! That hat,
   now, cost more than a penny. Such notions of upper-
   osity she's gettin'. [*Putting the hat on her head*] Oh,
   swank, what !   [*She replaces it in parcel.*

F*

Fluther. She's a pretty little Judy, all the same.

Mrs. Gogan. Ah, she is, an' she isn't. There's prettiness an' prettiness in it. I'm always sayin' that her skirts are a little too short for a married woman. An' to see her, sometimes of an evenin', in her glad-neck gown would make a body's blood run cold. I do be ashamed of me life before her husband. An' th' way she thries to be polite, with her " Good mornin', Mrs. Gogan," when she's goin' down, an' her " Good evenin', Mrs. Gogan," when she's comin' up. But there's politeness an' politeness in it.

Fluther. They seem to get on well together, all th' same.

Mrs. Gogan. Ah, they do, an' they don't. The pair o' them used to be like two turtle doves always billin' an' cooin'. You couldn't come into th' room but you'd feel, instinctive like, that they'd just been afther kissin' an' cuddlin' each other. . . . It often made me shiver, for, afther all, there's kissin' an' cuddlin' in it. But I'm thinkin' he's beginnin' to take things more quietly ; the mysthery of havin' a woman's a mysthery no longer. . . . She dhresses herself to keep him with her, but it's no use — afther a month or two, th' wondher of a woman wears off.

Fluther. I dunno, I dunno. Not wishin' to say anything derogatory, I think it's all a question of location : when a man finds th' wondher of one woman beginnin' to die, it's usually beginnin' to live in another.

Mrs. Gogan. She's always grumblin' about havin' to live in a tenement house. " I wouldn't like to spend me last hour in one, let alone live me life in a tenement," says she. " Vaults," says she, " that are hidin' th'

dead, instead of homes that are sheltherin' th' livin'."
" Many a good one," says I, " was reared in a tenement
house." Oh, you know, she's a well-up little lassie,
too ; able to make a shillin' go where another would
have to spend a pound. She's wipin' th' eyes of th'
Covey an' poor oul' Pether — everybody knows that
— screwin' every penny she can out o' them, in ordher
to turn th' place into a babby-house. An' she has
th' life frightened out o' them ; washin' their face,
combin' their hair, wipin' their feet, brushin' their
clothes, thrimmin' their nails, cleanin' their teeth —
God Almighty, you'd think th' poor men were undher-
goin' penal servitude.

Fluther [*with an exclamation of disgust*]. A-a-ah, that's
goin' beyond th' beyonds in a tenement house. That's
a little bit too derogatory.

[*Peter enters from room, Back, head elevated and resentful
fire in his eyes ; he is still in his singlet and trousers,
but is now wearing a pair of unlaced boots — possibly
to be decent in the presence of Mrs. Gogan. He places
the white shirt, which he has carried in on his arm, on
the back of a chair near the fire, and, going over to the
chest of drawers, he opens drawer after drawer, looking
for something ; as he fails to find it he closes each drawer
with a snap ; he pulls out pieces of linen neatly folded,
and bundles them back again any way.*

Peter [*in accents of anguish*]. Well, God Almighty, give me
patience !

[*He returns to room, Back, giving the shirt a vicious turn
as he passes.*

Mrs. Gogan. I wondher what he is foostherin' for now ?

Fluther. He's adornin' himself for th' meeting to-night.

[*Pulling a handbill from his pocket and reading*] " Great Demonstration an' torchlight procession around places in th' city sacred to th' memory of Irish Patriots, to be concluded be a meetin', at which will be taken an oath of fealty to th' Irish Republic.   Formation in Parnell Square at eight o'clock."   Well, they can hold it for Fluther.   I'm up th' pole ; no more dhrink for Fluther. It's three days now since I touched a dhrop, an' I feel a new man already.

Mrs. Gogan. Isn't oul' Peter a funny-lookin' little man ? . . . Like somethin' you'd pick off a Christmas Tree. . . . When he's dhressed up in his canonicals, you'd wondher where he'd been got.   God forgive me, when I see him in them, I always think he must ha' had a Mormon for a father !   He an' th' Covey can't abide each other ; th' pair o' them is always at it, thryin' to best each other.   There'll be blood dhrawn one o' these days.

Fluther. How is it that Clitheroe himself, now, doesn't have anythin' to do with th' Citizen Army ?   A couple o' months ago, an' you'd hardly ever see him without his gun, an' th' Red Hand o' Liberty Hall in his hat.

Mrs. Gogan. Just because he wasn't made a Captain of. He wasn't goin' to be in anything where he couldn't be conspishuous.   He was so cocksure o' being made one that he bought a Sam Browne belt, an' was always puttin' it on an' standin' at th' door showing it off, till th' man came an' put out th' street lamps on him.   God, I think he used to bring it to bed with him !   But I'm tellin' you herself was delighted that that cock didn't crow, for she's like a clockin' hen if he leaves her sight for a minute.

[*While she is talking, she takes up book after book from the table, looks into each of them in a near-sighted way, and then leaves them back. She now lifts up the sword, and proceeds to examine it.*

Mrs. Gogan. Be th' look of it, this must ha' been a general's sword. . . . All th' gold lace an' th' fine figaries on it. . . . Sure it's twiced too big for him.

Fluther. A-ah; it's a baby's rattle he ought to have, an' he as he is with thoughts tossin' in his head of what may happen to him on th' day o' judgement.

[*Peter has entered, and seeing Mrs. Gogan with the sword, goes over to her, pulls it resentfully out of her hands, and marches into the room, Back, without speaking.*

Mrs. Gogan [*as Peter whips the sword*]. Oh, excuse me ! . . . [*To Fluther*] Isn't he th' surly oul' rascal !

Fluther. Take no notice of him. . . . You'd think he was dumb, but when you get his goat, or he has a few jars up, he's vice versa.   [*He coughs.*

Mrs. Gogan [*she has now sidled over as far as the shirt hanging on the chair*]. Oh, you've got a cold on you, Fluther.

Fluther [*carelessly*]. Ah, it's only a little one.

Mrs. Gogan. You'd want to be careful, all th' same. I knew a woman, a big lump of a woman, red-faced an' round-bodied, a little awkward on her feet ; you'd think, to look at her, she could put out her two arms an' lift a two-storied house on th' top of her head ; got a ticklin' in her throat, an' a little cough, an' the' next mornin' she had a little catchin' in her chest, an' they had just time to wet her lips with a little rum, an' off she went.

[*She begins to look at and handle the shirt.*

Fluther [*a little nervously*]. It's only a little cold I have ; there's nothing derogatory wrong with me.

Mrs. Gogan. I dunno ; there's many a man this minute lowerin' a pint, thinkin' of a woman, or pickin' out a winner, or doin' work as you're doin', while th' hearse dhrawn be th' horses with the black plumes is dhrivin' up to his own hall door, an' a voice that he doesn't hear is muttherin' in his ear, " Earth to earth, an' ashes t' ashes, an' dust to dust."

Fluther [*faintly*]. A man in th' pink o' health should have a holy horror of allowin' thoughts o' death to be festherin' in his mind, for — [*with a frightened cough*] be God, I think I'm after gettin' a little catch in me chest that time — it's a creepy thing to be thinkin' about.

Mrs. Gogan. It is, an' it isn't ; it's both bad an' good. . . . It always gives meself a kind o' thresspassin' joy to feel meself movin' along in a mournin' coach, an' me thinkin' that, maybe, th' next funeral 'll be me own, an' glad, in a quiet way, that this is somebody else's.

Fluther. An' a curious kind of a gaspin' for breath — I hope there's nothin' derogatory wrong with me.

Mrs. Gogan [*examining the shirt*]. Frills on it, like a woman's petticoat.

Fluther. Suddenly gettin' hot, an' then, just as suddenly, gettin' cold.

Mrs. Gogan [*holding out the shirt towards Fluther*]. How would you like to be wearin' this Lord Mayor's night-dhress, Fluther ?

Fluther [*vehemently*]. Blast you an' your nightshirt ! Is a man fermentin' with fear to stick th' showin' off to him of a thing that looks like a shinin' shroud?

Mrs. Gogan. Oh, excuse me!
   [*Peter has again entered, and he pulls the shirt from the hands of Mrs. Gogan, replacing it on the chair. He returns to room.*

Peter [*as he goes out*]. Well, God Almighty, give me patience!

Mrs. Gogan [*to Peter*]. Oh, excuse me!
   [*There is heard a cheer from the men working outside on the street, followed by the clang of tools being thrown down, then silence. The glare of the gasolene light diminishes and finally goes out.*

Mrs. Gogan [*running into the back room to look out of the window*]. What's the men repairin' th' streets cheerin' for?

Fluther [*sitting down weakly on a chair*]. You can't sneeze but that oul' one wants to know th' why an' th' wherefore. . . . I feel as dizzy as bedamned! I hope I didn't give up th' beer too suddenly.
   [*The Covey comes in by door, Right. He is about twenty-five, tall, thin, with lines on his face that form a perpetual protest against life as he conceives it to be. Heavy seams fall from each side of nose, down around his lips, as if they were suspenders keeping his mouth from falling. He speaks in a slow, wailing drawl; more rapidly when he is excited. He is dressed in dungarees, and is wearing a vividly red tie. He flings his cap with a gesture of disgust on the table, and begins to take off his overalls.*

Mrs. Gogan [*to the Covey, as she runs back into the room*].
What's after happenin', Covey ?

The Covey [*with contempt*]. Th' job's stopped. They've
been mobilized to march in th' demonstration to-night
undher th' Plough an' th' Stars. Didn't you hear them
cheerin', th' mugs ! They have to renew their political
baptismal vows to be faithful in seculo seculorum.

Fluther [*forgetting his fear in his indignation*]. There's no
reason to bring religion into it. I think we ought to
have as great a regard for religion as we can, so as to
keep it out of as many things as possible.

The Covey [*pausing in the taking off of his dungarees*]. Oh,
you're one o' the boys that climb into religion as
high as a short Mass on Sunday mornin's ? I suppose
you'll be singin' songs o' Sion an' songs o' Tara at th'
meetin', too.

Fluther. We're all Irishmen, anyhow ; aren't we ?

The Covey [*with hand outstretched, and in a professional tone*].
Look here, comrade, there's no such thing as an Irishman, or an Englishman, or a German or a Turk ;
we're all only human bein's. Scientifically speakin',
it's all a question of the accidental gatherin' together of
mollycewels an' atoms.
  [*Peter comes in with a collar in his hand. He goes over to
  mirror, Left, and proceeds to try to put it on.*

Fluther. Mollycewels an' atoms ! D'ye think I'm goin'
to listen to you thryin' to juggle Fluther's mind with
complicated cunundhrums of mollycewels an' atoms ?

The Covey [*rather loudly*]. There's nothin' complicated in
it. There's no fear o' th' Church tellin' you that

mollycewels is a stickin' together of millions of atoms o' sodium, carbon, potassium o' iodide, etcetera, that, accordin' to th' way they're mixed, make a flower, a fish, a star that you see shinin' in th' sky, or a man with a big brain like me, or a man with a little brain like you !

Fluther [*more loudly still*]. There's no necessity to be raisin' your voice ; shoutin's no manifestin' forth of a growin' mind.

Peter [*struggling with his collar*]. God, give me patience with this thing. . . . She makes these collars as stiff with starch as a shinin' band o' solid steel ! She does it purposely to thry an' twart me. If I can't get it on th' singlet, how, in th' Name o' God, am I goin' to get it on th' shirt ?

The Covey [*loudly*]. There's no use o' arguin' with you ; it's education you want, comrade.

Fluther. The Covey an' God made th' world, I suppose, wha' ?

The Covey. When I hear some men talkin' I'm inclined to disbelieve that th' world's eight-hundhred million years old, for it's not long since th' fathers o' some o' them crawled out o' th' sheltherin' slime o' the sea.

Mrs. Gogan [*from room at back*]. There, they're afther formin' fours, an' now they're goin' to march away.

Fluther [*scornfully*]. Mollycewels ! [*He begins to untie his apron*] What about Adam an' Eve ?

The Covey. Well, what about them ?

Fluther [*fiercely*]. What about them, you ?

The Covey. Adam an' Eve ! Is that as far as you've got ? Are you still thinkin' there was nobody in th' world before Adam an' Eve ? [*Loudly*] Did you ever hear, man, of th' skeleton of th' man o' Java ?

Peter [*casting the collar from him*]. Blast it, blast it, blast it !

Fluther [*viciously folding his apron*]. Ah, you're not goin' to be let tap your rubbidge o' thoughts into th' mind o' Fluther.

The Covey. You're afraid to listen to th' thruth !

Fluther. Who's afraid ?

The Covey. You are !

Fluther. G'way, you wurum !

The Covey. Who's a worum ?

Fluther. You are, or you wouldn't talk th' way you're talkin'.

The Covey. Th' oul', ignorant savage leppin' up in you, when science shows you that th' head of your god is an empty one. Well, I hope you're enjoyin' th' blessin' o' havin' to live be th' sweat of your brow.

Fluther. You'll be kickin' an' yellin' for th' priest yet, me boyo. I'm not goin' to stand silent an' simple listenin' to a thick like you makin' a maddenin' mockery o' God Almighty. It 'ud be a nice derogatory thing on me conscience, an' me dyin', to look back in rememberin' shame of talkin' to a word-weavin' little ignorant yahoo of a red flag Socialist !

Mrs. Gogan [*she has returned to the front room, and has*

wandered around looking at things in general, and is now in front of the fireplace looking at the picture hanging over it. For God's sake, Fluther, dhrop it; there's always th' makin's of a row in th' mention of religion . . . [*Looking at picture*] God bless us, it's a naked woman!

Fluther [*coming over to look at it*]. What's undher it? [*Reading*] "Georgina: The Sleepin' Vennis". Oh, that's a terrible picture; oh, that's a shockin' picture! Oh, th' one that got that taken, she must have been a prime lassie!

Peter [*who also has come over to look, laughing, with his body bent at the waist, and his head slightly tilted back*]. Hee, hee, hee, hee, hee!

Fluther [*indignantly, to Peter*]. What are you hee, hee-in' for? That' a nice thing to be hee, hee-in' at. Where's your morality, man?

Mrs. Gogan. God forgive us, it's not right to be lookin' at it.

Fluther. It's nearly a derogatory thing to be in th' room where it is.

Mrs. Gogan [*giggling hysterically*]. I couldn't stop any longer in th' same room with three men, afther lookin' at it!   [*She goes out.*

[*The Covey, who has divested himself of his dungarees, throws them with a contemptuous motion on top of Peter's white shirt.*

Peter [*plaintively*]. Where are you throwin' them? Are you thryin' to twart an' torment me again?

The Covey. Who's thryin' to twart you?

Peter [*flinging the dungarees violently on the floor*]. You're not goin' to make me lose me temper, me young Covey.

The Covey [*flinging the white shirt on the floor*]. If you're Nora's pet, aself, you're not goin' to get your way in everything.

Peter [*plaintively, with his eyes looking up at the ceiling*]. I'll say nothin'. . . . I'll leave you to th' day when th' all-pitiful, all-merciful, all-lovin' God 'll be handin' you to th' angels to be rievin' an' roastin' you, tearin' an' tormentin' you, burnin' an' blastin' you !

The Covey. Aren't you th' little malignant oul' bastard, you lemon-whiskered oul' swine !

[*Peter runs to the sword, draws it, and makes for the Covey, who dodges him around the table ; Peter has no intention of striking, but the Covey wants to take no chances.*

The Covey [*dodging*]. Fluther, hold him, there. It's a nice thing to have a lunatic like this lashin' around with a lethal weapon !

[*The Covey darts out of the room, Right, slamming the door in the face of Peter.*

Peter [*battering and pulling at the door*]. Lemme out, lemme out ; isn't it a poor thing for a man who wouldn't say a word against his greatest enemy to have to listen to that Covey's twartin' animosities, shovin' poor, patient people into a lashin' out of curses that darken his soul with th' shadow of th' wrath of th' last day !

Fluther. Why d'ye take notice of him ? If he seen you didn't, he'd say nothin' derogatory.

Peter. I'll make him stop his laughin' an' leerin', jibin' an' jeerin' an' scarifyin' people with his corner-boy insinuations ! . . . He's always thryin' to rouse me : if it's not a song, it's a whistle ; if it isn't a whistle, it's a cough.   But you can taunt an' taunt — I'm laughin' at you ; he, hee, hee, hee, hee, heee !

The Covey [*singing through the keyhole*] :

Dear harp o' me counthry, in darkness I found thee,
The dark chain of silence had hung o'er thee long —

Peter [*frantically*]. Jasus, d'ye hear that ? D'ye hear him soundin' forth his divil-souled song o' provocation ?

The Covey [*singing as before*] :

When proudly, me own island harp, I unbound thee,
An' gave all thy chords to light, freedom an' song !

Peter [*battering at door*]. When I get out I'll do for you, I'll do for you, I'll do for you !

The Covey [*through the keyhole*]. Cuckoo-oo !
[*Nora enters by door, Right.   She is a young woman of twenty-two, alert, swift, full of nervous energy, and a little anxious to get on in the world.   The firm lines of her face are considerably opposed by a soft, amorous mouth and gentle eyes.   When her firmness fails her, she persuades with her feminine charm.   She is dressed in a tailor-made costume, and wears around her neck a silver fox fur.*

Nora [*running in and pushing Peter away from the door*]. Oh, can I not turn me back but th' two o' yous are at it like a pair o' fightin' cocks ! Uncle Peter . . . Uncle Peter . . . UNCLE PETER !

Peter [*vociferously*]. Oh, Uncle Peter, Uncle Peter be damned ! D'ye think I'm goin' to give a free pass to

th' young Covey to turn me whole life into a Holy
Manual o' penances an' martyrdoms ?

The Covey [*angrily rushing into the room*]. If you won't
exercise some sort o' conthrol over that Uncle Peter o'
yours, there'll be a funeral, an' it won't be me that'll
be in th' hearse !

Nora [*between Peter and the Covey, to the Covey*]. Are yous
always goin' to be tearin' down th' little bit of respectability that a body's thryin' to build up ?   Am I
always goin' to be havin' to nurse yous into th' hardy
habit o' thryin' to keep up a little bit of appearance ?

The Covey. Why weren't you here to see th' way he run
at me with th' sword ?

Peter. What did you call me a lemon-whiskered oul'
swine for ?

Nora. If th' two o' yous don't thry to make a generous
altheration in your goin's on, an' keep on thryin' t'
inaugurate th' customs o' th' rest o' th' house into
this place, yous can flit into other lodgin's where your
bowsey battlin' 'ill meet, maybe, with an encore.

Peter [*to Nora*]. Would you like to be called a lemon-
whiskered oul' swine ?

Nora. If you attempt to wag that sword of yours at anybody again, it'll have to be taken off you an' put in a
safe place away from babies that don't know th' danger
o' them things.

Peter [*at entrance to room, Back*]. Well, I'm not goin' to let
anybody call me a lemon-whiskered oul' swine.

                                                     [*He goes in.*

Fluther [*trying the door*]. Openin' an' shuttin' now with a well-mannered motion, like a door of a select bar in a high-class pub.

Nora [*to the Covey, as she lays table for tea*]. An', once for all, Willie, you'll have to thry to deliver yourself from th' desire of provokin' oul' Pether into a wild forgetfulness of what's proper an' allowable in a respectable home.

The Covey. Well, let him mind his own business, then. Yestherday, I caught him hee-hee-in' out of him an' he readin' bits out of Jenersky's *Thesis on th' Origin, Development, an' Consolidation of th' Evolutionary Idea of th' Proletariat.*

Nora. Now, let it end at that, for God's sake ; Jack 'll be in any minute, an' I'm not goin' to have th' quiet of his evenin' tossed about in an everlastin' uproar between you an' Uncle Pether. [*To Fluther*] Well, did you manage to settle th' lock, yet, Mr. Good ?

Fluther [*opening and shutting door*]. It's betther than a new one, now, Mrs. Clitheroe ; it's almost ready to open and shut of its own accord.

Nora [*giving him a coin*]. You're a whole man.   How many pints will that get you ?

Fluther [*seriously*]. Ne'er a one at all, Mrs. Clitheroe, for Fluther's on th' wather waggon now.   You could stan' where you're stannin' chantin', "Have a glass o' malt, Fluther ; Fluther, have a glass o' malt," till th' bells would be ringin' th' ould year out an' th' New Year in, an' you'd have as much chance o' movin' Fluther as a tune on a tin whistle would move a deaf man an' he dead.

[*As Nora is opening and shutting door, Mrs. Bessie Burgess appears at it. She is a woman of forty, vigorously built. Her face is a dogged one, hardened by toil, and a little coarsened by drink. She looks scornfully and viciously at Nora for a few moments before she speaks.*]

Bessie. Puttin' a new lock on her door . . . afraid her poor neighbours ud break through an' steal. . . . [*In a loud tone*] Maybe, now, they're a damn sight more honest than your ladyship . . . checkin' th' children playin' on th' stairs . . . gettin' on th' nerves of your ladyship. . . . Complainin' about Bessie Burgess singin' her hymns at night, when she has a few up. . . . [*She comes in half-way on the threshold, and screams*] Bessie Burgess 'll sing whenever she damn well likes !
[*Nora tries to shut door, but Bessie violently shoves it in, and, gripping Nora by the shoulders, shakes her.*]

Bessie. You little over-dressed throllope, you, for one pin I'd paste th' white face o' you !

Nora [*frightened*]. Fluther, Fluther !

Fluther [*running over and breaking the hold of Bessie from Nora*]. Now, now, Bessie, Bessie, leave poor Mrs. Clitheroe alone ; she'd do no one any harm, an' minds no one's business but her own.

Bessie. Why is she always thryin' to speak proud things, an' lookin' like a mighty one in th' congregation o' th' people !
[*Nora sinks frightened on to the couch as Jack Clitheroe enters. He is a tall, well-made fellow of twenty-five. His face has none of the strength of Nora's. It is a face in which is the desire for authority, without the power to attain it.*]

Clitheroe [*excitedly*]. What's up ? what's afther happenin' ?

Fluther. Nothin', Jack. Nothin'. It's all over now. Come on, Bessie, come on.

Clitheroe [*to Nora*]. What's wrong, Nora ? Did she say anything to you ?

Nora. She was bargin' out of her, an' I only told her to g'up ower o' that to her own place ; an' before I knew where I was, she flew at me like a tiger, an' thried to guzzle me !

Clitheroe [*going to door and speaking to Bessie*]. Get up to your own place, Mrs. Burgess, and don't you be interferin' with my wife, or it'll be th' worse for you. . . . Go on, go on !

Bessie [*as Clitheroe is pushing her out*]. Mind who you're pushin', now. . . . I attend me place o' worship, anyhow . . . not like some o' them that go to neither church, chapel nor meetin'-house. . . . If me son was home from th' threnches he'd see me righted.

[*Bessie and Fluther depart, and Clitheroe closes the door.*

Clitheroe [*going over to Nora, and putting his arm round her*]. There, don't mind that old bitch, Nora, darling ; I'll soon put a stop to her interferin'.

Nora. Some day or another, when I'm here be meself, she'll come in an' do somethin' desperate.

Clitheroe [*kissing her*]. Oh, sorra fear of her doin' anythin' desperate. I'll talk to her to-morrow when she's sober. A taste o' me mind that'll shock her into the sensibility of behavin' herself !

[*Nora gets up and settles the table. She sees the dungarees on the floor and stands looking at them, then she turns to the Covey, who is reading Jenersky's " Thesis " at the fire.*

Nora. Willie, is that th' place for your dungarees ?

The Covey [getting up and lifting them from the floor]. Ah, they won't do th' floor any harm, will they ?
> *[He carries them into room, Back.*

Nora [calling]. Uncle Peter, now, Uncle Peter ; tea's ready.
> *[Peter and the Covey come in from room, Back ; they all sit down to tea. Peter is in full dress of the Foresters : green coat, gold braided ; white breeches, top boots, frilled shirt. He carries the slouch hat, with the white ostrich plume, and the sword in his hands. They eat for a few moments in silence, the Covey furtively looking at Peter with scorn in his eyes. Peter knows it and is fidgety.*

The Covey [provokingly]. Another cut o' bread, Uncle Peter ?
> *[Peter maintains a dignified silence.*

Clitheroe. It's sure to be a great meetin' to-night. We ought to go, Nora.

Nora [decisively]. I won't go, Jack ; you can go if you wish.
> *[A pause.*

The Covey. D'ye want th' sugar, Uncle Peter ?

Peter [explosively]. Now, are you goin' to start your thryin' an' your twartin' again ?

Nora. Now, Uncle Peter, you musn't be so touchy ; Willie has only assed you if you wanted th' sugar.

Peter. He doesn't care a damn whether I want th' sugar or no. He's only thryin' to twart me !

Nora [*angrily, to the Covey*]. Can't you let him alone, Willie? If he wants the sugar, let him stretch his hand out an' get it himself!

The Covey [*to Peter*]. Now, if you want the sugar, you can stretch out your hand and get it yourself!

Clitheroe. To-night is th' first chance that Brennan has got of showing himself off since they made a Captain of him — why, God only knows. It'll be a treat to see him swankin' it at th' head of the Citizen Army carryin' th' flag of the Plough an' th' Stars. . . . [*Looking roguishly at Nora*] He was sweet on you, once, Nora?

Nora. He may have been. . . . I never liked him. I always thought he was a bit of a thick.

The Covey. They're bringin' nice disgrace on that banner now.

Clitheroe [*remonstratively*]. How are they bringin' disgrace on it?

The Covey [*snappily*]. Because it's a Labour flag, an' was never meant for politics. . . . What does th' design of th' field plough, bearin' on it th' stars of th' heavenly plough, mean, if it's not Communism? It's a flag that should only be used when we're buildin' th' barricades to fight for a Workers' Republic!

Peter [*with a puff of derision*]. P-phuh.

The Covey [*angrily*]. What are you phuhin' out o' you for? Your mind is th' mind of a mummy. [*Rising*] I betther go an' get a good place to have a look at Ireland's warriors passin' by.

        [*He goes into room, Left, and returns with his cap.*

Nora [*to the Covey*]. Oh, Willie, brush your clothes before you go.

The Covey. Oh, they'll do well enough.

Nora. Go an' brush them ; th' brush is in th' drawer there.

> [*The Covey goes to the drawer, muttering, gets the brush, and starts to brush his clothes.*

The Covey [*singing at Peter, as he does so*] :

> Oh, where's th' slave so lowly,
> Condemn'd to chains unholy,
> Who, could he burst his bonds at first,
> Would pine beneath them slowly ?
>
> We tread th' land that . . . bore us,
> Th' green flag glitters . . . o'er us,
> Th' friends we've tried are by our side,
> An' th' foe we hate . . . before us !

Peter [*leaping to his feet in a whirl of rage*]. Now, I'm tellin' you, me young Covey, once for all, that I'll not stick any longer these tittherin' taunts of yours, rovin' around to sing your slights an' slandhers, reddenin' th' mind of a man to th' thinkin' an' sayin' of things that sicken his soul with sin ! [*Hysterically ; lifting up a cup to fling at the Covey*] Be God, I'll——

Clitheroe [*catching his arm*]. Now then, none o' that, none o' that !

Nora. Uncle Pether, Uncle Pether, UNCLE PETHER !

The Covey [*at the door, about to go out*]. Isn't that th' malignant oul' varmint ! Lookin' like th' illegitimate son of an illegitimate child of a corporal in th' Mexican army !   [*He goes out.*

Peter [*plaintively*]. He's afther leavin' me now in such a state of agitation that I won't be able to do meself justice when I'm marchin' to th' meetin'.

Nora [*jumping up*]. Oh, for God's sake, here, buckle your sword on, and go to your meetin', so that we'll have at least one hour of peace !

[*She proceeds to belt on the sword.*

Clitheroe [*irritably*]. For God's sake hurry him up ou' o' this, Nora.

Peter. Are yous all goin' to thry to start to twart me now ?

Nora [*putting on his plumed hat*]. S-s-sh. Now, your hat's on, your house is thatched ; off you pop !

[*She gently pushes him from her.*

Peter [*going, and turning as he reaches the door*]. Now, if that young Covey——

Nora. Go on, go on. [*He goes.*

[*Clitheroe sits down in the lounge, lights a cigarette, and looks thoughtfully into the fire. Nora takes the things from the table, placing them on the chest of drawers. There is a pause, then she swiftly comes over to him and sits beside him.*

Nora [*softly*]. A penny for them, Jack !

Clitheroe. Me ? Oh, I was thinkin' of nothing.

Nora. You were thinkin' of th' . . . meetin' . . . Jack. When we were courtin' an' I wanted you to go, you'd say, " Oh, to hell with meetin's," an' that you felt lonely in cheerin' crowds when I was absent. An' we weren't a month married when you began that you couldn't keep away from them.

Clitheroe. Oh, that's enough about th' meetin'. It looks
as if you wanted me to go, th' way you're talkin'. You
were always at me to give up th' Citizen Army, an' I
gave it up ; surely that ought to satisfy you.

Nora. Ay, you gave it up — because you got th' sulks
when they didn't make a Captain of you. It wasn't for
my sake, Jack.

Clitheroe. For your sake or no, you're benefitin' by it,
aren't you ? I didn't forget this was your birthday,
did I ? [*He puts his arms around her*] And you liked your
new hat ; didn't you, didn't you ?

                              [*He kisses her rapidly several times.*

Nora [*panting*]. Jack, Jack ; please, Jack ! I thought you
were tired of that sort of thing long ago.

Clitheroe. Well, you're finding out now that I amn't tired
of it yet, anyhow. Mrs. Clitheroe doesn't want to be
kissed, sure she doesn't ? [*He kisses her again*] Little,
little red-lipped Nora !

Nora [*coquettishly removing his arm from around her*]. Oh,
yes, your little, little red-lipped Nora's a sweet little
girl when th' fit seizes you ; but your little, little red-
lipped Nora has to clean your boots every mornin', all
the same.

Clitheroe [*with a movement of irritation*]. Oh, well, if we're
goin' to be snotty !   [*A pause.*

Nora. It's lookin' like as if it was you that was goin' to
be . . . snotty ! Bridlin' up with bittherness, th'
minute a body attempts t'open her mouth.

Clitheroe. Is it any wondher, turnin' a tendher sayin' into
a meanin' o' malice an' spite !

Nora. It's hard for a body to be always keepin' her mind bent on makin' thoughts that'll be no longer than th' length of your own satisfaction.   [*A pause.*

Nora [*standing up*]. If we're goin' to dhribble th' time away sittin' here like a pair o' cranky mummies, I'd be as well sewin' or doin' something about th' place.
   [*She looks appealingly at him for a few moments ; he doesn't speak. She swiftly sits down beside him, and puts her arm around his neck.*

Nora [*imploringly*]. Ah, Jack, don't be so cross !

Clitheroe [*doggedly*]. Cross ? I'm not cross ; I'm not a bit cross. It was yourself started it.

Nora [*coaxingly*]. I didn't mean to say anything out o' the way. You take a body up too quickly, Jack. [*In an ordinary tone as if nothing of an angry nature had been said*] You didn't offer me me evenin' allowance yet.
   [*Clitheroe silently takes out a cigarette for her and himself and lights both.*

Nora [*trying to make conversation*]. How quiet th' house is now ; they must be all out.

Clitheroe [*rather shortly*]. I suppose so.

Nora [*rising from the seat*]. I'm longin' to show you me new hat, to see what you think of it. Would you like to see it ?

Clitheroe. Ah, I don't mind.
   [*Nora suppresses a sharp reply, hesitates for a moment, then gets the hat, puts it on, and stands before Clitheroe.*

Nora. Well, how does Mr. Clitheroe like me new hat ?

Clitheroe. It suits you, Nora, it does right enough.
[*He stands up, puts his hand beneath her chin, and tilts her head up. She looks at him roguishly. He bends down and kisses her.*

Nora. Here, sit down, an' don't let me hear another cross word out of you for th' rest o' the night.
[*They sit down.*

Clitheroe [*with his arms around her*]. Little, little, red-lipped Nora !

Nora [*with a coaxing movement of her body towards him*]. Jack !

Clitheroe [*tightening his arms around her*]. Well ?

Nora. You haven't sung me a song since our honeymoon. Sing me one now, do . . . please, Jack !

Clitheroe. What song ? " Since Maggie Went Away " ?

Nora. Ah, no, Jack, not that ; it's too sad. " When You said You Loved Me."
[*Clearing his throat, Clitheroe thinks for a moment, and then begins to sing. Nora, putting an arm around him, nestles her head on his breast and listens delightedly.*

Clitheroe [*singing verses following to the air of " When You and I were Young, Maggie "*] :

> Th' violets were scenting th' woods, Nora,
>   Displaying their charm to th' bee,
> When I first said I lov'd only you, Nora,
>   An' you said you lov'd only me !
>
> Th' chestnut blooms gleam'd through th' glade,
>   Nora,
>   A robin sang loud from a tree,
> When I first said I lov'd only you, Nora,
>   An' you said you lov'd only me !

Th' golden-rob'd daffodils shone, Nora,
  An' danc'd in th' breeze on th' lea,
When I first said I lov'd only you, Nora,
  An' you said you lov'd only me !

Th' trees, birds, an' bees sang a song, Nora,
  Of happier transports to be,
When I first said I lov'd only you, Nora,
  An' you said you lov'd only me !

> [*Nora kisses him.*
> [*A knock is heard at the door, Right ; a pause as they listen. Nora clings closely to Clitheroe. Another knock, more imperative than the first.*

Clitheroe. I wonder who can that be, now ?

Nora [*a little nervous*]. Take no notice of it, Jack ; they'll go away in a minute. [*Another knock, followed by a voice.*

Voice. Commandant Clitheroe, Commandant Clitheroe, are you there ? A message from General Jim Connolly.

Clitheroe. Damn it, it's Captain Brennan.

Nora [*anxiously*]. Don't mind him, don't mind, Jack. Don't break our happiness. . . . Pretend we're not in. Let us forget everything to-night but our two selves !

Clitheroe [*reassuringly*]. Don't be alarmed, darling ; I'll just see what he wants, an' send him about his business.

Nora [*tremulously*]. No, no. Please, Jack ; don't open it. Please, for your own little Nora's sake !

Clitheroe [*rising to open the door*]. Now don't be silly, Nora.
> [*Clitheroe opens door, and admits a young man in the full uniform of the Irish Citizen Army — green suit ; slouch green hat caught up at one side by a small Red Hand.*

C.P.—I   G

badge ; Sam Browne belt, with a revolver in the holster.
He carries a letter in his hand. When he comes in he
smartly salutes Clitheroe. The young man is Captain
Brennan.

Capt. Brennan [*giving the letter to Clitheroe*]. A dispatch
from General Connolly.

Clitheroe [*reading. While he is doing so, Brennan's eyes are*
fixed on Nora, who droops as she sits on the lounge]. " Commandant Clitheroe is to take command of the eighth
battalion of the I.C.A. which will assemble to proceed
to the meeting at nine o'clock. He is to see that all
units are provided with full equipment ; two days'
rations and fifty rounds of ammunition. At two
o'clock A.M. the army will leave Liberty Hall for a
reconnaissance attack on Dublin Castle. — Com.-Gen.
Connolly."

Clitheroe. I don't understand this. Why does General
Connolly call me Commandant ?

Capt. Brennan. Th' Staff appointed you Commandant,
and th' General agreed with their selection.

Clitheroe. When did this happen ?

Capt. Brennan. A fortnight ago.

Clitheroe. How is it word was never sent to me ?

Capt. Brennan. Word was sent to you. . . . I meself
brought it.

Clitheroe. Who did you give it to, then ?

Capt. Brennan [*after a pause*]. I think I gave it to Mrs.
Clitheroe, there.

Clitheroe. Nora, d'ye hear that ? [*Nora makes no answer.*

Clitheroe [*there is a note of hardness in his voice*]. Nora . . .
Captain Brennan says he brought a letter to me from
General Connolly, and that he gave it to you. . . .
Where is it ? What did you do with it ?

Nora [*running over to him, and pleadingly putting her arms
around him*]. Jack, please, Jack, don't go out to-night an'
I'll tell you ; I'll explain everything. . . . Send him
away, an' stay with your own little red-lipp'd Nora.

Clitheroe [*removing her arms from around him*]. None o' this
nonsense, now ; I want to know what you did with
th' letter ? [*Nora goes slowly to the lounge and sits down.*

Clitheroe [*angrily*]. Why didn't you give me th' letter ?
What did you do with it ? . . . [*He shakes her by the
shoulder*] What did you do with th' letter ?

Nora [*flaming up*]. I burned it, I burned it ! That's what
I did with it ! Is General Connolly an' th' Citizen
Army goin' to be your only care ? Is your home goin'
to be only a place to rest in ? Am I goin' to be only
somethin' to provide merry-makin' at night for you ?
Your vanity'll be th' ruin of you an' me yet. . . .
That's what's movin' you : because they've made an
officer of you, you'll make a glorious cause of what
you're doin', while your little red-lipp'd Nora can go
on sittin' here, makin' a companion of th' loneliness of
th' night !

Clitheroe [*fiercely*]. You burned it, did you ? [*He grips her
arm*] Well, me good lady——

Nora. Let go — you're hurtin' me !

Clitheroe. You deserve to be hurt. . . . Any letter that comes to me for th' future, take care that I get it. . . . D'ye hear — take care that I get it !

> [*He goes to the chest of drawers and takes out a Sam Browne belt, which he puts on, and then puts a revolver in the holster. He puts on his hat, and looks towards Nora. While this dialogue is proceeding, and while Clitheroe prepares himself, Brennan softly whistles " The Soldiers' Song".*

Clitheroe [*at door, about to go out*]. You needn't wait up for me ; if I'm in at all, it won't be before six in th' morning.

Nora [*bitterly*]. I don't care if you never come back !

Clitheroe [*to Capt. Brennan*]. Come along, Ned.

> [*They go out ; there is a pause. Nora pulls the new hat from her head and with a bitter movement flings it to the other end of the room. There is a gentle knock at door, Right, which opens, and Mollser comes into the room. She is about fifteen, but looks to be only about ten, for the ravages of consumption have shrivelled her up. She is pitifully worn, walks feebly, and frequently coughs. She goes over to Nora.*

Mollser [*to Nora*]. Mother's gone to th' meetin', an' I was feelin' terrible lonely, so I come down to see if you'd let me sit with you, thinkin' you mightn't be goin' yourself. . . . I do be terrible afraid I'll die sometime when I'm be meself. . . . I often envy you, Mrs. Clitheroe, seein' th' health you have, an' th' lovely place you have here, an' wondherin' if I'll ever be sthrong enough to be keepin' a home together for a man. Oh, this must be some more o' the Dublin Fusiliers flyin' off to the front.

[*Just before Mollser ceases to speak, there is heard in the distance the music of a brass band playing a regiment to the boat on the way to the front. The tune that is being played is " It's a Long Way to Tipperary" ; as the band comes to the chorus, the regiment is swinging into the street by Nora's house, and the voices of the soldiers can be heard lustily singing the chorus of the song.*

It's a long way to Tipperary, it's a long way to go ;
It's a long way to Tipperary, to th' sweetest girl I know !
Goodbye Piccadilly, farewell Leicester Square.
It's a long, long way to Tipperary, but my heart's right there !

[*Nora and Mollser remain silently listening. As the chorus ends and the music is faint in the distance again, Bessie Burgess appears at door, Right, which Mollser has left open.*

Bessie [*speaking in towards the room*]. There's th' men marchin' out into th' dhread dimness o' danger, while th' lice is crawlin' about feedin' on th' fatness o' the land ! But yous'll not escape from th' arrow that flieth be night, or th' sickness that wasteth be day. . . . An' ladyship an' all, as some o' them may be, they'll be scattered abroad, like th' dust in th' darkness !

[*Bessie goes away ; Nora steals over and quietly shuts the door. She comes back to the lounge and wearily throws herself on it beside Mollser.*

Mollser [*after a pause and a cough*]. Is there anybody goin', Mrs. Clitheroe, with a titther o' sense ?

CURTAIN

Act II

A commodious public-house at the corner of the street in which the meeting is being addressed from Platform No. 1. It is the south corner of the public-house that is visible to the audience. The counter, beginning at Back about one-fourth of the width of the space shown, comes across two-thirds of the length of the stage, and, taking a circular sweep, passes out of sight to Left. On the counter are beer-pulls, glasses, and a carafe. The other three-fourths of the Back is occupied by a tall, wide, two-paned window. Beside this window at the Right is a small, box-like, panelled snug. Next to the snug is a double swing door, the entrance to that particular end of the house. Farther on is a shelf on which customers may rest their drinks. Underneath the windows is a cushioned seat. Behind the counter at Back can be seen the shelves running the whole length of the counter. On these shelves can be seen the end (or the beginning) of rows of bottles. The Barman is seen wiping the part of the counter which is in view. Rosie is standing at the counter toying with what remains of a half of whisky in a wine-glass. She is a sturdy, well-shaped girl of twenty; pretty, and pert in manner. She is wearing a cream blouse, with an obviously suggestive glad neck; a grey tweed dress, brown stockings and shoes. The blouse and most of the dress are hidden by a black shawl. She has no hat, and in her hair is jauntily set a cheap, glittering, jewelled ornament. It is an hour later.

Barman [*wiping counter*]. Nothin' much doin' in your line to-night, Rosie ?

Rosie. Curse o' God on th' haporth, hardly, Tom. There

192

isn't much notice taken of a pretty petticoat of a night like this. . . . They're all in a holy mood. Th' solemn-lookin' dials on th' whole o' them an' they marchin' to th' meetin.' You'd think they were th' glorious company of th' saints, an' th' noble army of martyrs thrampin' through th' sthreets of paradise. They're all thinkin' of higher things than a girl's garthers. . . . It's a tremendous meetin' ; four plat-forms they have — there's one o' them just outside opposite th' window.

Barman. Oh, ay ; sure when th' speaker comes [*motion-ing with his hand*] to th' near end, here, you can see him plain, an' hear nearly everythin' he's spoutin' out of him.

Rosie. It's no joke thrying' to make up fifty-five shillin's a week for your keep an' laundhry, an' then taxin' you a quid for your own room if you bring home a friend for th' night. . . . If I could only put by a couple of quid for a swankier outfit, everythin' in th' garden ud look lovely——

Barman. Whisht, till we hear what he's sayin'.
[*Through the window is silhouetted the figure of a tall man who is speaking to the crowd. The Barman and Rosie look out of the window and listen.*

The Voice of the Man. It is a glorious thing to see arms in the hands of Irishmen. We must accustom ourselves to the thought of arms, we must accustom ourselves to the sight of arms, we must accustom ourselves to the use of arms. . . . Bloodshed is a cleansing and sancti-fying thing, and the nation that regards it as the final horror has lost its manhood. . . . There are many

things more horrible than bloodshed, and slavery is one
of them !

[*The figure moves away towards the Right, and is lost to
sight and hearing.*

Rosie. It's th' sacred thruth, mind you, what that man's
afther sayin'.

Barman. If I was only a little younger, I'd be plungin'
mad into th' middle of it !

Rosie [*who is still looking out of the window*]. Oh, here's the
two gems runnin' over again for their oil !

[*Peter and Fluther enter tumultuously. They are hot, and
full and hasty with the things they have seen and heard.
Emotion is bubbling up in them, so that when they drink,
and when they speak, they drink and speak with the
fullness of emotional passion. Peter leads the way to the
counter.*

Peter [*splutteringly to Barman*]. Two halves . . . [*To
Fluther*] A meetin' like this always makes me feel as
if I could dhrink Loch Erinn dhry !

Fluther. You couldn't feel any way else at a time like
this when th' spirit of a man is pulsin' to be out
fightin' for th' thruth with his feet thremblin' on th'
way, maybe to th' gallows, an' his ears tinglin' with
th' faint, far-away sound of burstin' rifle-shots that'll
maybe whip th' last little shock o' life out of him
that's left lingerin' in his body !

Peter. I felt a burnin' lump in me throat when I heard
th' band playin' " The Soldiers' Song", rememberin'
last hearin' it marchin' in military formation, with th'
people starin' on both sides at us, carryin' with us

th' pride an' resolution o' Dublin to th' grave of Wolfe Tone.

Fluther. Get th' Dublin men goin' an' they'll go on full force for anything that's thryin' to bar them away from what they're wantin', where th' slim thinkin' counthry boyo ud limp away from th' first faintest touch of compromization !

Peter [*hurriedly to the Barman*]. Two more, Tom ! . . . [*To Fluther*] Th' memory of all th' things that was done, an' all th' things that was suffered be th' people, was boomin' in me brain. . . . Every nerve in me body was quiverin' to do somethin' desperate !

Fluther. Jammed as I was in th' crowd, I listened to th' speeches pattherin' on th' people's head, like rain fallin' on th' corn ; every derogatory thought went out o' me mind, an' I said to meself, " You can die now, Fluther, for you've seen th' shadow-dhreams of th' past leppin' to life in th' bodies of livin' men that show, if we were without a titther o' courage for centuries, we're vice versa now ! " Looka here. [*He stretches out his arm under Peter's face and rolls up his sleeve.*] The blood was BOILIN' in me veins !

[*The silhouette of the tall figure again moves into the frame of the window speaking to the people.*

Peter [*unaware, in his enthusiasm, of the speaker's appearance, to Fluther*]. I was burnin' to dhraw me sword, an' wave an' wave it over me——

Fluther [*overwhelming Peter*]. Will you stop your blatherin' for a minute, man, an' let us hear what he's sayin' !

Voice of the Man. Comrade soldiers of the Irish Volunteers and of the Citizen Army, we rejoice in this terrible war. The old heart of the earth needed to be warmed with the red wine of the battlefields. . . . Such august homage was never offered to God as this : the homage of millions of lives given gladly for love of country. And we must be ready to pour out the same red wine in the same glorious sacrifice, for without shedding of blood there is no redemption !

> [*The figure moves out of sight and hearing.*

Fluther [*gulping down the drink that remains in his glass, and rushing out*]. Come on, man ; this is too good to be missed !

> [*Peter finishes his drink less rapidly, and as he is going out wiping his mouth with the back of his hand he runs into the Covey coming in. He immediately erects his body like a young cock, and with his chin thrust forward, and a look of venomous dignity on his face, he marches out.*

The Covey [*at counter*]. Give us a glass o' malt, for God's sake, till I stimulate meself from th' shock o' seein' th' sight that's afther goin' out !

Rosie [*all business, coming over to the counter, and standing near the Covey*]. Another one for me, Tommy ; [*to the Barman*] th' young gentleman's ordherin' it in th' corner of his eye.

> [*The Barman brings the drink for the Covey, and leaves it on the counter. Rosie whips it up.*

Barman. Ay, houl' on there, houl' on there, Rosie !

Rosie [*to the Barman*]. What are you houldin' on out o' you for ? Didn't you hear th' young gentleman say that he couldn't refuse anything to a nice little bird ? [*To the Covey*] Isn't that right, Jiggs ? [*The Covey says nothing.*] Didn't I know, Tommy, it would be all right ? It takes Rosie to size a young man up, an' tell th' thoughts that are thremblin' in his mind. Isn't that right, Jiggs ?

[*The Covey stirs uneasily, moves a little farther away, and pulls his cap over his eyes.*

Rosie [*moving after him*]. Great meetin' that's gettin' held outside. Well, it's up to us all, anyway, to fight for our freedom.

The Covey [*to Barman*]. Two more, please. [*To Rosie*] Freedom ! What's th' use o' freedom, if it's not economic freedom ?

Rosie [*emphasizing with extended arm and moving finger*]. I used them very words just before you come in. " A lot o' thricksters," says I, " that wouldn't know what freedom was if they got it from their mother." . . . [*To Barman*] Didn't I, Tommy ?

Barman. I disremember.

Rosie. No, you don't disremember. Remember you said, yourself, it was all " only a flash in th' pan." Well, " flash in th' pan, or no flash in th' pan," says I, " they're not goin' to get Rosie Redmond," says I, " to fight for freedom that wouldn't be worth winnin' in a raffle ! "

The Covey. There's only one freedom for th' workin' man : conthrol o' th' means o' production, rates of exchange, an' th' means of disthribution. [*Tapping Rosie on the shoulder*] Look here, comrade, I'll leave here to-morrow night for you a copy of Jenersky's *Thesis on the Origin, Development, an' Consolidation of the Evolutionary Idea of the Proletariat.*

Rosie [*throwing off her shawl on to the counter, and showing an exemplified glad neck, which reveals a good deal of a white bosom*]. If y'ass Rosie, it's heartbreakin' to see a young fella thinkin' of anything, or admirin' anything, but silk thransparent stockin's showin' off the shape of a little lassie's legs !

> [*The Covey, frightened, moves a little away.*

Rosie [*following on*]. Out in th' park in th' shade of a warm summery evenin', with your little darlin' bridie to be, kissin' an' cuddlin' [*she tries to put her arm around his neck*], kissin' an' cuddlin', ay ?

The Covey [*frightened*]. Ay, what are you doin' ? None o' that, now ; none o' that. I've something else to do besides shinannickin' afther Judies !

> [*He turns away, but Rosie follows, keeping face to face with him.*

Rosie. Oh, little duckey, oh, shy little duckey ! Never held a mot's hand, an' wouldn't know how to tittle a little Judy ! [*She clips him under the chin.*] Tittle him undher th' chin, tittle him undher th' chin !

The Covey [*breaking away and running out*]. Ay, go on, now ; I don't want to have any meddlin' with a lassie like you !

Rosie [*enraged*]. Jasus, it's in a monasthery some of us ought to be, spendin' our holidays kneelin' on our adorers, tellin' our beads, an' knockin' hell out of our buzzums !

The Covey [*outside*]. Cuckoo-oo !

> [*Peter and Fluther come in again, followed by Mrs. Gogan, carrying a baby in her arms. They go over to the counter.*

Peter [*with plaintive anger*]. It's terrible that young Covey can't let me pass without proddin' at me ! Did you hear him murmurin' " cuckoo " when we were passin' ?

Fluther [*irritably*]. I wouldn't be everlastin' cockin' me ear to hear every little whisper that was floatin' around about me ! It's my rule never to lose me temper till it would be dethrimental to keep it. There's nothin' derogatory in th' use o' th' word " cuckoo ", is there ?

Peter [*tearfully*]. It's not th' word ; it's th' way he says it : he never says it straight out, but murmurs it with curious quiverin' ripples, like variations on a flute !

Fluther. Ah, what odds if he gave it with variations on a thrombone ! [*To Mrs. Gogan*] What's yours goin' to be, ma'am ?

Mrs. Gogan. Ah, a half o' malt, Fluther.

Fluther [*to Barman*]. Three halves, Tommy.
                              [*The Barman brings the drinks.*

Mrs. Gogan [*drinking*]. The Foresthers' is a gorgeous dhress ! I don't think I've seen nicer, mind you, in a pantomime. . . . Th' loveliest part of th' dhress, I think, is th' osthrichess plume. . . . When yous are goin' along, an' I see them wavin' an' noddin' an' waggin', I seem to be lookin' at each of yous hangin' at th' end of a rope, your eyes bulgin' an' your legs twistin' an' jerkin', gaspin' an' gaspin' for breath while yous are thryin' to die for Ireland !

Fluther. If any o' them is hangin' at the end of a rope, it won't be for Ireland !

Peter. Are you goin' to start th' young Covey's game o' proddin' an' twartin' a man ? There's not many that's talkin' can say that for twenty-five years he never missed a pilgrimage to Bodenstown !

Fluther. You're always blowin' about goin' to Bodenstown. D'ye think no one but yourself ever went to Bodenstown ?

Peter [*plaintively*]. I'm not blowin' about it ; but there's not a year that I go there but I pluck a leaf off Tone's grave, an' this very day me prayer-book is nearly full of them.

Fluther [*scornfully*]. Then Fluther has a vice versa opinion of them that put ivy leaves into their prayer-books, scabbin' it on th' clergy, an' thryin' to out-do th' haloes o' th' saints be lookin' as if he was wearin' around his head a glittherin' aroree boree allis ! [*Fiercely*] Sure, I don't care a damn if you slep' in Bodenstown ! You can take your breakfast, dinner, an' tea on th' grave in Bodenstown, if you like, for Fluther !

Mrs. Gogan. Oh, don't start a fight, boys, for God's sake ; I was only sayin' what a nice costume it is — nicer than th' kilts, for, God forgive me, I always think th' kilts is hardly decent.

Fluther. Ah, sure, when you'd look at him, you'd wondher whether th' man was makin' fun o' th' costume, or th' costume was makin' fun o' th' man !

Barman. Now, then, thry to speak asy, will yous ? We don't want no shoutin' here.

[*The Covey followed by Bessie Burgess comes in. They go over to the opposite end of the counter, and direct their gaze on the other group.*

The Covey [*to Barman*]. Two glasses o' malt.

Peter. There he is, now ; I knew he wouldn't be long till he folleyed me in.

Bessie [*speaking to the Covey, but really at the other party*]. I can't for th' life o' me undherstand how they can call themselves Catholics, when they won't lift a finger to help poor little Catholic Belgium.

Mrs. Gogan [*raising her voice*]. What about poor little Catholic Ireland ?

Bessie [*over to Mrs. Gogan*]. You mind your own business, ma'am, an' stupefy your foolishness be gettin' dhrunk.

Peter [*anxiously*]. Take no notice of her ; pay no attention to her. She's just tormentin' herself towards havin' a row with somebody.

Bessie. There's a storm of anger tossin' in me heart, thinkin' of all th' poor Tommies, an' with them me own son, dhrenched in water an' soaked in blood, gropin' their way to a shattherin' death, in a shower o' shells ! Young men with th' sunny lust o' life beamin' in them, layin' down their white bodies, shredded into torn an' bloody pieces, on th' althar that God Himself has built for th' sacrifice of heroes !

Mrs. Gogan. Isn't it a nice thing to have to be listenin' to a lassie an' hangin' our heads in a dead silence, knowin' that some persons think more of a ball of malt than they do of th' blessed saints.

Fluther. Whisht ; she's always dangerous an' derogatory when she's well oiled. Th' safest way to hindher her from havin' any enjoyment out of her spite, is to dip our thoughts into the fact of her bein' a female person that has moved out of th' sight of ordinary sensible people.

Bessie. To look at some o' th' women that's knockin' about, now, is a thing to make a body sigh. . . . A woman on her own, dhrinkin' with a bevy o' men, is hardly an example to her sex. . . . A woman dhrinkin' with a woman is one thing, an' a woman dhrinkin' with herself is still a woman — flappers may be put in another category altogether — but a middle-aged married woman makin' herself th' centre of a circle of men is as a woman that is loud an' stubborn, whose feet abideth not in her own house.

The Covey [*to Bessie*]. When I think of all th' problems in front o' th' workers, it makes me sick to be lookin' at oul' codgers goin' about dhressed up like green-accoutred figures gone asthray out of a toyshop !

Peter. Gracious God, give me patience to be listenin' to that blasted young Covey proddin' at me from over at th' other end of th' shop !

Mrs. Gogan [*dipping her finger in the whisky, and moistening with it the lips of her baby*]. Cissie Gogan's a woman livin' for nigh on twenty-five years in her own room, an' beyond biddin' th' time o' day to her neighbours, never yet as much as nodded her head in th' direction of other people's business, while she knows some as are never content unless they're standin' senthry over other people's·doin's !

[*Bessie is about to reply, when the tall, dark figure is again silhouetted against the window, and the voice of the speaker is heard speaking passionately.*

Voice of Speaker. The last sixteen months have been the most glorious in the history of Europe. Heroism has come back to the earth. War is a terrible thing, but war is not an evil thing. People in Ireland dread war because they do not know it. Ireland has not known the exhilaration of war for over a hundred years. When war comes to Ireland she must welcome it as she would welcome the Angel of God !

[*The figure passes out of sight and hearing.*

The Covey [*towards all present*]. Dope, dope. There's only one war worth havin' : th' war for th' economic emancipation of th' proletariat.

Bessie. They may crow away out o' them ; but it ud be fitther for some o' them to mend their ways, an' cease from havin' scouts out watchin' for th' comin' of th' Saint Vincent de Paul man, for fear they'd be nailed lowerin' a pint of beer, mockin' th' man with an angel face, shinin' with th' glamour of deceit an' lies !

Mrs. Gogan. An' a certain lassie standin' stiff behind her own door with her ears cocked listenin' to what's being said, stuffed till she's sthrained with envy of a neighbour thryin' for a few little things that may be got be hard sthrivin' to keep up to th' letther an' th' law, an' th' practices of th' Church !

Peter [*to Mrs. Gogan*]. If I was you, Mrs. Gogan, I'd parry her jabbin' remarks be a powerful silence that'll keep her tantalizin' words from penethratin' into your feelin's. It's always betther to leave these people to th' vengeance o' God !

Bessie. Bessie Burgess doesn't put up to know much, never havin' a swaggerin' mind, thanks be to God, but goin' on packin' up knowledge accordin' to her conscience : precept upon precept, line upon line ; here a little, an' there a little. But [*with a passionate swing of her shawl*], thanks be to Christ, she knows when she

was got, where she was got, an' how she was got ;
while there's some she knows, decoratin' their finger
with a well-polished weddin' ring, would be hard put
to it if they were assed to show their weddin' lines !

Mrs. Gogan [plunging out into the centre of the floor in a wild
tempest of hysterical rage]. Y' oul' rip of a blasted liar, me
weddin' ring's been well earned be twenty years be th'
side o' me husband, now takin' his rest in heaven,
married to me be Father Dempsey, in th' Chapel o'
Saint Jude's, in th' Christmas Week of eighteen
hundhred an' ninety-five ; an' any kid, livin' or dead,
that Jinnie Gogan's had since, was got between th'
bordhers of th' Ten Commandments ! . . . An' that's
more than some o' you can say that are kep' from th'
dhread o' desthruction be a few drowsy virtues, that
th' first whisper of temptation lulls into a sleep, that'll
know one sin from another only on th' day of their
last anointin', an' that use th' innocent light o' th'
shinin' stars to dip into th' sins of a night's diversion !

Bessie [jumping out to face Mrs. Gogan, and bringing the palms
of her hands together in sharp claps to emphasize her remarks].
Liar to you, too, ma'am, y' oul' hardened thresspasser on
other people's good nature, wizenin' up your soul in
th' arts o' dodgeries, till every dhrop of respectability
in a female is dhried up in her, lookin' at your ready-
made manœuverin' with th' menkind !

Barman. Here, there ; here, there ; speak asy there. No
rowin' here, no rowin' here, now.

Fluther [trying to calm Mrs. Gogan]. Now Jinnie, Jinnie,
it's a derogatory thing to be smirchin' a night like this
with a row ; it's rompin' with th' feelin's of hope we
ought to be, instead o' bein' vice versa !

Peter [*trying to quiet Bessie*]. I'm terrible dawny, Mrs. Burgess, an' a fight leaves me weak for a long time aftherwards. . . . Please, Mrs. Burgess, before there's damage done, thry to have a little respect for yourself.

Bessie [*with a push of her hand that sends Peter tottering to the end of the shop*]. G'way, you little sermonizing, little yella-faced, little consequential, little pudgy, little bum, you !

Mrs. Gogan [*screaming*]. Fluther, leggo ! I'm not goin' to keep an unresistin' silence, an' her scattherin' her festherin' words in me face, stirrin' up every dhrop of decency in a respectable female, with her restless rally o' lies that would make a saint say his prayer backwards !

Bessie [*shouting*]. Ah, everybody knows well that th' best charity that can be shown to you is to hide th' thruth as much as our thrue worship of God Almighty will allow us !

Mrs. Gogan [*frantically*]. Here, houl' th' kid, one o' yous ; houl' th' kid for a minute ! There's nothin' for it but to show this lassie a lesson or two. . . . [*To Peter*] Here, houl' th' kid, you. [*Before Peter is aware of it, she places the infant in his arms.*]

Mrs. Gogan [*to Bessie, standing before her in a fighting attitude*]. Come on, now, me loyal lassie, dyin' with grief for little Catholic Belgium ! When Jinnie Gogan's done with you, you'll have a little leisure lyin' down to think an' pray for your king an' counthry !

Barman [*coming from behind the counter, getting between the women, and proceeding to push them towards the door*]. Here, now, since yous can't have a little friendly argument quietly, you'll get out o' this place in quick time. Go on, an' settle your differences somewhere else — I don't want to have another endorsement on me licence.

Peter [*anxiously, over to Mrs. Gogan*]. Here, take your kid back, ower this. How nicely I was picked, now, for it to be plumped into me arms !

The Covey. She knew who she was givin' it to, maybe.

Peter [*hotly to the Covey*]. Now, I'm givin' you fair warnin', me young Covey, to quit firin' your jibes an' jeers at me. . . . For one o' these days, I'll run out in front o' God Almighty an' take your sacred life !

Barman [*pushing Bessie out after Mrs. Gogan*]. Go on, now ; out you go.

Bessie [*as she goes out*]. If you think, me lassie, that Bessie Burgess has an untidy conscience, she'll soon show you to th' differ !

Peter [*leaving the baby down on the floor*]. Ay, be Jasus, wait there, till I give her back her youngster ! [*He runs to the door.*] Ay, there, ay ! [*He comes back.*] There, she's afther goin' without her kid. What are we goin' to do with it, now ?

The Covey. What are we goin' to do with it ? Bring it outside an' show everybody what you're afther findin' !

Peter [*in a panic to Fluther*]. Pick it up, you, Fluther, an' run afther her with it, will you ?

Fluther. What d'ye take Fluther for ? You must think Fluther's a right gom. D'ye think Fluther's like yourself, destitute of a titther of undherstandin' ?

Barman [*imperatively to Peter*]. Take it up, man, an' run out afther her with it, before she's gone too far. You're not goin' to leave th' bloody thing here, are you ?

Peter [*plaintively, as he lifts up the baby*]. Well, God Almighty, give me patience with all th' scorners, tormentors, an' twarters that are always an' ever thryin' to goad me into prayin' for their blindin' an' blastin' an' burnin' in th' world to come !

[*He goes out.*

Fluther. God, it's a relief to get rid o' that crowd. Women is terrible when they start to fight. There's no holdin' them back. [*To the Covey*] Are you goin' to have anything ?

The Covey. Ah, I don't mind if I have another half.

Fluther [*to Barman*]. Two more, Tommy, me son.

[*The Barman gets the drinks.*

Fluther. You know, there's no conthrollin' a woman when she loses her head.

[*Rosie enters and goes over to the counter on the side nearest to Fluther.*

Rosie [*to Barman*]. Divil a use o' havin' a thrim little leg on a night like this ; things was never worse. . . . Give us a half till to-morrow, Tom, duckey.

Barman [*coldly*]. No more to-night, Rosie ; you owe me for three already.

Rosie [*combatively*]. You'll be paid, won't you ?

Barman. I hope so.

Rosie. You hope so ! Is that th' way with you, now ?

Fluther [*to Barman*]. Give her one ; it'll be all right.

Rosie [*clapping Fluther on the back*]. Oul' sport !

Fluther. Th' meetin' should be soon over, now.

The Covey. Th' sooner th' betther. It's all a lot o' blasted nonsense, comrade.

Fluther. Oh, I wouldn't say it was all nonsense. Afther all, Fluther can remember th' time, an' him only a dawny chiselur, bein' taught at his mother's knee to be faithful to th' Shan Van Vok !

The Covey. That's all dope, comrade ; th' sort o' thing ·that workers are fed on be th' Boorzwawzee.

Fluther [*a little sharply*]. What's all dope ? Though I'm sayin' it that shouldn't : [*catching his cheek with his hand, and pulling down the flesh from the eye*] d'ye see that mark there, undher me eye ? . . . A sabre slice from a dragoon in O'Connell Street ! [*Thrusting his head forward towards Rosie*] Feel that dint in th' middle o' me nut !

Rosie [*rubbing Fluther's head, and winking at the Covey*]. My God, there's a holla !

Fluther [*putting on his hat with quiet pride*]. A skelp from a bobby's baton at a Labour meetin' in th' Phœnix Park !

The Covey. He must ha' hitten you in mistake. I don't know what you ever done for th' Labour movement.

Fluther [*loudly*]. D'ye not ? Maybe, then, I done as much, an' know as much about th' Labour movement as th' chancers that are blowin' about it !

Barman. Speak easy, Fluther, thry to speak easy.

The Covey. There's no necessity to get excited about it, comrade.

Fluther [*more loudly*]. Excited ? Who's gettin' excited ?

There's no one gettin' excited ! It would take something more than a thing like you to flutther a feather
o' Fluther. Blatherin', an', when all is said, you know
as much as th' rest in th' wind up !

The Covey. Well, let us put it to th' test, then, an' see
what you know about th' Labour movement : what's
the mechanism of exchange ?

Fluther [*roaring, because he feels he is beaten*]. How th' hell
do I know what it is ? There's nothin' about that in
th' rules of our Thrades Union !

Barman. For God's sake, thry to speak easy, Fluther.

The Covey. What does Karl Marx say about th' Relation
of Value to th' Cost o' Production ?

Fluther [*angrily*]. What th' hell do I care what he says ?
I'm Irishman enough not to lose me head be follyin'
foreigners !

Barman. Speak easy, Fluther.

The Covey. It's only waste o' time talkin' to you, comrade.

Fluther. Don't be comradin' me, mate. I'd be on me
last legs if I wanted you for a comrade.

Rosie [*to the Covey*]. It seems a highly rediculous thing to
hear a thing that's only an inch or two away from a
kid, swingin' heavy words about he doesn't know th'
meanin' of, an' uppishly thryin' to down a man like
Misther Fluther here, that's well flavoured in th'
knowledge of th' world he's livin' in.

The Covey [*savagely to Rosie*]. Nobody's askin' you to be
buttin' in with your prate. . . . I have you well
taped, me lassie. . . . Just you keep your opinions
for your own place. . . . It'll be a long time before

th' Covey takes any insthructions or reprimandin'
from a prostitute !

Rosie [*wild with humiliation*]. You louse, you louse, you !
. . . You're no man. . . . You're no man . . . I'm
a woman, anyhow, an' if I'm a prostitute aself, I have
me feelin's. . . . Thryin' to put his arm around me
a minute ago, an' givin' me th' glad eye, th' little
wrigglin' lump o' desolation turns on me now, because
he saw there was nothin' doin'. . . . You louse,
you ! If I was a man, or you were a woman, I'd bate
th' puss o' you !

Barman. Ay, Rosie, ay ! You'll have to shut your mouth
altogether, if you can't learn to speak easy !

Fluther [*to Rosie*]. Houl' on there, Rosie ; houl' on there.
There's no necessity to flutther yourself when you're
with Fluther. . . . Any lady that's in th' company
of Fluther is goin' to get a fair hunt. . . . This is
outside your province. . . . I'm not goin' to let you
demean yourself be talkin' to a tittherin' chancer.
. . . Leave this to Fluther — this is a man's job.
[*To the Covey*] Now, if you've anything to say, say it
to Fluther, an', let me tell you, you're not goin' to be
pass-remarkable to any lady in my company.

The Covey. Sure I don't care if you were runnin' all
night afther your Mary o' th' Curlin' Hair, but, when
you start tellin' luscious lies about what you done for
th' Labour movement, it's nearly time to show y'up !

Fluther [*fiercely*]. Is it you show Fluther up ? G'way,
man, I'd beat two o' you before me breakfast !

The Covey [*contemptuously*]. Tell us where you bury your
dead, will you ?

Fluther [*with his face stuck into the face of the Covey*]. Sing a little less on th' high note, or, when I'm done with you, you'll put a Christianable consthruction on things, I'm tellin' you !

The Covey. You're a big fella, you are.

Fluther [*tapping the Covey threateningly on the shoulder*]. Now, you're temptin' Providence when you're temptin' Fluther !

The Covey [*losing his temper, and bawling*]. Easy with them hands, there, easy with them hands ! You're startin' to take a little risk when you commence to paw the Covey !
   [*Fluther suddenly springs into the middle of the shop, flings his hat into the corner, whips off his coat, and begins to paw the air.*

Fluther [*roaring at the top of his voice*]. Come on, come on, you lowser ; put your mits up now, if there's a man's blood in you ! Be God, in a few minutes you'll see some snots flyin' around, I'm tellin' you. . . . When Fluther's done with you, you'll have a vice versa opinion of him ! Come on, now, come on !

Barman [*running from behind the counter and catching hold of the Covey*]. Here, out you go, me little bowsey. Because you got a couple o' halves you think you can act as you like. [*He pushes the Covey to the door*] Fluther's a friend o' mine, an' I'll not have him insulted.

The Covey [*struggling with the Barman*]. Ay, leggo, leggo there ; fair hunt, give a man a fair hunt ! One minute with him is all I ask ; one minute alone with him, while you're runnin' for th' priest an' th' doctor.

Fluther [*to the Barman*]. Let him go, let him go, Tom : let him open th' door to sudden death if he wants to !

Barman [*to the Covey*]. Go on, out you go an' do th' bowsey somewhere else.   [*He pushes the Covey out and comes back.*

Rosie [*getting Fluther's hat as he is putting on his coat*]. Be God, you put th' fear o' God in his heart that time ! I thought you'd have to be dug out of him. . . . Th' way you lepped out without any of your fancy side-steppin' ! " Men like Fluther," say I to meself, " is gettin' scarce nowadays."

Fluther [*with proud complacency*]. I wasn't goin' to let meself be malignified by a chancer. . . . He got a little bit too derogatory for Fluther. . . . Be God, to think of a cur like that comin' to talk to a man like me !

Rosie [*fixing on his hat*]. Did j'ever !

Fluther. He's lucky he got off safe. I hit a man last week, Rosie, an' he's fallin' yet !

Rosie. Sure, you'd ha' broken him in two if you'd ha' hitten him one clatther !

Fluther [*amorously, putting his arm around Rosie*]. Come on into th' snug, me little darlin', an' we'll have a few dhrinks before I see you home.

Rosie. Oh, Fluther, I'm afraid you're a terrible man for th' women.

   [*They go into the snug as Clitheroe, Captain Brennan, and Lieut. Langon of the Irish Volunteers enter hurriedly. Captain Brennan carries the banner of The Plough and*

*the Stars, and Lieut. Langon a green, white, and orange
Tri-colour. They are in a state of emotional excitement.
Their faces are flushed and their eyes sparkle ; they
speak rapidly, as if unaware of the meaning of what they
said. They have been mesmerized by the fervency of the
speeches.*

Clitheroe [*almost pantingly*]. Three glasses o' port !
[*The Barman brings the drinks.*

Capt. Brennan. We won't have long to wait now.

Lieut. Langon. Th' time is rotten ripe for revolution.

Clitheroe. You have a mother, Langon.

Lieut. Langon. Ireland is greater than a mother.

Capt. Brennan. You have a wife, Clitheroe.

Clitheroe. Ireland is greater than a wife.

Lieut. Langon. Th' time for Ireland's battle is now — th'
place for Ireland's battle is here.
[*The tall, dark figure again is silhouetted against the
window. The three men pause and listen.*

Voice of the Man. Our foes are strong, but strong as they
are, they cannot undo the miracles of God, who ripens
in the heart of young men the seeds sown by the young
men of a former generation. They think they have
pacified Ireland ; think they have foreseen everything ;
think they have provided against everything ; but the
fools, the fools, the fools ! — they have left us our
Fenian dead, and, while Ireland holds these graves,
Ireland, unfree, shall never be at peace !

Capt. Brennan [*catching up The Plough and the Stars*]. Im-
prisonment for th' Independence of Ireland !

Lieut. Langon [*catching up the Tri-colour*]. Wounds for th' Independence of Ireland !

Clitheroe. Death for th' Independence of Ireland !

The Three [*together*]. So help us God !

> [*They drink. A bugle blows the Assembly. They hurry out. A pause. Fluther and Rosie come out of the snug ; Rosie is linking Fluther, who is a little drunk. Both are in a merry mood.*

Rosie. Come on home, ower o' that, man. Are you afraid or what ? Are you goin' to come home, or are you not ?

Fluther. Of course I'm goin' home. What ud ail me that I wouldn't go ?

Rosie [*lovingly*]. Come on, then, oul' sport.

Officer's Voice [*giving command outside*]. Irish Volunteers, by th' right, quick march !

Rosie [*putting her arm round Fluther and singing*] :

> I once had a lover, a tailor, but he could do nothin' for me,
> An' then I fell in with a sailor as strong an' as wild as th' sea.
> We cuddled an' kissed with devotion, till th' night from th' mornin' had fled ;
> An' there, to our joy, a bright bouncin' boy
> Was dancin' a jig in th' bed !
>
> Dancin' a jig in th' bed, an' bawlin' for butther an' bread.
> An' there, to our joy, a bright bouncin' boy
> Was dancin' a jig in th' bed !

> [*They go out with their arms round each other.*

Clitheroe's Voice [*in command outside*]. Dublin Battalion of the Irish Citizen Army, by th' right, quick march !

CURTAIN

ACT III

*The corner house in a street of tenements : it is the home of the
Clitheroes. The house is a long, gaunt, five-story tenement ; its
brick front is chipped and scarred with age and neglect. The
wide and heavy hall door, flanked by two pillars, has a look of
having been charred by a fire in the distant past. The door
lurches a little to one side, disjointed by the continual and reckless
banging when it is being closed by most of the residents. The
diamond-paned fanlight is destitute of a single pane, the frame-
work alone remaining. The windows, except the two looking into
the front parlour [Clitheroe's room], are grimy, and are draped
with fluttering and soiled fragments of lace curtains. The front
parlour windows are hung with rich, comparatively, casement
cloth. Five stone steps lead from the door to the path on the
street. Branching on each side are railings to prevent people
from falling into the area. At the left corner of the house runs a
narrow lane, bisecting the street, and connecting it with another
of the same kind. At the corner of the lane is a street lamp.*

*As the house is revealed, Mrs. Gogan is seen helping Mollser
to a chair, which stands on the path beside the railings, at the
left side of the steps. She then wraps a shawl around Mollser's
shoulders. It is some months later.*

Mrs. Gogan [*arranging shawl around Mollser*]. Th' sun'll do
you all th' good in th' world. A few more weeks o'
this weather, an' there's no knowin' how well you'll
be. . . . Are you comfy, now ?

Mollser [*weakly and wearily*]. Yis, ma ; I'm all right.

Mrs. Gogan. How are you feelin' ?

Mollser. Betther, ma, betther. If th' horrible sinkin' feelin' ud go, I'd be all right.

Mrs. Gogan. Ah, I wouldn't put much pass on that. Your stomach maybe's out of ordher. . . . Is th' poor breathin' any betther, d'ye think ?

Mollser. Yis, yis, ma ; a lot betther.

Mrs. Gogan. Well, that's somethin' anyhow. . . . With th' help o' God, you'll be on th' mend from this out. . . . D'your legs feel any sthronger undher you, d'ye think ?

Mollser [*irritably*]. I can't tell, ma. I think so. . . . A little.

Mrs. Gogan. Well, a little aself is somethin'. . . . I thought I heard you coughin' a little more than usual last night. . . . D'ye think you were ?

Mollser. I wasn't, ma, I wasn't.

Mrs. Gogan. I thought I heard you, for I was kep' awake all night with th' shootin'. An' thinkin' o' that madman, Fluther, runnin' about through th' night lookin' for Nora Clitheroe to bring her back when he heard she'd gone to folly her husband, an' in dhread any minute he might come staggerin' in covered with bandages, splashed all over with th' red of his own blood, an' givin' us barely time to bring th' priest to hear th' last whisper of his final confession, as his soul was passin' through th' dark doorway o' death into th' way o' th' wondherin' dead. . . . You don't feel cold, do you ?

Mollser. No, ma ; I'm all right.

Mrs. Gogan. Keep your chest well covered, for that's th'

delicate spot in you . . . if there's any danger, I'll whip you in again. . . . [*Looking up the street*] Oh, here's th' Covey an' oul' Pether hurryin' along. God Almighty, sthrange things is happenin' when them two is pullin' together.

[*The Covey and Peter come in, breathless and excited.*]

Mrs. Gogan [*to the two men*]. Were yous far up th' town? Did yous see any sign o' Fluther or Nora? How is things lookin'? I hear they're blazin' away out o' th' G.P.O. That th' Tommies is sthretched in heaps around Nelson's Pillar an' th' Parnell Statue, an' that th' pavin' sets in O'Connell Street is nearly covered be pools o' blood.

Peter. We seen no sign o' Nora or Fluther anywhere.

Mrs. Gogan. We should ha' held her back be main force from goin' to look for her husband. . . . God knows what's happened to her — I'm always seein' her sthretched on her back in some hospital, moanin' with th' pain of a bullet in her vitals, an' nuns thryin' to get her to take a last look at th' crucifix!

The Covey. We can do nothin'. You can't stick your nose into O'Connell Street, an' Tyler's is on fire.

Peter. An' we seen th' Lancers——

The Covey [*interrupting*]. Throttin' along, heads in th' air; spurs an' sabres jinglin', an' lances quiverin', an' lookin' as if they were assin' themselves, " Where's these blighters, till we get a prod at them? " when there was a volley from th' Post Office that stretched half o' them, an' sent th' rest gallopin' away wondherin' how far they'd have to go before they'd feel safe.

Peter [*rubbing his hands*]. " Damn it," says I to meself, " this looks like business ! "

The Covey. An' then out comes General Pearse an' his staff, an', standin' in th' middle o' th' street, he reads th' Proclamation.

Mrs. Gogan. What proclamation ?

Peter. Declarin' an Irish Republic.

Mrs. Gogan. Go to God !

Peter. The gunboat *Helga's* shellin' Liberty Hall, an' I hear the people livin' on th' quays had to crawl on their bellies to Mass with th' bullets that were flyin' around from Boland's Mills.

Mrs. Gogan. God bless us, what's goin' to be th' end of it all !

Bessie [*looking out of the top window*]. Maybe yous are satisfied now ; maybe yous are satisfied now. Go on an' get guns if yous are men — Johnny get your gun, get your gun, get your gun ! Yous are all nicely shanghaied now ; th' boyo hasn't a sword on his thigh now ! Oh, yous are all nicely shanghaied now !

Mrs. Cogan [*warningly to Peter and the Covey*]. S-s-sh, don't answer her. She's th' right oul' Orange bitch ! She's been chantin' " Rule, Britannia " all th' mornin'.

Peter. I hope Fluther hasn't met with any accident, he's such a wild card.

Mrs. Gogan. God grant it ; but last night I dreamt I seen gettin' carried into th' house a sthretcher with a figure lyin' on it, stiff an' still, dhressed in th' habit of Saint Francis. An, then, I heard th' murmurs of a crowd no one could see sayin' th' litany for th' dead ; an'

then it got so dark that nothin' was seen but th' white
face of th' corpse, gleamin' like a white wather-lily
floatin' on th' top of a dark lake. Then a tiny whisper
thrickled into me ear, sayin', "Isn't the face very
like th' face o' Fluther?" an' then, with a thremblin'
flutther, th' dead lips opened, an', although I couldn't
hear, I knew they were sayin', "Poor oul' Fluther,
afther havin' handed in his gun at last, his shakin' soul
moored in th' place where th' wicked are at rest an' th'
weary cease from throublin'."

Peter [who has put on a pair of spectacles, and has been looking
down the street]. Here they are, be God, here they are ;
just afther turnin' th' corner — Nora an' Fluther !

The Covey. She must be wounded or something — he
seems to be carryin' her.

    [Fluther and Nora enter. Fluther has his arm around her
    and is half leading, half carrying her in. Her eyes are
    dim and hollow, her face pale and strained-looking ; her
    hair is tossed, and her clothes are dusty.

Mrs. Gogan [running over to them]. God bless us, is it
wounded y'are, Mrs. Clitheroe, or what ?

Fluther. Ah, she's all right, Mrs. Gogan ; only worn out
from thravellin' an' want o' sleep. A night's rest,
now, an' she'll be as fit as a fiddle. Bring her in, an'
make her lie down.

Mrs. Gogan [to Nora]. Did you hear e'er a whisper o' Mr.
Clitheroe ?

Nora [wearily]. I could find him nowhere, Mrs. Gogan.
None o' them would tell me where he was. They told
me I shamed my husband an' th' women of Ireland be
carryin' on as I was. . . . They said th' women must

C.P.—I   H

learn to be brave an' cease to be cowardly. . . . Me who risked more for love than they would risk for hate. . . . [*Raising her voice in hysterical protest*] My Jack will be killed, my Jack will be killed ! . . . He is to be butchered as a sacrifice to th' dead !

Bessie [*from upper window*]. Yous are all nicely shanghaied now ! Sorra mend th' lasses that have been kissin' an' cuddlin' their boys into th' sheddin' of blood ! . . . Fillin' their minds with fairy tales that had no beginnin', but, please God, 'll have a bloody quick endin' ! . . . Turnin' bitther into sweet, an' sweet into bitther. . . . Stabbin' in th' back th' men that are dyin' in th' threnches for them ! It's a bad thing for any one that thries to jilt th' Ten Commandments, for judgements are prepared for scorners an' sthripes for th' back o' fools ! [*Going away from window as she sings :*]

> Rule, Britannia, Britannia rules th' waves,
> Britons never, never, never shall be slaves !

Fluther [*with a roar up at the window*]. Y'ignorant oul' throllope, you !

Mrs. Gogan [*to Nora*]. He'll come home safe enough to you, you'll find, Mrs. Clitheroe ; afther all, there's a power o' women that's handed over sons an' husbands to take a runnin' risk in th' fight they're wagin'.

Nora. I can't help thinkin' every shot fired 'll be fired at Jack, an' every shot fired at Jack 'll be fired at me. What do I care for th' others ? I can think only of me own self. . . . An' there's no woman gives a son or a husband to be killed — if they say it, they're lyin', lyin', against God, Nature, an' against themselves ! . . . One blasted hussy at a barricade told me to go home an' not be thryin' to dishearten th' men. . . .

That I wasn't worthy to bear a son to a man that was out fightin' for freedom. . . . I clawed at her, an' smashed her in th' face till we were separated. . . . I was pushed down th' street, an' I cursed them — cursed the rebel ruffians an' Volunteers that had dhragged me ravin' mad into th' sthreets to seek me husband !

Peter. You'll have to have patience, Nora. We all have to put up with twarthers an' tormentors in this world.

The Covey. If they were fightin' for anything worth while, I wouldn't mind.

Fluther [*to Nora*]. Nothin' derogatory 'll happen to Mr. Clitheroe. You'll find, now, in th' finish up it'll be vice versa.

Nora. Oh, I know that wherever he is, he's thinkin' of wantin' to be with me. I know he's longin' to be passin' his hand through me hair, to be caressin' me neck, to fondle me hand an' to feel me kisses clingin' to his mouth. . . . An' he stands wherever he is because he's brave ? [*Vehemently*] No, but because he's a coward, a coward, a coward !

Mrs. Gogan. Oh, they're not cowards anyway.

Nora [*with denunciatory anger*]. I tell you they're afraid to say they're afraid ! . . . Oh, I saw it, I saw it, Mrs. Cogan. . . . At th' barricade in North King Street I saw fear glowin' in all their eyes. . . . An' in th' middle o' th' sthreet was somethin' huddled up in a horrible tangled heap. . . . His face was jammed again th' stones, an' his arm was twisted round his back. . . . An' every twist of his body was a cry against th' terrible thing that had happened to him. . . . An' I saw they were afraid to look at it. . . .

An' some o' them laughed at me, but th' laugh was a frightened one. . . . An' some o' them shouted at me, but th' shout had in it th' shiver o' fear. . . . I tell you they were afraid, afraid, afraid !

Mrs. Gogan [*leading her towards the house*]. Come on in, dear. If you'd been a little longer together, th' wrench asundher wouldn't have been so sharp.

Nora. Th' agony I'm in since he left me has thrust away every rough thing he done, an' every unkind word he spoke ; only th' blossoms that grew out of our lives are before me now ; shakin' their colours before me face, an' breathin' their sweet scent on every thought springin' up in me mind, till, sometimes, Mrs. Gogan, sometimes I think I'm goin' mad !

Mrs. Gogan. You'll be a lot betther when you have a little lie down.

Nora [*turning towards Fluther as she is going in*]. I don't know what I'd have done, only for Fluther. I'd have been lyin' in th' streets, only for him. . . . [*As she goes in*] They have dhriven away th' little happiness life had to spare for me. He has gone from me for ever, for ever. . . . Oh, Jack, Jack, Jack !

> [*She is led in by Mrs. Gogan as Bessie comes out with a shawl around her shoulders. She passes by them with her head in the air. When they have gone in, she gives a mug of milk to Mollser silently.*]

Fluther. Which of yous has th' tossers ?

The Covey. I have.

Bessie [*as she is passing them to go down the street*]. You an' your Leadhers an' their sham-battle soldiers has landed a body in a nice way, havin' to go an' ferret out a bit

o' bread God knows where. . . . Why aren't yous in
th' G.P.O. if yous are men ? It's paler an' paler yous
are gettin'. . . . A lot o' vipers, that's what th' Irish
people is !   [*She goes out.*

Fluther. Never mind her. . . . [*To the Covey*] Make a
start an' keep us from th' sin o' idleness. [*To Mollser*]
Well, how are you to-day, Mollser, oul' son ? What
are you dhrinkin', milk ?

Mollser. Grand, Fluther, grand, thanks. Yis, milk.

Fluther. You couldn't get a betther thing down you. . . .
This turn-up has done one good thing, anyhow ; you
can't get dhrink anywhere, an' if it lasts a week, I'll be
so used to it that I won't think of a pint.

The Covey [*who has taken from his pocket two worn coins and a
thin strip of wood about four inches long*]. What's th'
bettin' ?

Peter. Heads, a juice.

Fluther. Harps, a tanner.
   [*The Covey places the coins on the strip of wood, and flips
   them up into the air. As they jingle on the ground the
   distant boom of a big gun is heard. They stand for a
   moment listening.*

Fluther. What th' hell's that ?

The Covey. It's like th' boom of a big gun !

Fluther. Surely to God they're not goin' to use artillery
on us ?

The Covey [*scornfully*]. Not goin' ! [*Vehemently*] Wouldn't
they use anything on us, man ?

Fluther. Aw, holy Christ, that's not playin' th' game !

Peter [*plaintively*]. What would happen if a shell landed here now ?

The Covey [*ironically*]. You'd be off to heaven in a fiery chariot.

Peter. In spite of all th' warnin's that's ringin' around us, are you goin' to start your pickin' at me again ?

Fluther. Go on, toss them again, toss them again. . . . Harps, a tanner.

Peter. Heads, a juice.   [*The Covey tosses the coins.*

Fluther [*as the coins fall*]. Let them roll, let them roll. Heads, be God !
> [*Bessie runs in excitedly. She has a new hat on her head, a fox fur round her neck over her shawl, three umbrellas under her right arm, and a box of biscuits under her left. She speaks rapidly and breathlessly.*

Bessie. They're breakin' into th' shops, they're breakin' into th' shops ! Smashin' th' windows, battherin' in th' doors, an' whippin' away everything ! An' th' Volunteers is firin' on them. I seen two men an' a lassie pushin' a piano down th' sthreet, an' th' sweat rollin' off them thryin' to get it up on th' pavement ; an' an oul' wan that must ha' been seventy lookin' as if she'd dhrop every minute with th' dint o' heart beatin', thryin' to pull a big double bed out of a broken shop-window ! I was goin' to wait till I dhressed meself from th' skin out.

Mollser [*to Bessie, as she is going in*]. Help me in, Bessie ; I'm feelin' curious.
> [*Bessie leaves the looted things in the house, and, rapidly returning, helps Mollser in.*

The Covey. Th' selfishness of that one — she waited till she got all she could carry before she'd come to tell anyone !

Fluther [*running over to the door of the house and shouting in to Bessie*]. Ay, Bessie, did you hear of e'er a pub gettin' a shake up ?

Bessie [*inside*]. I didn't hear o' none.

Fluther [*in a burst of enthusiasm*]. Well, you're goin' to hear of one soon !

The Covey. Come on, man, an' don't be wastin' time.

Peter [*to them as they are about to run off*]. Ay, ay, are you goin' to leave me here ?

Fluther. Are you goin' to leave yourself here ?

Peter [*anxiously*]. Didn't yous hear her sayin' they were firin' on them ?

The Covey and Fluther [*together*]. Well ?

Peter. Supposin' I happened to be potted ?

Fluther. We'd give you a Christian burial, anyhow.

The Covey [*ironically*]. Dhressed up in your regimentals.

Peter [*to the Covey, passionately*]. May th' all-lovin' God give you a hot knock one o' these days, me young Covey, tuthorin' Fluther up now to be tiltin' at me, an' crossin' me with his mockeries an' jibin' !

 [*A fashionably dressed, middle-aged, stout woman comes hurriedly in, and makes for the group. She is almost fainting with fear.*

The Woman. For Gawd's sake, will one of you kind men show any safe way for me to get to Wrathmines ? . . .

I was foolish enough to visit a friend, thinking the howl thing was a joke, and now I cawn't get a car or a tram to take me home — isn't it awful?

Fluther. I'm afraid, ma'am, one way is as safe as another.

Woman. And what am I gowing to do? Oh, isn't this awful? . . . I'm so different from others. . . . The mowment I hear a shot, my legs give way under me — I cawn't stir, I'm paralysed — isn't it awful?

Fluther [*moving away*]. It's a derogatory way to be, right enough, ma'am.

Woman [*catching Fluther's coat*]. Creeping along the street there, with my head down and my eyes half shut, a bullet whizzed past within an inch of my nowse. . . . I had to lean against the wall for a long time, gasping for breath — I nearly passed away — it was awful! . . . I wonder, would you kind men come some of the way and see me safe?

Fluther. I have to go away, ma'am, to thry an' save a few things from th' burnin' buildin's.

The Covey. Come on, then, or there won't be anything left to save. [*The Covey and Fluther hurry away.*

Woman [*to Peter*]. Wasn't it an awful thing for me to leave my friend's house? Wasn't it an idiotic thing to do? . . . I haven't the slightest idea where I am. . . . You have a kind face, sir. Could you possibly come and pilot me in the direction of Wrathmines?

Peter [*indignantly*]. D'ye think I'm goin' to risk me life throttin' in front of you? An' maybe get a bullet that would gimme a game leg or something that would leave me a jibe an' a jeer to Fluther an' th' young Covey for th' rest o' me days !

[*With an indignant toss of his head he walks into the house.*

The Woman [*going out*]. I know I'll fall down in a dead faint if I hear another shot go off anyway near me — isn't it awful !

[*Mrs. Gogan comes out of the house pushing a pram before her. As she enters the street, Bessie rushes out, follows Mrs. Gogan, and catches hold of the pram, stopping Mrs. Gogan's progress.*

Bessie. Here, where are you goin' with that ? How quick you were, me lady, to clap your eyes on th' pram. . . . Maybe you don't know that Mrs. Sullivan, before she went to spend Easther with her people in Dunboyne, gave me sthrict injunctions to give an accasional look to see if it was still standin' where it was left in th' corner of th' lobby.

Mrs. Gogan. That remark of yours, Mrs. Bessie Burgess, requires a little considheration, seein' that th' pram was left on our lobby, an' not on yours ; a foot or two a little to th' left of th' jamb of me own room door ; nor is it needful to mention th' name of th' person that gave a squint to see if it was there th' first thing in th' mornin', an' th' last thing in th' stillness o' th' night ; never failin' to realize that her eyes couldn't be goin' wrong, be sthretchin' out her arm an' runnin' her hand over th' pram, to make sure that th' sight was no deception ! Moreover, somethin's tellin' me that th' runnin' hurry of an inthrest you're takin' in it now is a sudden ambition to use th' pram for a purpose that a loyal woman of law an' ordher would stagger away from !

[*She gives the pram a sudden push that pulls Bessie forward.*

H*

Bessie [*still holding the pram*]. There's not as much as one body in th' house that doesn't know that it wasn't Bessie Burgess that was always shakin' her voice complainin' about people leavin' bassinettes in th' way of them that, week in an' week out, had to pay their rent, an' always had to find a regular accommodation for her own furniture in her own room. . . . An' as for law an' ordher, puttin' aside th' harp an' shamrock, Bessie Burgess 'll have as much respect as she wants for th' lion an' unicorn !

Peter [*appearing at the door*]. I think I'll go with th' pair of yous an' see th' fun. A fella might as well chance it, anyhow.

Mrs. Gogan [*taking no notice of Peter, and pushing the pram on another step*]. Take your rovin' lumps o' hands from pattin' th' bassinette, if you please, ma'am ; an', steppin' from th' threshold of good manners, let me tell you, Mrs. Burgess, that's it's a fat wondher to Jennie Gogan that a lady-like singer o' hymns like yourself would lower her thoughts from sky-thinkin' to sthretch out her arm in a sly-seekin' way to pinch anything dhriven asthray in th' confusion of th' battle our boys is makin' for th' freedom of their counthry !

Peter [*laughing and rubbing his hands together*]. Hee, hee, hee, hee, hee ! I'll go with th' pair o' yous an' give yous a hand.

Mrs. Gogan [*with a rapid turn of her head as she shoves the pram forward*]. Get up in th' prambulator an' we'll wheel you down.

Bessie [*to Mrs. Gogan*]. Poverty an' hardship has sent Bessie Burgess to abide with sthrange company, but she

always knew them she had to live with from backside
to breakfast time ; an' she can tell them, always
havin' had a Christian kinch on her conscience, that a
passion for thievin' an' pinchin' would find her soul a
foreign place to live in, an' that her present intention is
quite th' lofty-hearted one of pickin' up anything
shaken up an' scatthered about in th' loose confusion
of a general plundher !

[*By this time they have disappeared from view. Peter is
following, when the boom of a big gun in the distance
brings him to a quick halt.*]

Peter. God Almighty, that's th' big gun again ! God
forbid any harm would happen to them, but sorra
mind I'd mind if they met with a dhrop in their mad
endeyvours to plundher an' desthroy.

[*He looks down the street for a moment, then runs to the
hall door of the house, which is open, and shuts it with a
vicious pull ; he then goes to the chair in which Mollser
had sat, sits down, takes out his pipe, lights it and
begins to smoke with his head carried at a haughty angle.
The Covey comes staggering in with a ten-stone sack of
flour on his back. On the top of the sack is a ham. He
goes over to the door, pushes it with his head, and finds
he can't open it ; he turns slightly in the direction of
Peter.*]

The Covey [*to Peter*]. Who shut th' door ? . . . [*He kicks
at it*] Here, come on an' open it, will you ? This isn't
a mot's hand-bag I've got on me back.

Peter. Now, me young Covey, d'ye think I'm goin' to be
your lackey ?

The Covey [*angrily*]. Will you open th' door, y'oul'——

Peter [*shouting*]. Don't be assin' me to open any door,

don't be assin' me to open any door for you. . . . Makin' a shame an' a sin o' th' cause that good men are fightin' for. . . . Oh, God forgive th' people that, instead o' burnishin' th' work th' boys is doin' to-day with quiet honesty an' patience, is revilin' their sacrifices with a riot of lootin' an' roguery !

The Covey. Isn't your own eyes leppin' out o' your head with envy that you haven't th' guts to ketch a few o' th' things that God is givin' to His chosen people ? . . . Y'oul' hypocrite, if everyone was blind you'd steal a cross off an ass's back !

Peter [*very calmly*]. You're not going to make me lose me temper ; you can go on with your proddin' as long as you like ; goad an' goad an' goad away ; hee, hee, heee ! I'll not lose me temper.

> [*Somebody opens door and the Covey goes in.*

The Covey [*inside, mockingly*]. Cuckoo-oo !

Peter [*running to the door and shouting in a blaze of passion as he follows the Covey in*]. You lean, long, lanky lath of a lowsey bastard. . . . [*Following him in*] Lowsey bastard, lowsey bastard !

> [*Bessie and Mrs. Gogan enter, the pride of a great joy illuminating their faces. Bessie is pushing the pram, which is filled with clothes and boots ; on the top of the boots and clothes is a fancy table, which Mrs. Gogan is holding on with her left hand, while with her right hand she holds a chair on the top of her head. They are heard talking to each other before they enter.*

Mrs. Gogan [*outside*]. I don't remember ever havin' seen such lovely pairs as them, [*they appear*] with th' pointed toes an' th' cuban heels.

Bessie. They'll go grand with th' dhresses we're afther liftin', when we've stitched a sthray bit o' silk to lift th' bodices up a little bit higher, so as to shake th' shame out o' them, an' make them fit for women that hasn't lost themselves in th' nakedness o' th' times.

[*They fussily carry in the chair, the table, and some of the other goods. They return to bring in the rest.*]

Peter [*at door, sourly to Mrs. Gogan*]. Ay, you. Mollser looks as if she was goin' to faint, an' your youngster is roarin' in convulsions in her lap.

Mrs. Gogan [*snappily*]. She's never any other way but faintin' !

[*She goes to go in with some things in her arms, when a shot from a rifle rings out. She and Bessie make a bolt for the door, which Peter, in a panic, tries to shut before they have got inside.*]

Mrs. Gogan. Ay, ay, ay, you cowardly oul' fool, what are you thryin' to shut th' door on us for ?

[*They retreat tumultuously inside. A pause ; then Captain Brennan comes in supporting Lieutenant Langon, whose arm is around Brennan's neck. Langon's face, which is ghastly white, is momentarily convulsed with spasms of agony. He is in a state of collapse, and Brennan is almost carrying him. After a few moments Clitheroe, pale, and in a state of calm nervousness, follows, looking back in the direction from which he came, a rifle, held at the ready, in his hands.*]

Capt. Brennan [*savagely to Clitheroe*]. Why did you fire over their heads ? Why didn't you fire to kill?

Clitheroe. No, no, Bill ; bad as they are they're Irish men an' women.

Capt. Brennan [*savagely*]. Irish be damned ! Attackin' an' mobbin' th' men that are riskin' their lives for them. If these slum lice gather at our heels again, plug one o' them, or I'll soon shock them with a shot or two meself !

Lieut. Langon [*moaningly*]. My God, is there ne'er an ambulance knockin' around anywhere ? . . . Th' stomach is ripped out o' me ; I feel it — o-o-oh, Christ !

Capt. Brennan. Keep th' heart up, Jim ; we'll soon get help, now.

> [*Nora rushes wildly out of the house and flings her arms round the neck of Clitheroe with a fierce and joyous insistence. Her hair is down, her face is haggard, but her eyes are agleam with the light of happy relief.*

Nora. Jack, Jack, Jack ; God be thanked . . . be thanked. . . . He has been kind and merciful to His poor handmaiden. . . . My Jack, my own Jack, that I thought was lost is found, that I thought was dead is alive again ! . . . Oh, God be praised for ever, evermore ! . . . My poor Jack. . . . Kiss me, kiss me, Jack, kiss your own Nora !

Clitheroe [*kissing her, and speaking brokenly*]. My Nora ; my little, beautiful Nora, I wish to God I'd never left you.

Nora. It doesn't matter — not now, not now, Jack. It will make us dearer than ever to each other. . . . Kiss me, kiss me again.

Clitheroe. Now, for God's sake, Nora, don't make a scene.

Nora. I won't, I won't ; I promise, I promise, Jack ;

honest to God. I'll be silent an' brave to bear th' joy
of feelin' you safe in my arms again. . . . It's hard
to force away th' tears of happiness at th' end of an
awful agony.

Bessie [*from the upper window*]. Th' Minsthrel Boys aren't
feelin' very comfortable now. Th' big guns has knocked
all th' harps out of their hands. General Clitheroe 'd
rather be unlacin' his wife's bodice than standin'
at a barricade . . . An' th' professor of chicken-
butcherin' there, finds he's up against somethin' a
little tougher even than his own chickens, an' that's
sayin' a lot !

Capt. Brennan [*up to Bessie*]. Shut up, y'oul' hag !

Bessie [*down to Brennan*]. Choke th' chicken, choke th'
chicken, choke th' chicken !

Lieut. Langon. For God's sake, Bill, bring me some place
where me wound 'll be looked afther. . . . Am I to
die before anything is done to save me ?

Capt. Brennan [*to Clitheroe*]. Come on, Jack. We've got to
get help for Jim, here — have you no thought for his
pain an' danger ?

Bessie. Choke th' chicken, choke th' chicken, choke th'
chicken !

Clitheroe [*to Nora*]. Loosen me, darling, let me go.

Nora [*clinging to him*]. No, no, no, I'll not let you go !
Come on, come up to our home, Jack, my sweetheart,
my lover, my husband, an' we'll forget th' last few
terrible days ! . . . I look tired now, but a few hours
of happy rest in your arms will bring back th' bloom

of freshness again, an' you will be glad, you will be glad, glad . . . glad!

Lieut. Langon. Oh, if I'd kep' down only a little longer, I mightn't ha' been hit! Everyone else escapin', an' me gettin' me belly ripped asundher! . . . I couldn't scream, couldn't even scream. . . . D'ye think I'm really badly wounded, Bill? Me clothes seem to be all soakin' wet. . . . It's blood . . . My God, it must be me own blood!

Capt. Brennan [*to Clitheroe*]. Go on, Jack, bid her good-bye with another kiss, an' be done with it! D'ye want Langon to die in me arms while you're dallyin' with your Nora?

Clitheroe [*to Nora*]. I must go, I must go, Nora. I'm sorry we met at all. . . . It couldn't be helped — all other ways were blocked be th' British. . . . Let me go, can't you, Nora? D'ye want me to be unthrue to me comrades?

Nora. No, I won't let you go. . . . I want you to be thrue to me, Jack. . . . I'm your dearest comrade; I'm your thruest comrade. . . . They only want th' comfort of havin' you in th' same danger as them-selves. . . . Oh, Jack, I can't let you go!

Clitheroe. You must, Nora, you must.

Nora. All last night at th' barricades I sought you, Jack. . . . I didn't think of th' danger — I could only think of you. . . . I asked for you everywhere. . . . Some o' them laughed. . . . I was pushed away, but I shoved back. . . . Some o' them even sthruck me. . . . an' I screamed an' screamed your name!

Clitheroe [*in fear her action would give him future shame*].

What possessed you to make a show of yourself, like
that ? . . . What way d'ye think I'll feel when I'm
told my wife was bawlin' for me at th' barricades ?
What are you more than any other woman ?

Nora. No more, maybe ; but you are more to me
than any other man, Jack. . . . I didn't mean any
harm, honestly, Jack. . . . I couldn't help it. . . . I
shouldn't have told you. . . . My love for you made
me mad with terror.

Clitheroe [*angrily*]. They'll say now that I sent you out
th' way I'd have an excuse to bring you home. . . .
Are you goin' to turn all th' risks I'm takin' into a
laugh ?

Lieut. Langon. Let me lie down, let me lie down, Bill ;
th' pain would be easier, maybe, lyin' down. . . . Oh,
God, have mercy on me !

Capt. Brennan [*to Langon*]. A few steps more, Jim, a few
steps more ; thry to stick it for a few steps more.

Lieut. Langon. Oh, I can't, I can't, I can't !

Capt. Brennan [*to Clitheroe*]. Are you comin', man, or are
you goin' to make an arrangement for another honeymoon ? . . . If you want to act th' renegade, say so,
an' we'll be off !

Bessie [*from above*]. Runnin' from th' Tommies — choke
th' chicken. Runnin' from th' Tommies — choke th'
chicken !

Clitheroe [*savagely to Brennan*]. Damn you, man, who
wants to act th' renegade ? [*To Nora*] Here, let go
your hold ; let go, I say !

Nora [*clinging to Clitheroe, and indicating Brennan*]. Look,
Jack, look at th' anger in his face ; look at th' fear

glintin' in his eyes. . . . He himself's afraid, afraid, afraid ! . . . He wants you to go th' way he'll have th' chance of death sthrikin' you an' missin' him ! . . . Turn round an' look at him, Jack, look at him, look at him ! . . . His very soul is cold . . . shiverin' with th' thought of what may happen to him. . . . It is his fear that is thryin' to frighten you from recognizin' th' same fear that is in your own heart !

Clitheroe [*struggling to release himself from Nora*]. Damn you, woman, will you let me go !

Capt. Brennan [*fiercely, to Clitheroe*]. Why are you beggin' her to let you go ? Are you afraid of her, or what ? Break her hold on you, man, or go up, an' sit on her lap !   [*Clitheroe trying roughly to break her hold.*

Nora [*imploringly*]. Oh, Jack. . . . Jack. . . . Jack !

Lieut. Langon [*agonisingly*]. Brennan, a priest ; I'm dyin', I think, I'm dyin' !

Clitheroe [*to Nora*]. If you won't do it quietly, I'll have to make you ! [*To Brennan*] Here, hold this gun, you, for a minute.   [*He hands the gun to Brennan.*

Nora [*pitifully*]. Please, Jack. . . . You're hurting me, Jack. . . . Honestly. . . . Oh, you're hurting . . . me ! . . . I won't, I won't, I won't ! . . . Oh, Jack, I gave you everything you asked of me. . . . Don't fling me from you, now !
       [*He roughly loosens her grip, and pushes her away from him. Nora sinks to the ground and lies there.*

Nora [*weakly*]. Ah, Jack. . . . Jack. . . . Jack !

Clitheroe [*taking the gun back from Brennan*]. Come on, come on.

[*They go out.   Bessie looks at Nora lying on the street, for a few moments, then, leaving the window, she comes out, runs over to Nora, lifts her up in her arms, and carries her swiftly into the house.   A short pause, then down the street is heard a wild, drunken yell ; it comes nearer, and Fluther enters, frenzied, wild-eyed, mad, roaring drunk. In his arms is an earthen half-gallon jar of whisky ; streaming from one of the pockets of his coat is the arm of a new tunic shirt ; on his head is a woman's vivid blue hat with gold lacing, all of which he has looted.*

Fluther [*singing in a frenzy*] :

Fluther's a jolly good fella ! . . . Fluther's a jolly good
fella !
Up th' rebels ! . . . That nobody can deny !

[*He beats on the door.*
Get us a mug or a jug, or somethin', some o' yous, one
o' yous, will yous, before I lay one o' yous out ! . . .
[*Looking down the street*] Bang an' fire away for all Fluther
cares. . . . [*Banging at door*] Come down an' open th'
door, some of yous, one o' yous, will yous, before I
lay some o' yous out ! . . . Th' whole city can topple
home to hell, for Fluther !

[*Inside the house is heard a scream from Nora, followed by a moan.*

Fluther [*singing furiously*] :

That nobody can deny, that nobody can deny,
For Fluther's a jolly good fella, Fluther's a jolly good fella,
Fluther's a jolly good fella . . . Up th' rebels ! That
nobody can deny !

[*His frantic movements cause him to spill some of the whisky out of the jar.*
Blast you, Fluther, don't be spillin' th' precious
liquor ! [*He kicks at the door.*] Ay, give us a mug or a

jug, or somethin', one o' yous, some o' yous, will yous, before I lay one o' yous out !

[*The door suddenly opens, and Bessie, coming out, grips him by the collar.*

Bessie [*indignantly*]. You bowsey, come in ower o' that. . . . I'll thrim your thricks o' dhrunken dancin' for you, an' none of us knowin' how soon we'll bump into a world we were never in before !

Fluther [*as she is pulling him in*]. Ay, th' jar, th' jar, th' jar !

[*A short pause, then again is heard a scream of pain from Nora. The door opens and Mrs. Gogan and Bessie are seen standing at it.*

Bessie. Fluther would go, only he's too dhrunk. . . . Oh, God, isn't it a pity he's so dhrunk ! We'll have to thry to get a docthor somewhere.

Mrs. Gogan. I'd be afraid to go. . . . Besides, Mollser's terrible bad. I don't think you'll get a docthor to come. It's hardly any use goin'.

Bessie [*determinedly*]. I'll risk it. . . . Give her a little of Fluther's whisky. . . . It's th' fright that's brought it on her so soon. . . . Go on back to her, you.

[*Mrs. Gogan goes in, and Bessie softly closes the door. She is moving forward, when the sound of some rifle shots, and the tok, tok, tok of a distant machine-gun bring her to a sudden halt. She hesitates for a moment, then she tightens her shawl round her, as if it were a shield, then she firmly and swiftly goes out.*

Bessie [*as she goes out*]. Oh, God, be Thou my help in time o' throuble. An' shelter me safely in th' shadow of Thy wings !

CURTAIN

ACT IV

The living-room of Bessie Burgess. It is one of two small attic rooms [the other, used as a bedroom, is to the Left], the ceiling slopes up towards the back, giving to the apartment a look of compressed confinement. In the centre of the ceiling is a small skylight. There is an unmistakable air of poverty bordering on destitution. The paper on the walls is torn and soiled, particularly near the fire where the cooking is done, and near the washstand where the washing is done. The fireplace is to the Left. A small armchair near fire. One small window at Back. A pane of this window is starred by the entrance of a bullet. Under the window to the Right is an oak coffin standing on two kitchen chairs. Near the coffin is a home-manufactured stool, on which are two lighted candles. Beside the window is a worn-out dresser on which is a small quantity of delf. Tattered remains of cheap lace curtains drape the window. Standing near the window on Left is a brass standard-lamp with a fancy shade ; hanging on the wall near the same window is a vividly crimson silk dress, both of which have been looted. A door on Left leading to the bedroom. Another opposite giving a way to the rest of the house. To the Left of this door a common washstand. A tin kettle, very black, and an old saucepan inside the fender. There is no light in the room but that given from the two candles and the fire. The dusk has well fallen, and the glare of the burning buildings in the town can be seen through the window, in the distant sky. The Covey and Fluther have been playing cards, sitting on the floor by the light of the candles on the stool near the coffin. When the curtain rises the Covey is shuffling the cards, Peter is sitting in a stiff, dignified way

239

beside him, and Fluther is kneeling beside the window, cautiously looking out. It is a few days later.

Fluther [*furtively peeping out of the window*]. Give them a good shuffling. . . . Th' sky's gettin' reddher an' reddher. . . . You'd think it was afire. . . . Half o' th' city must be burnin'.

The Covey. If I was you, Fluther, I'd keep away from that window. . . . It's dangerous, an', besides, if they see you, you'll only bring a nose on th' house.

Peter. Yes ; an' he knows we had to leave our own place th' way they were riddlin' it with machine-gun fire. . . . He'll keep on pimpin' an' pimpin' there, till we have to fly out o' this place too.

Fluther [*ironically*]. If they make any attack here, we'll send you out in your green an' glory uniform, shakin' your sword over your head, an' they'll fly before you as th' Danes flew before Brian Boru !

The Covey [*placing the cards on the floor, after shuffling them*]. Come on, an' cut.
> [*Fluther comes over, sits on floor, and cuts the cards.*

The Covey [*having dealt the cards*]. Spuds up again.
> [*Nora moans feebly in room on Left.*

Fluther. There, she's at it again. She's been quiet for a long time, all th' same.

The Covey. She was quiet before, sure, an' she broke out again worse than ever. . . . What was led that time ?

Peter. Thray o' Hearts, Thray o' Hearts, Thray o' Hearts.

Fluther. It's damned hard lines to think of her dead-born kiddie lyin' there in th' arms o' poor little Mollser. Mollser snuffed it sudden too, afther all.

The Covey. Sure she never got any care. How could she get it, an' th' mother out day an' night lookin' for work, an' her consumptive husband leavin' her with a baby to be born before he died !

Voices in a lilting chant to the Left in a distant street. Red Cr . . . oss, Red Cr . . . oss ! . . . Ambu . . . lance, Ambu . . . lance !

The Covey [to Fluther]. Your deal, Fluther.

Fluther [shuffling and dealing the cards]. It'll take a lot out o' Nora — if she'll ever be th' same.

The Covey. Th' docthor thinks she'll never be th' same ; thinks she'll be a little touched here. [*He touches his forehead.*] She's ramblin' a lot ; thinkin' she's out in th' counthry with Jack ; or gettin' his dinner ready for him before he comes home ; or yellin' for her kiddie. All that, though, might be th' chloroform she got. . . . I don't know what we'd have done only for oul' Bessie : up with her for th' past three nights, hand runnin'.

Fluther. I always knew there was never anything really derogatory wrong with poor oul' Bessie. [*To Peter, who is taking a trick*] Ay, houl' on, there, don't be so damn quick — that's my thrick.

Peter. What's your thrick ? It's my thrick, man.

Fluther [loudly]. How is it your thrick ?

Peter [answering as loudly]. Didn't I lead th' deuce !

Fluther. You must be gettin' blind, man ; don't you see th' ace ?

Bessie [*appearing at door of room, Left ; in a tense whisper*].
D'ye want to waken her again on me, when she's just
gone asleep ? If she wakes will yous come an' mind
her ? If I hear a whisper out o' one o' yous again, I'll
. . . gut yous !

The Covey [*in a whisper*]. S-s-s-h. She can hear anything
above a whisper.

Peter [*looking up at the ceiling*]. Th' gentle an' merciful
God 'll give th' pair o' yous a scawldin' an' a scarifyin'
one o' these days !
  [*Fluther takes a bottle of whisky from his pocket, and takes a
  drink.*

The Covey [*to Fluther*]. Why don't you spread that out,
man, an' thry to keep a sup for to-morrow ?

Fluther. Spread it out ? Keep a sup for to-morrow ?
How th' hell does a fella know there'll be any to-
morrow ? If I'm goin' to be whipped away, let me be
whipped away when it's empty, an' not when it's half
full ! [*To Bessie, who has seated herself in an armchair at
the fire*] How is she, now, Bessie ?

Bessie. I left her sleeping quietly. When I'm listenin' to
her babblin', I think she'll never be much betther than
she is. Her eyes have a hauntin' way of lookin' in
instead of lookin' out, as if her mind had been lost
alive in madly minglin' memories of th' past. . . .
[*Sleepily*] Crushin' her thoughts . . . together . . . in
a fierce . . . an' fanciful . . . [*she nods her head and
starts wakefully*] idea that dead things are livin', an'
livin' things are dead. . . . [*With a start*] Was that
a scream I heard her give ? [*Reassured*] Blessed God, I
think I hear her screamin' every minute ! An' it's
only there with me that I'm able to keep awake.

The Covey. She'll sleep, maybe, for a long time, now. Ten there.

Fluther. Ten here. If she gets a long sleep, she might be all right. Peter's th' lone five.

The Covey. Whisht! I think I hear somebody movin' below. Whoever it is, he's comin' up.

A pause. Then the door opens and Captain Brennan comes into the room. He has changed his uniform for a suit of civvies. His eyes droop with the heaviness of exhaustion; his face is pallid and drawn. His clothes are dusty and stained here and there with mud. He leans heavily on the back of a chair as he stands.

Capt. Brennan. Mrs. Clitheroe; where's Mrs. Clitheroe? I was told I'd find her here.

Bessie. What d'ye want with Mrs. Clitheroe?

Capt. Brennan. I've a message, a last message for her from her husband.

Bessie. Killed! He's not killed, is he!

Capt. Brennan [*sinking stiffly and painfully on to a chair*]. In th' Imperial Hotel; we fought till th' place was in flames. He was shot through th' arm, an' then through th' lung. . . . I could do nothin' for him — only watch his breath comin' an' goin' in quick, jerky gasps, an' a tiny sthream o' blood thricklin' out of his mouth, down over his lower lip. . . . I said a prayer for th' dyin', an' twined his Rosary beads around his fingers. . . . Then I had to leave him to save meself. . . . [*He shows some holes in his coat*] Look at th' way a machine-gun tore at me coat, as I belted out o' th' buildin' an' darted across th' sthreet for shelter. . . .

An' then, I seen The Plough an' th' Stars fallin' like a shot as th' roof crashed in, an' where I'd left poor Jack was nothin' but a leppin' spout o' flame !

Bessie [*with partly repressed vehemence*]. Ay, you left him ! You twined his Rosary beads round his fingers, an' then you run like a hare to get out o' danger !

Capt. Brennan. I took me chance as well as him. . . . He took it like a man.   His last whisper was to " Tell Nora to be brave ; that I'm ready to meet my God, an' that I'm proud to die for Ireland."   An' when our General heard it he said that " Commandant Clitheroe's end was a gleam of glory."   Mrs. Clitheroe's grief will be a joy when she realizes that she has had a hero for a husband.

Bessie. If you only seen her, you'd know to th' differ.
[*Nora appears at door, Left.   She is clad only in her nightdress ;   her hair, uncared for some days, is hanging in disorder over her shoulders.   Her pale face looks paler still because of a vivid red spot on the tip of each cheek. Her eyes are glimmering with the light of incipient insanity ;   her hands are nervously fiddling with her nightgown.   She halts at the door for a moment, looks vacantly around the room, and then comes slowly in.   The rest do not notice her till she speaks.*

Nora [*in a quiet and monotonous tone*]. No . . . Not there, Jack. . . . I can feel comfortable only in our own familiar place beneath th' bramble tree. . . . We must be walking for a long time ; I feel very, very tired. . . . Have we to go farther, or have we passed it by ? [*Passing her hand across her eyes*] Curious mist on my eyes. . . . Why don't you hold my hand, Jack. . . . [*Excitedly*] No, no, Jack, it's not.   Can't you see it's a goldfinch. Look at th' black-satiny wings with th' gold bars, an' th' splash of crimson on its head. . . . [*Wearily*] Something ails me, something ails me. . . . Don't kiss me like that; you take my breath away, Jack. . . . Why do you frown at me? . . . You're going away, and [*frightened*] I can't follow you. Something's keeping me from moving. . . . [*Crying out*] Jack, Jack, Jack!

Bessie [*who has gone over and caught Nora's arm*]. Now, Mrs. Clitheroe, you're a terrible woman to get up out of bed. . . . You'll get cold if you stay here in them clothes.

Nora. Cold? I'm feelin' very cold; it's chilly out here in th' counthry. . . . [*Looking around frightened*] What place is this? Where am I?

Bessie [*coaxingly*]. You're all right, Nora; you're with friends, an' in a safe place. Don't you know your uncle an' your cousin, an' poor oul' Fluther?

Peter [*about to go over to Nora*]. Nora, darlin', now——

Fluther [*pulling him back*]. Now, leave her to Bessie, man. A crowd 'll only make her worse.

Nora [*thoughtfully*]. There is something I want to remember, an' I can't. [*With agony*] I can't, I can't, I can't! My head, my head! [*Suddenly breaking from Bessie, and running over to the men, and gripping Fluther by the shoulders*] Where is it? Where's my baby? Tell me where you've put it, where've you hidden it? My baby, my baby; I want my baby! My head, my poor head. . . . Oh, I can't tell what is wrong with me. [*Screaming*] Give him to me, give me my husband!

Bessie. Blessin' o' God on us, isn't this pitiful!

Nora [*struggling with Bessie*]. I won't go away for you ;
I won't. Not till you give me back my husband.
[*Screaming*] Murderers, that's what yous are ; mur-
derers, murderers !

Bessie. S-s-sh. We'll bring Mr. Clitheroe back to you,
if you'll only lie down an' stop quiet. . . . [*Trying to
lead her in*] Come on, now, Nora, an' I'll sing something to you.

Nora. I feel as if my life was thryin' to force its way
out of my body. . . . I can hardly breathe . . . I'm
frightened, I'm frightened, I'm frightened ! For
God's sake, don't leave me, Bessie. Hold my hand,
put your arms around me !

Fluther [*to Brennan*]. Now you can see th' way she is,
man.

Peter. An' what way would she be if she heard Jack had
gone west ?

The Covey [*to Peter*]. Shut up, you, man !

Bessie [*to Nora*]. We'll have to be brave, an' let patience
clip away th' heaviness of th' slow-movin' hours,
rememberin' that sorrow may endure for th' night, but
joy cometh in th' mornin'. . . . Come on in, an' I'll
sing to you, an' you'll rest quietly.

Nora [*stopping suddenly on her way to the room*]. Jack an' me
are goin' out somewhere this evenin'. Where I can't
tell. Isn't it curious I can't remember. . . . Maura,
Maura, Jack, if th' baby's a girl ; any name you like,
if th' baby's a boy ! . . . He's there. [*Screaming*]
He's there, an' they won't give him back to me !

Bessie. S-ss-s-h, darlin', s-ssh. I won't sing to you, if
you're not quiet.

Nora [*nervously holding Bessie*]. Hold my hand, hold my hand, an' sing to me, sing to me !

Bessie. Come in an' lie down, an' I'll sing to you.

Nora [*vehemently*]. Sing to me, sing to me ; sing, sing !

Bessie [*singing as she leads Nora into room*] :

> Lead, kindly light, amid th' encircling gloom,
>> Lead Thou me on.
> Th' night is dark an' I am far from home,
>> Lead Thou me on.
> Keep Thou my feet, I do not ask to see
> Th' distant scene — one step enough for me.
>
> So long that Thou hast blessed me, sure Thou still
>> Wilt lead me on ;

[They go in.

Bessie [*singing in room*] :

> O'er moor an' fen, o'er crag an' torrent, till
>> Th' night is gone.
> An' in th' morn those angel faces smile
> That I have lov'd long since, an' lost awhile !

The Covey [*to Brennan*]. Now that you've seen how bad she is, an' that we daren't tell her what has happened till she's betther, you'd best be slippin' back to where you come from.

Capt. Brennan. There's no chance o' slippin' back now, for th' military are everywhere : a fly couldn't get through. I'd never have got here, only I managed to change me uniform for what I'm wearin'. . . . I'll have to take me chance, an' thry to lie low here for a while.

The Covey [*frightened*]. There's no place here to lie low. Th' Tommies 'll be hoppin' in here, any minute !

Peter [*aghast*]. An' then we'd all be shanghaied !

The Covey. Be God, there's enough afther happenin' to us !

Fluther [*warningly, as he listens*]. Whisht, whisht, th' whole o' yous. I think I heard th' clang of a rifle butt on th' floor of th' hall below. [*All alertness.*] Here, come on with th' cards again. I'll deal.

[*He shuffles and deals the cards to all.*

Fluther. Clubs up. [*To Brennan*] Thry to keep your hands from shakin', man. You lead, Peter. [*As Peter throws out a card*] Four o' Hearts led.

[*The door opens and Corporal Stoddart of the Wiltshires enters in full war kit ; steel helmet, rifle and bayonet, and trench tool. He looks round the room. A pause and a palpable silence.*

Fluther [*breaking the silence*]. Two tens an' a five.

Corporal Stoddart. 'Ello. [*Indicating the coffin*] This the stiff ?

The Covey. Yis.

Corporal Stoddart. Who's gowing with it ? Ownly one allowed to gow with it, you know.

The Covey. I dunno.

Corporal Stoddart. You dunnow ?

The Covey. I dunno.

Bessie [*coming into the room*]. She's afther slippin' off to sleep again, thanks be to God. I'm hardly able to keep me own eyes open. [*To the soldier*] Oh, are yous goin' to take away poor little Mollser ?

Corporal Stoddart. Ay ; 'oo's agowing with 'er ?

Bessie. Oh, th' poor mother, o' course. God help her, it's a terrible blow to her !

Fluther. A terrible blow ? Sure, she's in her element now, woman, mixin' earth to earth, an' ashes t'ashes an' dust to dust, an' revellin' in plumes an' hearses, last days an' judgements !

Bessie [*falling into chair by the fire*]. God bless us ! I'm jaded !

Corporal Stoddart. Was she plugged ?

The Covey. Ah, no ; died o' consumption.

Corporal Stoddart. Ow, is that all ? Thought she moight 'ave been plugged.

The Covey. Is that all ? Isn't it enough ? D'ye know, comrade, that more die o' consumption than are killed in th' wars ? An' it's all because of th' system we're livin' undher ?

Corporal Stoddart. Ow, I know. I'm a Sowcialist moiself, but I 'as to do my dooty.

The Covey [*ironically*]. Dooty ! Th' only dooty of a Socialist is th' emancipation of th' workers.

Corporal Stoddart. Ow, a man's a man, an 'e 'as to foight for 'is country, 'asn't 'e ?

Fluther [*aggressively*]. You're not fightin' for your counthry here, are you ?

Peter [*anxiously, to Fluther*]. Ay, ay, Fluther, none o' that, none o' that !

The Covey. Fight for your counthry ! Did y'ever read, comrade, Jenersky's *Thesis on the Origin, Development, an' Consolidation of th' Evolutionary Idea of the Proletariat* ?

Corporal Stoddart. Ow, cheese it, Paddy, cheese it !

Bessie [*sleepily*]. How is things in th' town, Tommy ?

Corporal Stoddart. Ow, I fink it's nearly hover. We've got 'em surrounded, and we're clowsing in on the bloighters. Ow, it was only a little bit of a dawg-foight.

[*The sharp ping of the sniper's rifle is heard, followed by a squeal of pain.*

Voices to the Left in a chant. Red Cr . . . oss, Red Cr . . . oss ! Ambu . . . lance, Ambu . . . lance !

Corporal Stoddart [*excitedly*]. Christ, that's another of our men 'it by that blawsted sniper ! 'E's knocking abaht 'ere, somewheres. Gawd, when we gets th' bloighter, we'll give 'im the cold steel, we will. We'll jab the belly aht of 'im, we will !

[*Mrs. Gogan comes in tearfully, and a little proud of the importance of being directly connected with death.*

Mrs. Gogan [*to Fluther*]. I'll never forget what you done for me, Fluther, goin' around at th' risk of your life settlin' everything with th' undhertaker an' th' cemetery people. When all me own were afraid to put their noses out, you plunged like a good one through hummin' bullets, an' they knockin' fire out o' th' road, tinklin' through th' frightened windows, an' splashin' themselves to pieces on th' walls ! An' you'll find, that Mollser, in th' happy place she's gone to, won't forget to whisper, now an' again, th' name o' Fluther.

Corporal Stoddart. Git it aht, mother, git it aht.

Bessie [*from the chair*]. It's excusin' me you'll be, Mrs.

Gogan, for not stannin' up, seein' I'm shaky on me feet for want of a little sleep, an' not desirin' to show any disrespect to poor little Mollser.

Fluther. Sure, we all know, Bessie, that it's vice versa with you.

Mrs. Gogan [*to Bessie*]. Indeed, it's meself that has well chronicled, Mrs. Burgess, all your gentle hurryin's to me little Mollser, when she was alive, bringin' her somethin' to dhrink, or somethin' t'eat, an' never passin' her without liftin' up her heart with a delicate word o' kindness.

Corporal Stoddart [*impatiently, but kindly*]. Git it aht, git it aht, mother.

[*The Covey, Fluther, Brennan, and Peter carry out the coffin, followed by Mrs. Gogan.*

Corporal Stoddart [*to Bessie, who is almost asleep*]. 'Ow many men is in this 'ere 'ouse? [*No answer. Loudly*] 'Ow many men is in this 'ere 'ouse?

Bessie [*waking with a start*]. God, I was nearly asleep! . . . How many men? Didn't you see them?

Corporal Stoddart. Are they all that are in the 'ouse?

Bessie. Oh, there's none higher up, but there may be more lower down. Why?

Corporal Stoddart. All men in the district 'as to be rounded up. Somebody's giving 'elp to the snipers, and we 'as to take precautions. If I 'ad my woy, I'd make 'em all join hup, and do their bit! But I suppowse they and you are all Shinners.

Bessie [*who has been sinking into sleep, waking up to a sleepy vehemence*]. Bessie Burgess is no Shinner, an' never had no thruck with anything spotted be th' fingers o' th' Fenians ; but always made it her business to harness herself for Church whenever she knew that God Save the King was goin' to be sung at t'end of th' service ; whose only son went to th' front in th' first contingent of the Dublin Fusiliers, an' that's on his way home carryin' a shatthered arm that he got fightin' for his King an' counthry !

> [*Her head sinks slowly forward again. Peter comes into the room ; his body is stiffened and his face is wearing a comically indignant look. He walks to and fro at the back of the room, evidently repressing a violent desire to speak angrily. He is followed in by Fluther, the Covey, and Brennan, who slinks into an obscure corner of the room, nervous of notice.*

Fluther [*after an embarrassing pause*]. Th' air in th' sthreet outside's shakin' with the firin' o' rifles an' machine-guns. It must be a hot shop in th' middle o' th' scrap.

Corporal Stoddart. We're pumping lead in on 'em from every side, now ; they'll soon be shoving up th' white flag.

Peter [*with a shout*]. I'm tellin' you either o' yous two lowsers 'ud make a betther hearse-man than Peter ; proddin' an' pokin' at me an' I helpin' to carry out a corpse !

Fluther. It wasn't a very derogatory thing for th' Covey to say that you'd make a fancy hearse-man, was it ?

Peter [*furiously*]. A pair o' redjesthered bowseys pondherin' from mornin' till night on how they'll get a chance to break a gap through th' quiet nature of a man that's always endeavourin' to chase out of him any sthray thought of venom against his fella-man !

The Covey. Oh, shut it, shut it, shut it !

Peter. As long as I'm a livin' man, responsible for me thoughts, words, an' deeds to th' Man above, I'll feel meself instituted to fight again' th' sliddherin' ways of a pair o' picaroons, whisperin', concurrin', concoctin', an' conspirin' together to rendher me unconscious of th' life I'm thryin' to live !

Corporal Stoddart [*dumbfounded*]. What's wrong, Daddy ; wot 'ave they done to you ?

Peter [*savagely to the Corporal*]. You mind your own business! What's it got to do with you, what's wrong with me ?

Bessie [*in a sleepy murmur*]. Will yous thry to conthrol yourselves into quietness ? Yous'll waken her . . . up . . . on . . . me . . . again.   [*She sleeps.*

Fluther. Come on, boys, to th' cards again, an' never mind him.

Corporal Stoddart. No use of you gowing to start cawds ; you'll be gowing out of 'ere, soon as Sergeant comes.

Fluther. Goin' out o' here ? An' why're we goin' out o' here ?

Corporal Stoddart. All men in district to be rounded up, and 'eld in till the scrap is hover.

Fluther. An' where're we goin' to be held in ?

Corporal Stoddart. They're puttin 'em in a church.

The Covey. A church ?

Fluther. What sort of a church ? Is it a Protestan' Church ?

Corporal Stoddart. I dunnow ; I suppowse so.

Fluther [*dismayed*]. Be God, it'll be a nice thing to be stuck all night in a Protestan' Church !

Corporal Stoddart. Bring the cawds ; you moight get a chance of a goime.

Fluther. Ah, no, that wouldn't do. . . . I wondher ? [*After a moment's thought*] Ah, I don't think we'd be doin' anything derogatory be playin' cards in a Protestan' Church.

Corporal Stoddart. If I was you I'd bring a little snack with me ; you moight be glad of it before the mawning. [*Sings*] :

> I do loike a snoice mince poy,
> I do loike a snoice mince poy !

[*The snap of the sniper's rifle rings out again, followed simultaneously by a scream of pain. Corporal Stoddart goes pale, and brings his rifle to the ready, listening.*

Voices chanting to the Right. Red Cro . . . ss, Red Cro . . . ss ! Ambu . . . lance, Ambu . . . lance !
[*Sergeant Tinley comes rapidly in, pale, agitated, and fiercely angry.*

Corporal Stoddart [*to Sergeant*]. One of hour men 'it, Sergeant ?

Sergeant Tinley. Private Taylor ; got 'it roight through the chest, 'e did ; an 'ole in front of 'im as 'ow you could put your fist through, and 'arf 'is back blown awoy ! Dum-dum bullets they're using. Gang of Hassassins potting at us from behind roofs. That's not playing the goime : why down't they come into the owpen and foight fair !

Fluther [*unable to stand the slight*]. Fight fair ! A few hundhred scrawls o' chaps with a couple o' guns an' Rosary beads, again' a hundhred thousand thrained men with horse, fut. an' artillery . . . an' he wants us to fight fair ! [*To Sergeant*] D'ye want us to come out in our skins an' throw stones ?

Sergeant Tinley [*to Corporal*]. Are these four all that are 'ere ?

Corporal Stoddart. Four ; that's all, Sergeant.

Sergeant Tinley [*vindictively*]. Come on, then ; get the blighters aht. [*To the men*] 'Ere, 'op it aht ! Aht into the streets with you, and if a snoiper sends another of our men west, you gow with 'im ! [*He catches Fluther by the shoulder*] Gow on, git aht !

Fluther. Eh, who are you chuckin', eh ?

Sergeant Tinley [*roughly*]. Gow on, git aht, you blighter.

Fluther. Who are you callin' a blighter to, eh ? I'm a Dublin man, born an' bred in th' city, see ?

Sergeant Tinley. I down't care if you were Broin Buroo ; git aht, git aht.

Fluther [*halting as he is going out*]. Jasus, you an' your guns ! Leave them down, an' I'd beat th' two o' yous without sweatin' !

[*Peter, Brennan, the Covey, and Fluther, followed by the soldiers, go out. Bessie is sleeping heavily on the chair by the fire. After a pause, Nora appears at door, Left, in her nightdress. Remaining at door for a few moments she looks vaguely around the room. She then comes in quietly, goes over to the fire, pokes it, and puts the kettle on. She thinks for a few moments, pressing her hand to her forehead. She looks questioningly at the fire, and then at the press at back. She goes to the press, opens it, takes out a soiled cloth and spreads it on the table. She then places things for tea on the table.*

Nora. I imagine th' room looks very odd somehow. . . . I was nearly forgetting Jack's tea. . . . Ah, I think I'll have everything done before he gets in. . . . [*She lilts gently, as she arranges the table.*]

> Th' violets were scenting th' woods, Nora,
>   Displaying their charms to th' bee,
> When I first said I lov'd only you, Nora,
>   An' you said you lov'd only me.
>
> Th' chestnut blooms gleam'd through th' glade,
>   Nora,
>   A robin sang loud from a tree,
> When I first said I lov'd only you, Nora,
>   An' you said you lov'd only me.

[*She pauses suddenly, and glances round the room.*

Nora [*doubtfully*]. I can't help feelin' this room very strange. . . . What is it? . . . What is it? . . . I must think. . . . I must thry to remember. . . .

Voices chanting in a distant street. Ambu . . . lance, Ambu . . . lance ! Red Cro . . . ss, Red Cro . . . ss !

Nora [*startled and listening for a moment, then resuming the arrangement of the table*] :

Trees, birds, an' bees sang a song, Nora,
    Of happier transports to be,
When I first said I lov'd only you, Nora,
    An' you said you lov'd only me.

[*A burst of rifle fire is heard in a street near by, followed by the rapid rok, tok, tok of a machine-gun.*

Nora [*staring in front of her and screaming*]. Jack, Jack, Jack! My baby, my baby, my baby!

Bessie [*waking with a start*]. You divil, are you afther gettin' out o' bed again!
    [*She rises and runs towards Nora, who rushes to the window, which she frantically opens.*

Nora [*at window, screaming*]. Jack, Jack, for God's sake, come to me!

Soldiers [*outside, shouting*]. Git away, git away from that window, there!

Bessie [*seizing hold of Nora*]. Come away, come away, woman, from that window!

Nora [*struggling with Bessie*]. Where is it; where have you hidden it? Oh, Jack, Jack, where are you?

Bessie [*imploringly*]. Mrs. Clitheroe, for God's sake, come away!

Nora [*fiercely*]. I won't; he's below. Let . . . me . . . go! You're thryin' to keep me from me husband. I'll follow him. Jack, Jack, come to your Nora!

Bessie. Hus-s-sh, Nora, Nora! He'll be here in a minute. I'll bring him to you, if you'll only be quiet — honest to God, I will.
    [*With a great effort Bessie pushes Nora away from the*

window, the force used causing her to stagger against it herself. Two rifle shots ring out in quick succession. Bessie jerks her body convulsively ; stands stiffly for a moment, a look of agonized astonishment on her face, then she staggers forward, leaning heavily on the table with her hands.

Bessie [*with an arrested scream of fear and pain*]. Merciful God, I'm shot, I'm shot, I'm shot ! . . . Th' life's pourin' out o' me ! [*To Nora*] I've got this through . . . through you . . . through you, you bitch, you ! . . . O God, have mercy on me ! . . . [*To Nora*] You wouldn't stop quiet, no, you wouldn't, you wouldn't, blast you ! Look at what I'm afther gettin', look at what I'm afther gettin' . . . I'm bleedin' to death, an' no one's here to stop th' flowin' blood ! [*Calling*] Mrs. Gogan, Mrs. Gogan ! Fluther, Fluther, for God's sake, somebody, a doctor, a doctor !
    [*She staggers frightened towards the door, to seek for aid, but, weakening half-way across the room, she sinks to her knees, and bending forward, supports herself with her hands resting on the floor. Nora is standing rigidly with her back to the wall opposite, her trembling hands held out a little from the sides of her body, her lips quivering, her breast heaving, staring wildly at the figure of Bessie.*

Nora [*in a breathless whisper*]. Jack, I'm frightened. . . . I'm frightened, Jack. . . . Oh, Jack, where are you ?

Bessie [*moaningly*]. This is what's afther comin' on me for nursin' you day an' night. . . . I was a fool, a fool, a fool ! Get me a dhrink o' wather, you jade, will you ? There's a fire burnin' in me blood ! [*Pleadingly*] Nora, Nora, dear, for God's sake, run out an' get Mrs. Gogan, or Fluther, or somebody to bring a doctor, quick, quick, quick ! [*As Nora does not stir*] Blast you, stir yourself, before I'm gone !

Nora. Oh, Jack, Jack, where are you ?

Bessie [*in a whispered moan*]. Jesus Christ, me sight's goin' ! It's all dark, dark ! Nora, hold me hand !
    [*Bessie's body lists over and she sinks into a prostrate position on the floor.*

Bessie. I'm dyin', I'm dyin' . . . I feel it. . . . Oh God, oh God ! [*She feebly sings*]

> I do believe, I will believe
>   That Jesus died for me ;
> That on th' cross He shed His blood,
>   From sin to set me free. . . .

> I do believe . . . I will believe
>   . . . Jesus died . . . me ;
> . . . th' cross He shed . . . blood,
>   From sin . . . free.

    [*She ceases singing, and lies stretched out, still and very rigid. A pause. Then Mrs. Gogan runs hastily in.*

Mrs. Gogan [*quivering with fright*]. Blessed be God, what's afther happenin' ? [*To Nora*] What's wrong, child, what's wrong ? [*She sees Bessie, runs to her and bends over the body*] Bessie, Bessie ! [*She shakes the body*] Mrs. Burgess, Mrs. Burgess ! [*She feels Bessie's forehead*] My God, she's as cold as death. They're afther murdherin' th' poor inoffensive woman !
    [*Sergeant Tinley and Corporal Stoddart enter agitatedly, their rifles at the ready.*

Sergeant Tinley [*excitedly*]. This is the 'ouse. That's the window !

I*

Nora [*pressing back against the wall*]. Hide it, hide it ; cover it up, cover it up !

Sergeant Tinley [*going over to the body*]. 'Ere, what's this ? Who's this ? [*Looking at Bessie*] Oh Gawd, we've plugged one of the women of the 'ouse.

Corporal Stoddart. Whoy the 'ell did she gow to the window ? Is she dead ?

Sergeant Tinley. Oh, dead as bedamned. Well, we couldn't afford to toike any chawnces.

Nora [*screaming*]. Hide it, hide it ; don't let me see it ! Take me away, take me away, Mrs. Gogan !
   [*Mrs. Gogan runs into room, Left, and runs out again with a sheet which she spreads over the body of Bessie.*

Mrs. Gogan [*as she spreads the sheet*]. Oh, God help her, th' poor woman, she's stiffenin' out as hard as she can ! Her face has written on it th' shock o' sudden agony, an' her hands is whitenin' into th' smooth shininess of wax.

Nora [*whimperingly*]. Take me away, take me away ; don't leave me here to be lookin' an' lookin' at it !

Mrs. Gogan [*going over to Nora and putting her arm around her*]. Come on with me, dear, an' you can doss in poor Mollser's bed, till we gather some neighbours to come an' give th' last friendly touches to Bessie in th' lonely layin' of her out.
                    [*Mrs. Gogan and Nora go slowly out.*

Corporal Stoddart [*who has been looking around, to Sergeant Tinley*]. Tea here, Sergeant. Wot abaht a cup of scald ?

Sergeant Tinley. Pour it aht, Stoddart, pour it aht. I could scoff hanything just now.

> [*Corporal Stoddart pours out two cups of tea, and the two soldiers begin to drink. In the distance is heard a bitter burst of rifle and machine-gun fire, interspersed with the boom, boom of artillery. The glare in the sky seen through the window flares into a fuller and a deeper red.*

Sergeant Tinley. There gows the general attack on the Powst Office.

Voices in a distant street. Ambu . . . lance, Ambu . . . lance ! Red Cro . . . ss, Red Cro . . . ss !

> [*The voices of soldiers at a barricade outside the house are heard singing :*

> They were summoned from the 'illside,
> They were called in from the glen,
> And the country found 'em ready
> At the stirring call for men.
> Let not tears add to their 'ardship,
> As the soldiers pass along,
> And although our 'eart is breaking,
> Make it sing this cheery song.

Sergeant Tinley and Corporal Stoddart [*joining in the chorus, as they sip the tea*] :

> Keep the 'owme fires burning,
> While your 'earts are yearning ;
> Though your lads are far away
> They dream of 'owme ;
> There's a silver loining
> Through the dark cloud shoining,
> Turn the dark cloud inside out,
> Till the boys come 'owme !

CURTAIN

THE END OF THE BEGINNING

A Comedy in One Act

CHARACTERS IN THE PLAY

DARRY BERRILL. *About fifty-five; stocky, obstinate, with a pretty big belly. He is completely bald, except for a tuft of grey hair just above the forehead.*

BARRY DERRILL, *Darry's neighbour. Same age as Darry. Thin, easy-going, big moustache, and is very near-sighted.*

LIZZIE BERRILL, *Darry's wife. About forty-five. A good woman about the house, but that's about all.*

A big, comfortable kitchen. Steep stairs, almost like a ladder, leading to upper room, top right. Huge fireplace, right. Some chairs, one heavy, with rubbered castors. Small settee, and table. Chest of drawers, left, on top of which stands a gramophone. Door back, and to left of door a window. To right of door, a dresser, on which is, as well as delf, a large clock of the alarm type. To right of dresser, on a nail, hangs a whip; to the left of dresser hangs a mandolin. On table, a quantity of unwashed delf. To right of fireplace, a lumber room. The room, at night, is lighted by an electric bulb, hanging from centre of ceiling. It is a fine early autumn evening, with the sun low in the heavens. On wall, back, a large red card on which " Do It Now" is written in white letters. A sink under the window.

Darry [*at door of room above. He is shaving, and his chin is covered with lather*]. This shaving water's dead cold, woman. D'ye hear me? This shaving water's dead cold.

Lizzie [*busy about the room — quietly*]. Come down and heat it, then.

Darry [*scornfully*]. Too much to do, I suppose. I'd do all that has to be done here, three times over, 'n when all was finished, I'd be sighing for something to do.

Lizzie. If you had half of what I have to do here, at the end of the evening you'd be picked up dead out of the debris.

Darry. I would?

Lizzie. You would.

Darry. Sure ?

Lizzie. Certain.

Darry. If I only had half to do ?

Lizzie. Or less.

Darry. I'd be picked up out of the debris ?

Lizzie. Out of the middle of it.

Darry. Dead ?

Lizzie. As a mackerel.

Darry [*fiercely*]. I'm always challenging you to change places for a few hours, but you won't do it. I'd show you what a sinecure of a job you had here, while I'm sweating out in the fields.

Lizzie. Go out 'n finish the mowing of the meadow. It'll take you only half an hour or so, 'n there's plenty of light in the sky still.

Darry [*who has been shaving himself during this argument*]. The meadow'll do to be done to-morrow. Why don't you let me do what's to be done in the house, an' you go 'n mow the meadow ? Why don't you do that ? 'don't you do that ? 'you do that ? Agony to look at you ; agony to listen to you ; agony, agony to be anywhere near you.

Lizzie. I'd just like to see you doing what's to be done about the house — I'd just like to see you.

Darry. What is there to be done about the house — will you tell us that ?

Lizzie. There's the pig 'n the heifer 'n the hens to be

fed 'n tended. There's ironing, cooking, washing, 'n sewing to be done.

Darry. Sewing! An' only a button back 'n front of me so that it's next thing to a miracle that my trousers are kept from starting the neighbours talking.

Lizzie. If you say much more, I'll go 'n mow the meadow, 'n leave you to see what you can make of the house-work.

Darry [*angrily*]. Buzz off, buzz off, then, an' I'll show you how the work of a house is done. Done quietly; done with speed, 'n without a whisper of fuss in its doing. Buzz off, if you want to, 'n I'll show you 'n all your sex how the work of a house is done!

[*Lizzie violently pulls off a jazz-coloured overall she is wearing, and flings it on the floor.*

Lizzie [*furiously*]. Put that on you, 'n do what remains to be done about the house, while I go an' mow the meadow. Get into it, 'n show the world an' your poor wife the wonders you can do when you're under a woman's overall.

Darry [*a little frightened*]. Oh, I'll manage all right.

Lizzie. An' don't you let that Alice Lanigan in here while I'm away either, d'ye hear?

Darry. What Alice Lanigan?

Lizzie [*in a temper*]. What Alice Lanigan! The Alice Lanigan I caught you chattering to yesterday, when you should have been mowing the meadow. The Alice Lanigan that's setting you on to nag at me about the little I have to do in the house. The Alice Lanigan that's goading you into the idea that if you were a little slimmer round the belly, you'd be a shevaleer, an's getting you to do physical jerks. The Alice Lanigan that's on the margin of fifty, 'n assembles herself together as if she was a girl in her teens, jutting out her bust when she's coming in, 'n jutting out her behind when she's going out, like the Lady of Shalott, to catch the men — that's the Alice Lanigan I mean.

Darry. I don't be thinking of Alice Lanigan.

Lizzie. I've seen you, when you thought I slumbered 'n slept, naked, with nothing at all on you, doing your physical jerks in front of the looking-glass, 'n that, too, when the lessons of a Mission were still hot in your heart — an' all for Alice Lanigan. Maybe you don't know that she has a kid who has never had a pat on the head from a father.

Darry. You buzz off now, 'n I'll show how the work of a house is done.

Lizzie [*while she is putting a broad-brimmed hat on her head, pulling a pair of old gloves over her hands, and taking down a whip hanging from a nail in the wall*]. I'm telling you it's a dangerous thing to shake hands with Alice Lanigan, even with a priest giving the introduction. The day'll come soon when you'll know she's making mechanical toys of you 'n that other old fool, Barry Derrill, who's so near-sighted that he can't see the sky, unless the moon's shining in it !

Darry. Cheerio.

Lizzie [*at the door*]. I'm going now, 'n we'll see how you do the work of the house.

Darry. Hail 'n farewell to you. An' mind you, this'll be only the beginning of things.

Lizzie. God grant that it won't be the end, an' that when I come back, I'll at least find the four walls standing.

[*She goes out. Darry strolls to the door, and watches her going down the road.*

Darry [*scornfully to himself*]. Mow the meadow ! Well, let her see her folly out.

[*As he shuts the door, the clock in the distant Town Hall strikes eight. Darry returns, glances at the clock on the dresser, notices that it has stopped, takes it up, puts his ear against it, shakes it, begins to wind it, finds it difficult to turn, puts added strength into the turning, and a whirring rattle, like a strong spring breaking, comes from the inside of the clock. He hastily replaces the clock on the dresser. After a few seconds' thought, he takes it up again, removes the back, and part of a big, broken spring darts out, which he hurriedly crams in again, and puts the clock back on the dresser.*

Darry. Lizzie again !

[*He catches sight of the gramophone, looks at it, thinks for a second, goes over to the chest of drawers, takes some records from behind it, and fixes one on the disc of the gramophone. He takes off his waistcoat, loosens his braces, stands stiff, strokes his thighs, pats his belly, and tries to push it back a little. He starts the gramophone going, runs to the centre of the room, and lies down on the broad of his back. The gramophone begins to give directions for physical exercises, to which Darry listens and, awkwardly, clumsily, and puffingly, tries to follow the movements detailed in the words spoken by the gramophone when the music commences.*

Gramophone. Lie on back ; hands behind the head ; feet together — are you ready ? Bend the right knee ;

draw it into the waistline, towards the chest — commence !

[*Darry is too slow, or the gramophone is too quick, for he can't keep up with the time of the music. When he finds that he is behind the time of the music, Darry increases his speed by partial performance of the movements, and so gets into touch with the time, but presently, blowing and panting, he is out of time again by a beat or two. He climbs stiffly on to his feet, goes over to gramophone, and puts the indicator to " Slow".*

Darry. Phuh. Too quick, too damn quick altogether.

[*He starts the gramophone going, runs to the centre of the room, and again lies down on the broad of his back. When the music begins he goes through the movements as before ; but the music is playing so slowly now that he finds it impossible to go slowly enough to keep to the time of the tune. When he finds himself in front of a beat, he stops and puffs and waits for the beat to catch up with him before he recommences. As he is going through these movements, the door opens, and Barry Derrill comes into the room. He has a mandolin under his arm, and is wearing wide-rimmed, thick-lensed spectacles.*

Barry [*briskly*]. Come 'n kiss me sweet 'n twenty — what the hell are you trying to do ?

Darry. Can't you see what I'm trying to do ? Take off your spectacles 'n get a closer look. Keeping meself fit 'n flexible — that's what I'm trying to do.

Barry. The rhythm's too slow, man ; tense your muscles ; you're not tun'd into the movements properly, man.

Darry. The indicator must have shifted. Slip over 'n put it to the point marked medium, 'n then get down here 'n give us a hand.

Barry. What about the prologue of playing the song we're to sing at the Town Hall concert ?

Darry. Get down 'n have five minutes of this, first ; we'll both sing the better for it.

Barry [*dubiously*]. Never done it to music, 'n I wouldn't be able to keep in touch with the — with the measure.

Darry. The music makes it easier, man.   Keep your eye on me, 'n move when I move.

> [*Barry reluctantly takes off his coat and waistcoat, goes over to the gramophone, puts his nose against the instrument, and puts the indicator to " Fast ".*

Darry. To do this thing properly you'd want to be wearing shorts.   Right ;   now keep in touch with the rhythm, or you'll mar everything.   Start her off, and stretch yourself down.

> [*Barry starts the gramophone, runs over and lies down opposite to Darry, so that the soles of their feet are only a few inches apart.*

Gramophone [*very rapidly*]. Lie on back ;   hands behind the head ;   feet together — are you ready ?   Bend the right knee ;   draw it into the waistline towards the chest ; breathe out — commence !

> [*The tempo of the tune forces them to do the exercises in a frantic way, till it dawns on Darry, who is nearly exhausted, that there's something wrong.   He stops while Barry goes on manfully.*

Darry [*scornfully*]. Eh, eh, there, wait a minute, wait a minute, man.   Don't you see anything wrong ?

Barry [*stopping*]. No ;   what's wrong ?

Darry [*testily*]. Aw, what's wrong !   We're congestin'

ourselves with speed ; that's what's wrong. You must have jammed the indicator hard to Fast. [*He gets up, goes to the gramophone, and puts it right.*] We're entertainin' ourselves, an' not tryin' to say the Rosary.

[*He comes back and stretches himself again on the floor. The music begins and the two men commence the exercises. After a few moments, Darry slows down a little, misses several beats, and tries to blame Barry.*

Darry [*excitedly keeping up the movements, but out of time, as he talks*]. Try to keep the proper rhythm up, man. [*He hums the tune of " Coming thro' the Rye".*] Dad th' didee dah th' diddy dah th' diddy dee — that way, man. Dah th' diddy dah th' diddy [*rapidly*]. Keep your eye on me. Dah th' diddy dee.

[*After a few moments Darry is out of time and breathless ; he stops and sits up to complain, but he really wants to get a rest.*

Darry [*with aggravated patience*]. Barry, you're spoiling the whole thing by getting out of time. Don't let your arms and legs go limber, tense your muscles. Three beats to the bar, see ? Now !

[*They start again ; Darry is soon behind time, blowing and puffing out of him. Barry keeps to the beat of the tune splendidly.*

Darry [*angrily*]. You're going too damn quick altogether, now, man !

Barry. No I'm not — I'm there to the tick every time.

Darry [*violently*]. There to the tick — how is it you're not in the line with me, then, if you're there to the tick ? I don't know whether you're in front of me or behind me. Are you too stiff or what ?

Barry. I'm there to the second every time.   It's you that's missin' a beat in the bar.

Darry [*indignantly, stopping to talk, while Barry goes on*]. I'm missin' it because I'm trying to foster you into the right balance 'n rhythm of the movements.   That's why I'm missin' it. [*Loudly*] An' I'm wastin' me time !

Barry [*sharply*]. I'm doin' me best, amn't I ?

Darry [*more sharply still*]. Your best's a hell of a way behind what's wanted.   It's pitiful 'n painful to be watchin' you, man.   [*He stands up and looks at Barry, who keeps going.*] Eh, eh, you'll do yourself an injury, Barry.   Get up 'n we'll do the song.   [*As Barry goes on*] Oh, get up 'n we'll do the song.
 [*Barry gets up reluctantly, and Darry goes over and stops the gramophone.*

Barry. I was doin' it well enough, if you'd let me alone.

Darry [*scornfully*]. Yes ;   like the Londonderry Air play'd in march time.
 [*They get their mandolins and stand side by side at the back.*

Darry. Now we walk in a semicircle down to the front, 'n bow, you remember ?   Ready ?

Barry. Yep.

Darry. Go !
 [*They both step off to the right, take a few steps, and then they halt.*

Barry. Something wrong ;   we don't go round the same way, do we ?

Darry [*testily*]. Of course there's something wrong ;   of course we don't go round the same way.   Can't you try to remember, Barry? You're to go to the left, to the left.

Barry. I remember distinctly I was to go to the right.

Darry [*irritably*]. Oh, don't be such an egotist, Barry. Now think for a minute. [*A pause.*] Now make up your mind — d'ye want to go to the left or the right?

Barry [*testily*]. Oh, left, right — any way.

Darry. Left, then. Go.
  [*They march round, one to the right, the other to the left, meet in the front, and bow.*

Darry. You start, Barry, my boy.

Barry [*singing*].
  One summer eve a handsome man met a handsome maiden strolling,

Darry.
  Down where the bees were hummin' an' the wild flowers gaily growing ;

Barry.
  Said she, We'll sit down here a while, all selfish thoughts controlling,

Darry.
  Down where the bees are hummin' an' the wild flowers gaily growing :

Barry.
  Said she, We'll meditate on things, things high 'n edifying,
  How all things live 'n have their day 'n end their day by dying.
  He put his hand on her white breast an' murmur'd, Life is trying,

Darry.

Down where· the bees are hummin' an' the wild
flowers gaily growing.

Barry.

The moon glanc'd down 'n wonder'd what the pair of
them were doing,

Darry.

Down where the bees were hummin' an' the wild
flowers gaily growing ;

Barry.

Then th' moon murmur'd, I feel hot, 'n fear a storm
is brewing,

Darry.

Down where the bees are hummin' an' the wild
flowers gaily growing.

Barry.

She talk'd so well of things so high, he started to
reward her,

The moon ran in behind a cloud, for there was none
to guard her.

I'll take that off, she said, you'd ruin the lace that's
round the border,

Darry.

Down where the bees are hummin' an' the wild
flowers gaily growing.

Barry.

White-featur'd 'n thin goodie-goodies rush around
excited,

Darry.

Down where the bees are hummin' an' the wild
flowers gaily growing ;

Barry.
  Proclaiming that the dignity of living has been
  blighted,

Darry.
  Down where the bees are hummin' an' the wild
  flowers gaily growing.

Barry.
  But when the light is soft 'n dim, discovery disarming.
  The modest moon behind the clouds, young maidens,
  coy 'n charming,
  Still cuddle men who cuddle them, 'n carry on alarm-
  ing,

Darry.
  Down where the bees are hummin' an' the wild
  flowers gaily growing.
    [*When the song has ended, Darry cocks his ear and listens.*

Barry. Shall we try it once more ?

Darry. Shush, shut up, can't you ?
    [*Darry goes over to the door, opens it, and listens intently.
    There is heard the rattling whirr caused by the steady and
    regular movement of a mowing machine. The distant
    Town Hall clock strikes nine.*

Darry [*hastily putting the mandolin away*]. I forgot. I'll
  have to get going.

Barry. Get going at what ?

Darry. House-work. [*He begins to get into the overall left
  off by Lizzie.*] I dared her, an' she left me to do the
  work of the house while she was mowing the meadow.
  If it isn't done when she comes back, then sweet good-
  bye to the status I had in the home. [*He finds it difficult*

to get the overall on.] Dih dih dih, where's the back
'n where's the front, 'n which is which is the bottom
'n which is the top ?

Barry. Take it quietly, take it quietly, Darry.

Darry [*resentfully*]. Take it quietly ?   An' the time
galloping by ?   I can't stand up on a chair 'n say to
the sun, stand thou still there, over the meadow th'
missus is mowing, can I ?

Barry. I know damn well you can't, but you're not going
to expedite matters by rushing around in a hurry.

Darry [*he has struggled into the overall*]. Expedite matters !
It doesn't seem to strike you that when you do things
quickly, things are quickly done.   Expedite matters !
I suppose loitering to look at you lying on the broad
of your back, jiggling your legs about, was one way of
expediting matters ;   an' listening to you plucking
curious sounds out of a mandolin, an' singing a ques-
tionable song, was another way of expediting matters ?

Barry. You pioneered me into doing two of them yourself.

Darry [*busy with the pot on the fire*]. I pioneered you into
doing them !   Barry Derrill, there's such a thing in
the world as a libel.   You came strutting in with a
mandolin under your arm, didn't you ?

Barry. I did, but——

Darry. An' you sang your song.

Barry. Yes, but——

Darry. When you waltz'd in, I was doing callisthenics,
wasn't I ?

Barry. I know you were ; but all the same——

Darry. An' you flung yourself down on the floor, and got yourself into a tangle trying to do them too, didn't you ?

Barry. Hold on a second——

Darry. Now, I can't carry the conversation into a debate, for I have to get going. So if you can't give a hand, go, 'n let me do the things that have to be done, in an orderly 'n quiet way.

Barry. 'Course I'll give a hand — only waiting to be asked.

Darry [*looking at the clock, suddenly*]. Is the clock stopped ?

Barry [*taking up clock and putting it close to his ear*]. There's no ticking, 'n it's hours slow.

Darry. Lizzie again ! Forgot to wind it. Give the key a few turns, Barry, an' put the hands on to half-past nine.

   [*Barry starts to wind the clock. Darry goes over to table, gets a basin of water, begins to wash the delf, humming to himself the air of the song, " Down where the bees are humming ". Barry winds and winds away, but no sign is given of a tightening of the spring inside. He looks puzzled, winds again, and is about to silently put the clock back where he found it, when Darry turns and looks at him questioningly.*

Darry. You've broken the damn thing, have you ?

Barry. I didn't touch it.

Darry. Didn't touch it ? Amn't I after looking at you twisting an' tearing at it for nearly an hour ? [*He comes over to Barry.*] Show me that. [*He takes the clock from Barry and opens the back, and the spring darts out.*] Didn't touch it. Oh, for God's sake be more careful when you're handling things in this house! Dih dih dih. [*He pushes the spring back, and slaps the clock down on the dresser.*] You must have the hands of a gorilla, man. Here, come over 'n wipe while I wash.

[*A slight pause while the two of them work at the delf. Darry anxiously watches Barry, who, being very near-sighted, holds everything he wipes close up to his spectacles.*

Darry [*suddenly*]. Look out, look out, there — you're not leaving that jug on the table at all; you're depositing it in the air, man!

Barry [*peering down at the table*]. Am I? Don't be afraid, I won't let anything drop.

Darry [*humming the song*]. Dum dah de de dum da dee dee dum dah dee dee dee dah ah dum.

Barry [*swinging his arm to the tune*]. Down where the bees are hummin' an' the wild flowers gaily growing.

Darry. Fine swing, you know. Dum dah dee dee dum dah dee dee dum dah dee dee dee dah ah dum.

Barry [*swinging his arm*]. Down where the bees are hummin' —

[*Barry's arm sends the jug flying off the table on to the floor.*

Darry [*yelling*]. You snaky - arm'd candle - power - ey'd elephant, look at what you're after doing!

Barry [*heatedly*]. It's only a tiny jug, anyhow, 'n you can hardly see the pieces on the floor!

Darry [*just as heatedly*]. An' if I let you do much more, they would soon be big enough to bury us ! Sit down, sit down in the corner there ; do nothing, say nothing, an', if I could, I'd put a safety curtain round you. For God's sake, touch nothing while I run out an' give the spuds to the pig.

[*Darry dashes over to the fire, whips the pot off, and runs out. He leaves the door open, and again the rattling whirr of a mowing machine can be heard. Barry sits dejectedly in a corner. After a few moments a bump is heard outside, followed by a yell from Darry, who, a second later, comes rushing madly in, a bloody handkerchief pressed to his nose. He flings himself flat on the floor on his back, elevating his nose as much as possible.*

Darry. Get me something cold to put down the back of my neck, quick !

Barry [*frightened*]. What the hell did you do to yourself ?

Darry. I didn't bend low enough when I was going in, 'n I gave myself such a—oh, such a bang on my nose on the concrete. Get something cold, man, to shove down the back of my neck 'n stop the bleeding !

Barry. Keep the nose sticking up in the air as high as you can. I don't know where to get something cold to shove down the back of your neck. I knew this rushing round wouldn't expedite matters.

Darry [*with a moan of resentment as he hears " expedite matters "*]. Oh, pull yourself together, man, 'n remember we're in the middle of an emergency.

Barry. A little block of ice, now, would come in handy.

Darry. A little — oh, a little block of ice ! An' will you tell us where you're going to get a little block of ice ?   An', even if we had one, how could you fasten it down the back of my neck ?   Eh ?   Can't you answer — where are you going to get a block of ice ?

Barry. How the hell do I know where I'm going to get it ?

Darry. D'ye expect me to keep lying here till the winter comes ?

[*During this dialogue Barry is moving round the room aimlessly, peering into drawers, rattling the delf on the dresser with his nose as he looks along the shelves.*

Darry [*as he hears the crockery rattling*]. Mind, mind, or you'll break something.   I must be losing a lot of blood, Barry, an' I won't be able to keep my nose sticking up in the air much longer.   Can't you find anything ?

Barry. I can see nothing.

Darry. Run upstairs 'n get the key of the big shed that's hanging on the wall, somewhere over the mantelpiece at the far end of the room.   Go quick, man !

[*Barry runs upstairs, goes into room, comes out again, and looks down at Darry.*

Darry [*up to him*]. Did you get it ?

Barry, Where's the switch ?   It's as dark as pitch in there.

[*Darry, with a moan of exasperation, sits up, but immediately plunges down on his back again.*

Darry. Starts pumping out again the minute I sit up. [*To Barry*] There's no switch in that room.   We can't have a switch in every corner of the room just to suit you !   You've only got to move down the centre of

the room till you come to the fireplace ; then brush
your hand over the mantelpiece, along the wall, till
you feel the key hanging there.

[*Barry goes back into the room.   After a few seconds'
silence, there is a crash of falling crockery.   Darry, after
a second of silent consternation, sits up with a jerk, but
immediately plunges down on his back again.*

Darry [*sinking supine on the floor*]. What has he done now ;
oh, what has he done now ?   [*Shouting up to Barry*] Eh,
you up there — what have you done now ?

Barry [*sticking his head out of door above*] Nothing much —
the washhand-stand fell over.

Darry [*angrily*]. Nothing much.   It sounded a hell of a
lot, then.   You're the kind of man if you're not
chained up, 'll pull everything in the house asundher !
Come down, come down, 'n stop down, or that delicate
little hand of yours 'll smash everything in the house !

Barry. My eyes are used to the darkness, now, 'n I can
see.   I'll get the key for you.

[*He goes back into the room, leaving Darry speechless.   After
a few seconds, he comes out of the room in a sweat of fright
and anger, one hand tightly clasped over the other.   He
rushes down the stairs, and begins to pull the things out
of the chest of drawers, every other moment leaving off to
clasp one hand over the other.*

Barry [*frantically*]. Get your own key, get your own key.
Half slaughtering myself for your sake !   Why don't
you keep your razor-blades in a safe place, an' not
leave them scattered about in heaps all over the mantelpiece ?   Where is there a bit of old rag till I bind up
my wounds ?   Get your own key yourself, I'm tellin'
you.

Darry. Amn't I nicely handicapped, wanting help an' having only the help of a half-blind man ?

Barry. D'ye know I'm nearly after mowing my fingers off with your blasted razor-blades ? [*Coming near to Darry, with a handkerchief in his hand, and showing the injured fingers to him*] Look at them, uh, look at them — one looks as if only a thin thread of flesh was keeping it on.   How am I going to play the mandolin now ?

Darry. You'd play it better if all your fingers were off.

Barry [*keeping the wounded hand in the air, and holding out the handkerchief to Darry with the other*]. Here, get a grip of this 'n help me to bind up me wounds.
   [*Barry kneels down beside the prostrate Darry, who takes the handkerchief and proceeds to tie it round Barry's wounded fingers.*

Darry [*keeping his nose well up in the air*]. You give that an unexpected honour, if you call that a wound !
   [*Darry ties the handkerchief round Barry's hand, who stands looking at it.*

Barry [*reflectively*]. Won't be able to do much for you with it now.

Darry. It'll limit your capacity for breakin' things.
                                                              [*A pause.*

Darry. Slip out, Barry, old son, 'n see if the heifer's safe on the bank beside the house.
   [*Barry goes outside the door and stands looking up towards the top of the house.   The light has been fading, and it is getting dark.   Again can be heard the whirr of the mowing machine, and the Town Hall clock strikes ten.*

Barry. I think I can hear her croppin' the grass all right, but it doesn't seem wise to leave her there 'n the dusk fallin'.

Darry [*testily*]. I can't do anything till this bleeding stops, can I ?

Barry. The spuds are all scattered about here where you let them fall when you were runnin' in.

Darry [*moaning*]. 'N can't you get the broom 'n sweep them up into a corner, 'n not be trampling them into the ground ; you see the state I'm in !
　　[*Barry gets the broom and starts to sweep outside the door.*

Barry [*in to Darry*]. How's it now ?

Darry [*cautiously sitting up*]. It's nearly stopped now, but I'll have to go cautious.
　　[*Barry, sweeping with one hand, manages to bring the broom-handle into contact with the window, and breaks a pane. A silent pause.*

Barry [*as if he didn't know*]. What's that, what's that ?

Darry [*in an agony of anger*]. What's that, what's that ! Can't you see, man, that you're after thrustin' the handle of the broom through one of the windows ?

Barry [*peering down at the hole in the window*]. That's curious, now, for I never felt the handle touchin' the window ; but there's a hole in it, right enough.

Darry [*with angry mockery*]. No, you wouldn't feel it touchin' it, either. A hole in it — of course there's a hole in it ! My God Almighty, I've a destroyin' angel in the house !

Barry. Well, not much use of lookin' at it now.

Darry [*vehemently*]. Oh, come in, come in, come in, man.

Didn't you hear the clock strikin' ten? I'll have to get goin' now.

[*He gets up gingerly, feeling his nose, and still keeping it at a high angle.*

Barry [*introducing another subject*]. Hadn't you better stable the heifer before you do anything?

Darry [*violently*]. Haven't I to clean out the cowhouse first before I stable her, man? With your exercisin', 'n your singin', 'n your great 'n godly gift of expeditin' matters, I haven't made a bit of headway! I hadn't a chance to give her the graze she needs, so let her get all she can on the bank at the back of the house.

Barry. Supposing she wanders to the edge of the bank 'n tumbles off?

Darry. I don't know what to do about that.

Barry. Couldn't you tie her to something?

Darry [*angrily*]. There's nothing to tie her to, man.

Barry. What about putting a rope down the chimney 'n tying it to something in the room?

Darry [*after a few seconds' thought*]. That's a good idea, Barry. There's a rope outside, an' I'll sling one end round her neck, let the other end down the chimney, an' tie it to a chair. Wait here a second 'n get it when it comes down.

[*Darry rushes out. After a few moments his voice is heard faintly from above calling, "Hello, hello!" Barry, who has his head a little up the chimney, the smoke making him cough, answers, "Righto, let her come." The rope comes down; Barry catches the end and pulls it into the room. Darry returns, and they tie the rope to a chair.*

Barry. Put the chair at the far end of the room, an' if the heifer wanders too far, we'll see the chair moving across the room.

Darry [*with enthusiasm*]. Now you're beginnin' to use your brains at last, Barry, me boy. [*He shifts the chair to the far end of the room.*] Now we can get goin' 'n get everything shipshape before the missus toddles back. Let's put on the light and see what we're doin'.
   [*He snaps down the switch, but no light comes into the bulb.*

Darry [*annoyed*]. Dih dih dih — must be the meter again.
       [*He hurries into the lumber room, stepping over the rope.*

Barry [*speaking in to Darry*]. I wouldn't do much tamperin' with that.

Darry [*inside room — emphatically*]. Oh, I know what I'm doin'.
   [*Darry rushes out again, snaps down the switch, but no light comes.*

Darry [*irritably*]. Must be the blasted bulb. [*He rushes to a drawer.*] There's a bulb here, somewhere, we've had for a long time, 'n never used. [*He takes one from the drawer.*] Here we are. [*He pulls a chair to the centre of the room, stands on it, takes off the old bulb, and gives it to Barry.*] See if you can see anything wrong with it.

Barry [*holding it to his nose*]. Can't see anything.

Darry. Leave it down, leave it down.

Barry. Sure the one you're fixing's the right voltage?

Darry [*stopping to look at Barry*]. Course it's the right voltage. Why wouldn't it be the right voltage?

Barry. If it wasn't, it might fuse.

Darry. Fuse? No fear of it fusing.

> [*He starts to work again.*
>
> [*The chair to which the rope is tied begins to move across the floor.*

Barry [*startled*]. Look out, look out — the heifer's moving !

Darry, Catch hold of it, catch hold of it, before she disappears up the chimney !

> [*Barry catches the chair, but the strain is too much, and he is pulled along. Darry jumps down off the chair, leaves the bulb on the table, catches hold of the rope, and helps Barry to tug the chair back to the far end of the room.*

Darry. You sit on the chair, 'n then she can't move without our knowledge.

> [*Barry sits on the chair ; Darry mounts the chair again, and starts to fix the bulb. The chair begins to move with Barry sitting on it.*

Barry [*excitedly*]. Eh, quick again, get down, the heifer's movin' !

> [*Darry jumps down again, and the two of them pull the chair back to its place.*

Darry. The missus'll be back 'n nothin' done but damage.

> [*He gets up again and fixes the bulb ; there is a flash, and the room is darker than ever.*

Barry [*like a prophet*]. I warned you, Darry ; I saw it comin'.

Darry [*forcibly*]. What are you blatherin' about ? We're no worse off than we were before we fixed it. There's a drum of oil in the lumber room, 'n if there's any left in it we can light the lamps. You light the one hangin' on the wall, while I see how we stand.

[*He runs into the lumber room. Barry takes the lamp from the wall, removes the chimney, and tries to light the wick, but he can't see it, and holds the match anywhere but near the wick. Darry comes out of cellar.*]

Darry [*jubilantly*]. Plenty of oil in it. Aw, you're not holding the match within a mile of the wick, man. Show it to me, show it to me.

[*He takes the match from Barry, and lights the lamp.*]

Darry. Out with you now, 'n get one of the old lamps you'll find on one of the shelves to the right in the shed at the back of the yard.

Barry. How'll I see ?

Darry. Strike a match 'n look. You'll see them staring at you. I'll take a canful of oil from the drum to put in it when you bring it back, 'n then we'll have lashin's of light.

Barry [*going out by door*]. I know I won't be able to see.

[*Darry, with a can that has a long snout on it, runs back into the lumber room. Barry has left the door open, and the rattling whirr of the mowing machine can be heard again. There is a slight pause. Suddenly Darry rushes out of the lumber room over to the open door.*]

Darry [*shouting madly*]. Barry, Barry, come here quick, man ! I turned the key of the tap too much, 'n it slipped out of me hand into a heap of rubbish 'n I can't turn off the cock, 'n I can't find the key in the dark. Come quick, man, or there won't be a drop of oil left in the drum !

[*He rushes wildly back into the lumber room.   Another slight pause.   He rushes out again, with the drum in his arms, his thumb pressed to the tap outlet, and runs over to the door.*

Darry [*calling madly*]. Eh, Barry, Barry, d'ye hear me callin' you, man ? I won't be able to keep this oil in much longer.   Have you fallen asleep, or what ?
   [*There is heard outside a rattle, followed by a crash of falling pots, tins, and tools ; then a dead silence for a moment.*

Darry [*staggering against the wall*]. Aw, Mother o' God, what's he after doin' now !

Barry [*outside, in a loud voice of great distress*]. Darry, oh, Darry, I'm after nearly destroyin' meself !   Where's the doorway ? — I can't see !

Darry [*going over and standing in the doorway*]. Here, here, man ; no, to the left.   [*As Barry staggers in, dusty and frightened*] What ruin are you after causin' now ?

Barry [*moaningly*]. I'm after gettin' an awful shock !

Darry [*appealingly*]. Pull yourself together, for God's sake, man, 'n tell us what's happened.

Barry [*as he sinks down on a chair*]. The blasted lamps were on top of the top shelf ; there was nothing to stand on ; I had to climb upon the shelves, and climbing up, the shelves 'n all that was on them came down on top of me !
   [*Darry goes over and rests the drum in the sink, his hand still pressed over the outlet of the tap.*

Darry. 'N why did you climb the shelves ?   What did you want to do that for ?   Couldn't you see, you sap, that they weren't fixed well in the wall ? Why did you insist on climbing the shelves ?

Barry. I was just tryin' to expedite matters.

Darry [*with a wail*]. Tryin' to expedite matters. Oh, there'll be a nice panorama of ruin in front of Lizzie when she comes back !

Barry. 'N me spectacles were sent flyin' when the shelves fell.

Darry. 'N why didn't you grab them before they fell to the ground ?

Barry [*hotly*]. How could I grab them 'n they fallin', when I was fallin' too !

Darry [*impatiently*]. Well, get the lamp then, 'n look for the lost key in the lumber room.

Barry. 'N maybe let it fall, 'n set the house on fire ?

Darry [*woefully*]. Oh, amn't I in a nice predic— The chair, the chair — the heifer's movin' !

[*The chair to which the rope is tied begins to move across the floor. Barry catches it, tugs manfully, but he is carried on towards the fireplace.*

Barry [*anxiously*]. Give us a hand, give us a hand, or I'll be up the chimney !

[*Darry leaving the drum, runs over to Barry's side, grips the rope in front of Barry, and, to get a safer hold, takes the rope off the chair and puts it round him under his arms. With great pulling, they get the rope a little back. The oil flows from the drum into the sink unnoticed.*

Darry [*panting*]. Keep a strain, or we'll be up the chimney !

Barry. How'm I goin' to get home to-night without me spectacles ?

Darry [*loudly*]. Keep a sthrain on her, man, keep a sthrain on her ; we have to get this straightened out first, before we can brood over your spectacles !

Barry [*suddenly noticing the oil drum*]. The oil, the oil !
  [*He lets go of the rope, and runs over to the oil drum. Darry disappears up the chimney.*

Barry [*lifting the drum and shaking it*]. Not a drop left in it, not a single drop ! What're we goin' to do n——
                    [*He turns and sees that Darry has disappeared.*

Lizzie [*speaking outside in a voice of horror*]. The heifer, the heifer !

Darry [*calling out*]. Lizzie, Lizzie !
  [*Lizzie rushes in as Darry falls down the chimney. He crawls out from the fireplace on his hands and knees, and halts there, exhausted and sooty.*

Lizzie [*horrified*]. What in the Name of God has happened ?

Darry [*to Lizzie*]. Now you see the result of havin' your own way ! Why the hell didn't you hold on to the rope when you took it off the heifer, so that I wouldn't come down with a bump ?

Lizzie. How'd I know you were hangin' on the other end ?

Darry [*indignantly*]. You didn't know — my God, woman, can you do nothin' right !

CURTAIN

K*

MUSIC FOR SONG IN
"THE END OF THE BEGINNING"

DOWN WHERE THE BEES ARE HUMMING

A POUND ON DEMAND

A Sketch in One Act

CHARACTERS IN THE PLAY

A GIRL, *in charge of Pimblico Sub-Post Office*
JERRY, *a working man*
SAMMY, *another*
A POLICEMAN

SCENE

A Sub-Post Office on a late autumn evening

A Post Office. *There is a counter to the right which comes out for about four yards, turning at right angles, and running to the back. That part of the counter facing front is railed, and has in the centre a small, bracketed window for selling stamps. Above the window is a card on which is the word* STAMPS. *There is a swing-door in the centre at the back. To the right of the door a window having the words* POST OFFICE *on it to face towards the street. To the left is a table-ledge for the convenience of those who want to write letters, telegrams, fill in forms, or make out postal orders. Blotting-paper, quill pens, inkwells are on the ledge. Above ledge at back a telephone booth. Notices, such as, Save Saving Certificates and Saving Certificates will Save you; Buy by Telephone; Post often and Post early; Cardinal Virtues: Temperance, Prudence, Fortitude, Payment of Income Tax.*

Behind the counter, sitting on a high stool beside a desk, is a Girl, sorting and examining documents, and doing the routine work of a Post Office. Behind counter, on the left, a door. It is six o'clock or so in the evening of an autumn day; the sun is low in the sky, and his red light is flooding in through the window.

The swing-door suddenly opens and Jerry, pressing his body against the door to keep it open, while he holds Sammy, who is drunk, steady with his right hand, appears to view with an anxious and hopeful look on his face. Jerry is dressed in cement-soiled working clothes, and his trousers are bound under the knees with cords. He is about forty years of age. His friend, Sammy, is a workman too, and is dressed in the same way. Jerry wears a large tweed cap, and Sammy wears a brown trilby much the worse for wear. Sammy is in a state of maudlin drunkenness, and his reddish face is one wide, silly grin.

Jerry [*holding on to Sammy and calling in to the Girl*]. Yous do
Post Office Savin's Bank business here, don't you, miss ?
> [*Before the Girl has time to reply, Sammy lurches away
> from the door, pulling Jerry with him, and the door
> swings shut again. The Girl looks round, but sees only
> the swinging door. A pause. The door opens again, and
> Jerry, holding Sammy with a firmer grip, appears and
> speaks in to the Girl.*

Jerry [*to the Girl*]. Savin's Bank's business's's done here,
miss, isn't it ?
> [*Sammy lurches again, pulling Jerry with him, so that the
> door again swings shut. Again the Girl looks round and
> sees only the swinging door. She keeps her eyes on it. A
> pause. The door opens again and the two men appear,
> this time with Jerry behind Sammy, pushing him, and
> looking round him as he speaks in to the Girl.*

Jerry [*looking round Sammy as he speaks in to the Girl*]. Savin's
Bank business's's done here, isn't it, miss ?

Girl [*suspiciously*]. Yes.

Jerry [*exultantly to Sammy*]. I told you, Sammy, this is a
Post Office where Savin's Bank business's's done. In
we go.

Sammy [*looking round vacantly*]. Where ?

Jerry. In there, in here, can't you see ? We're in port,
Sammy — Post Office where Savin's Bank business's's
done.

Sammy [*vacantly*]. Where ?

Jerry [*appealingly*]. Aw, pull yourself together, Sammy.
Remember the mission we're on ; don't let a fella down
now. Remember what we want.

Sammy [*vacantly*]. Want nothin'.

Jerry [*irritably*]. Try to remember, man — pound on demand — remember ?

Sammy [*stiffening*]. Pound on demand, wanna pound on demand.

Jerry. Why're you sayin' you want nothin', then ? Don't make a fool of me when it comes to the push. You've only to sign a form — the young lady 'll give it to you.

Sammy. Sign no form ; don't wanna form.

Jerry [*irritably*]. You can't get your pound, man, till you sign a form. That's the way they do Savin's Bank business's, see ? Sign a form askin' a pound on demand, 'n hand it over to the young lady, see ?

Sammy. Wanna drink.

Jerry. You've no money for a dhrink. Can't get a dhrink till you get your pound on demand. [*Guiding Sammy over to the counter.*] Thry to keep your composure while we're doing the business.

> [*The pair come to the counter.*

Jerry [*in a wheedling way to the Girl*]. He wants a pound on demand, missie ; [*to Sammy*] don't you, Sammy — a pound on demand ? [*To the Girl*] Give's the form, missie, till he pops his name down on it.

Girl [*to Sammy — ignoring Jerry*]. What can I do for you, sir ?

Sammy [*vacantly*]. Wha' ?
> [*A stoutish Woman of about forty comes in by the door with a minor kind of a rush, and hurries over to the counter. She stares for a moment at the two men.*

Woman [*to the Girl*]. If I wrote a letter 'n posted it to catch the seven fifty-nine P.M. collection, would it get to Tarraringapatam on Friday before twelve fifty-four in the afternoon, please ?

Girl [*trying to collect her wits together*]. What collection, madam ?

Woman [*stiffly*]. I said the seven fifty-nine P.M. collection, I think.

Jerry [*impatiently*]. Gie's the little form, missie.

Sammy [*drunkenly breaking into song*]. Jush a song at twilight, when the lights 're slow——

Jerry [*remonstrating*]. Eh, eh, there, Sammy !

Sammy [*a little subdued*]. 'N the flickerin' shadowish softly——

Jerry [*emphatically*]. Eh, Sammy, eh !

Sammy [*ending it softly*]. Come 'n go.

Girl [*to the Woman*]. The destination of the letter, madam, please ?

Woman. Tarraringapatam.

Girl. Where exactly is that place or locality, madam ?

Sammy. Nex' parish but one t' ourish.

Woman [*indignantly, to Sammy*]. Keep your funny remarks to yourself, please. [*To the Girl*] Tarraringapatam's in the most southern part of Burma.

Jerry [*to the Girl*]. Fork over the form for the pound on demand, will you, missie ? Before me pal gets too tired to sign.

Girl [*to Jerry*]. One minute, please.

Sammy [*hammering on counter with his hand*]. A pound en deman', wanna pound en deman'.

Woman [*to the Girl*]. Will a letter posted to catch the seven fifty-nine get to Tarraringapatam on Friday before twelve fifty-four in the afternoon?

Girl. I'm afraid I couldn't say, madam.

Jerry [*briskly, to the Woman*]. Young lady doesn't know. [*To the Girl*] Pound on demand form, miss.

Woman [*indignantly, to Jerry*]. Be good enough, sir, to confine your attention to your own business, will you? [*To the Girl*] Will you find out?

Jerry [*to the Woman*]. You can't be let monopolize the time 'n attention of an office for the use of the public at large, can you?

Sammy [*briskly*]. Ish she tryin' to shtir up trouble, or wha'?

Woman [*to Sammy*]. I'm making an ordinary enquiry at a public office, and I will not tolerate interference.

Girl [*who has been running her finger along a list of names of places hanging on a card behind the counter*]. What name, again, please?

Woman [*with dignity*]. Tarraringapatam.

Girl [*looking at the list*]. Not on the list, madam.

Jerry [*ironically*]. Bus stop in the jungle, miss.

Woman. It must be there.

Girl [*to the Woman*]. Not on the list. [*To Sammy*] What can I do for you, sir?

Jerry [*confidentially*]. Just wants a pound on demand, miss.

Girl [*sharply, to Jerry*]. Let the gentleman speak for himself. [*To Sammy*] What is it, please?

Sammy. Ish she tryin' to shtir up trouble, or wha'?

Jerry [*loudly, to Sammy*]. Young lady's askin' if you want a pound on demand.

Sammy [*wakening up a little*]. Yeh, wha'? Wanna a pound on demand, yeh.

Jerry [*briskly*]. Give's the form, 'n I'll get him to sling his name down, missie.

Girl [*to Sammy*]. Can I have your bank-book, please?

Jerry [*briskly*]. Bank-book, bank-book, Sammy; young lady wants the bank-book.

> [*Sammy looks vacantly at the Girl and at Jerry.*

Jerry [*briskly*]. Get a move on. [*He puts a hand in Sammy's breast-pocket.*] Bank-book, bank-book, Sammy, me son; young lady wants bank-book.

> [*He takes the book from Sammy's pocket, and hands it to the Girl.*

Girl [*to Woman, who is standing beside the counter*]. Sorry, madam, but I can't tell you what you want to know — the name's not on the list. [*She looks at the bank-book Jerry has given to her.*] Which is Mr. Adams?

Jerry [*gaily indicating his friend*]. This is him, miss, all alive 'n full of beans.

Sammy [*delightedly*]. Jusht a song at twilight when the lights aresh slow——

Jerry [*interrupting*]. Shush — young lady doesn't like singing in her office, Sammy.

Sammy [*drunkenly*]. Sammy doesn't care about any young ladyish ; don't care 'bout offish or young ladyish.

Woman [*going over indignantly to ledge to write her letter*]. A finely appointed Post Office, I must say, that can't give you even a hint about the commonest postal regulation !
[*The Girl slowly gets a form and reluctantly hands it out towards Sammy, but Jerry takes it out of her hand, and hurries Sammy over to the writing-ledge opposite.*

Girl [*warningly*]. The depositor must sign himself ; and his signature must correspond with that in the book.
[*The woman is writing her letter, and is taking up a great deal of space. She is right in the middle of the ledge with writing materials spread round on each side of her. Jerry leads Sammy to the space on her right, looks at it, then leads Sammy round to the space on her left.*

Jerry. Now you've only just to gather the pen into your mit 'n slap down the old name on to the form.
[*Jerry spreads the form on the ledge, gets an old pen and puts it into Sammy's hand, who lets it fall to the floor.*

Jerry [*with irritation, as he picks it up, and places it again in Sammy's hand*]. Try to keep a grip on it, man, 'n don't be spillin' it all over the place. [*Sammy grips it like a sword.*] Aw, not that way. Don't go to the opposite extreme. [*Arranging pen.*] Nice 'n lightly between the finger 'n thumb. That way, see ? [*Speaking over to the Girl.*] He's not used to this kind of thing, miss, but he'll be all right in a minute.

Sammy [*standing still and looking vacantly at the wall*]. Wanna poun' on demand.

Jerry [*encouragingly*]. Go on, bend your back 'n write your name. [*To the Woman who is writing her letter*] Mind movin' over as far as you can, ma'am, to give him room to write his name — he wants a pound on demand ?

[*The Woman looks indignant, but moves a little away. Sammy bends down, gets the pen to the paper, slips and slides along the ledge, nearly knocking the Woman down.*

Jerry [*in dismay*]. Aw, Sammy, eh, eh. Look at the form, man. Can't you keep your balance for a second ?

Woman [*indignantly*]. This is a nice way to be scattered about, writing an important letter to Tarraringapatam ! [*To the Girl*] Aren't you going to exercise a little control here, please ?

Jerry [*to the Woman*]. He's sawl right, he's sawl right, ma'am.

Woman [*angrily*]. No, it's not all right ; it's anything but all right. [*Violently, to Sammy*] Remember you're in a Post Office, sir !

Sammy [*with drunken indignatiom*]. Posht Offish ! What's a Posht Offish ? Haven't to take me shoes from off me feet in a Posht Offish, have I ?

Jerry [*soothingly*]. It's sawl right. No one wants you to take your shoes from off your feet. Here, lean on the ledge till I get a new form.

[*He puts Sammy leaning against the ledge and goes over to get another form.*

Sammy [*meandering over to the Woman*]. Shuh want me to take me shoes from offish me feet ?

Jerry [*to the Girl*]. Slip us another form, missie.

Sammy [*close to the Woman — emphatically*]. Shuh hear me

talkin' to you ?   Shuh want me to take me shoish from off me feet ?

Jerry [*impatiently to the Girl*].   Give's the form, miss, before he begins to get lively.

Girl [*busy at work*].   Oh, just a minute.   I gave you one a moment ago.

Sammy [*close to the Woman*].   You push off, ma'am, please ; thish plaish is occupied.   Have to write me namish ; need spaish ; wanna pound on demand.   [*The Woman ignores him.*]   Push off when you're warned, can't you ? Thish plaish ish occupied.

Jerry [*speaking over to Sammy from the counter*].   Eh, eh, Sammy, there, control yourself, man.   [*To the Girl*] Hurry up, miss.   Steady, Sam !

Sammy [*more emphatically, as the Woman ignores him*].   Shuh hear me talkin' to you ?   Told you I wanted spaish. Push off, now — this plaish is occupied.

Jerry [*over to Sammy, in a warning voice*].   Sammy ! Steady !

Woman [*indignantly to Sammy*].   How dare you tell me to push off ?   I'll have you know this is a public office, and I am engaged in important business.

Sammy [*aggressively*].   Shuh don't want a pound on demanish, so push off before I call the polish.

Jerry [*facing towards the Girl*].   Calm, Sammy, calm.
   [*Sammy pushes the Woman as she is writing her letter, but she indignantly pushes back, and he finds it hard to keep his feet.   He recovers and returns to the charge, pushes her again, but she pushes him more violently than before, sending him more than half-way towards the door ;*

by a great effort he recovers and staggers back to the Woman with a look of determination on his face.

Jerry [*to the Girl, as Sammy is staggering about — which Jerry does not see*]. For God's sake, give's a form, missie.

Sammy [*pushing the Woman*]. I have you taped, me lassie ; wanta wash what're we doin' : I have you taped, but I'll block you, me lassie !
[*He pushes the Woman, who pushes him back ; he tries to recover, but she follows him up, and pushes again so that Sammy staggers to the door, hits it, the door opens, Sammy staggers out into the street, and the door closes again. The Woman goes back to the writing of her letter.*

Jerry [*who is ignorant of Sammy's disappearance, rapping impatiently on the counter*]. Eh, miss, missie, the form, miss, eh, the form, missie.

Girl [*impatiently slapping down a form on the counter*]. That's the last you'll get.

Jerry [*combatively*]. Oh, don't get too cocky, miss, for, after all, you're only a servant to the public. [*Tapping his chest*] It's the like of me that pays your wages. You're just here to serve the interests of the public, so don't get too cocky.

Girl [*tartly*]. I don't want any impertinence, please.

Jerry [*hotly*]. You'll do what's here to do accordin' to regulations. I wonder what'd happen if I sent in a chit of a complaint to the Postmaster-General ?
[*He turns round to go over to the writing-ledge and finds that Sammy has disappeared.*

Jarry [*staring round in bewilderment*]. Where's he gone ?

Eh, where did Sammy go? [*He runs over to the Woman.*]
Why the hell didn't you keep an eye on him when you
knew he had a few up?

> [*He rushes to the door, pushes it open and runs out.*

Woman [*to the Girl*]. Nice pair of drunken scoundrels.
What are the police doing?

> [*The door swings open and Jerry enters, dragging Sammy in
> after him.*

Jerry [*indignantly, to the Girl*]. Eh, will you speak to that
lady over there, 'n keep her from interferin' with people
transactin' public business?

> [*He leads Sammy back to the writing-ledge, spreads the form
> on the ledge for him, and carefully places a pen in his hand.*

Sammy [*as he is being led over*]. Have that lasshie taped;
thash lasshie over there, have her taped, so I have.

Jerry [*placing the pen in Sammy's hand*]. Get your mit
goin', Sammy, get your mit goin'. [*Sammy does not
stir.*] Aw, get down to it, man.

Sammy. Can't bend.

Jerry. Why can't you bend?

Sammy. Can't bend, can't stand; wanna chair.

Jerry [*impatiently*]. Hold on tight, then, while I get you
one. Hold tight, now.

> [*Sammy grips the writing-ledge grimly, as he stares over at
> the Woman who is writing at the other end. Jerry runs
> to the counter, acting and speaking so impetuously that the
> Girl does what is asked of her before she realizes what is
> happening.*

Jerry [*rapidly to the Girl*]. The stool, missie, a lend of the
stool; he can write his name safer sittin'; quick,
missie !

[*The Girl hands over a high stool, Jerry runs over to Sammy with the stool, helps Sammy to sit on it, settles the form, and again puts the pen in his hand. Sammy protrudes his tongue, and seems to find his coat in the way.*

Jerry. Oul' coat in the way, eh? Take it off, then, so's it won't clog your movements; young lady won't mind.

[*After a good deal of pulling, Sammy, with the help of Jerry, gets off his coat.*

Woman [*sarcastically, staring at the pair*]. Why don't you pull down the blinds and keep the light from hurting his eyes?

[*Sammy gives a violent movement of anger, sweeping pen, ink, and form to the ground. Holding precariously to the ledge, he tilts his seat, slides over towards the Woman, and brings his face as close to hers as possible.*

Sammy [*angrily to the Woman*]. Thish ish a Post Offish, see.? No one allowed interfere with men hash businish to do. Wasn't reared yesterday, 'n I have you taped, me lasshie!

Jerry [*indignantly, to the Woman*]. Whyja go 'n cause a commotion just as the man was doin' nicely? You've no right to interfere with men transactin' public business. [*Over to the Girl*] See that, miss, see the way she interfered the minute the man was just doin' nicely?

Girl [*calmly*]. I didn't see the lady interfering in any way.

Jerry [*indignantly*]. Well, if you hadda had your eyes open, you'd ha' seen it. There doesn't seem to be any proper conthrol in the place at all.

[*While Jerry is speaking, the Girl goes to the telephone, dials a number and listens. Jerry helps Sammy back to his original position on the stool.*

Girl [*at the telephone*]. Hello; Pimblico Post Office speaking; send down one of your little boys, will you? Yes, at once, please.

[*She replaces the receiver and stands watching the two men, glancing, now and again, at the door.*

Jerry [*when he has settled Sammy*]. Now don't fall asundher any more, for God's sake. [*To the Woman*] 'N no more of your condescendin' remarks, please, see?

Woman [*vehemently*]. One word more from either of you, 'n I'll go straight out 'n bring in a policeman!

[*There are a few moments dead silence.*

Sammy [*breaking out excitedly*]. Ja hear what she said? Ja hear? Bring a policeman in. That's what we get for trustin' people. What do I care for the poleish? Speak up, Jerry, 'n be a man — do I or do I not care for the poleish?

Jerry [*soothingly*]. No, never; everyone who knows Sammy, knows that.

Sammy. Not if they were round me in dozens — do I or do I not?

Jerry. Not a word, Sammy, not a word; we rest silent about them things.

Sammy. Not a word. We don't rush round tellin' things; but we know, don't we, Jerry?

Jerry. Not a word. Don't let your nerves get jangled now. Slip your name down.

Sammy. Not another word. Poleeish! Do I or do I not care for the poleeish — you know, Jerry?

Jerry. Not a word — go on, get your name down.

Sammy [*excitedly*]. Let her send for the poleeish! Wouldn't be long till they didn't know what was happenin'. Poleeish to the right of me, 'n to the left of me, 'n nothing left of them in the end but silver buttons for souvenirs!

Jerry. Rags, bones, 'n buttons, wha'? Go on — slip your name down.

> [*The door opens and a huge Policeman enters. He walks slowly in, goes over to the counter, looks at the Girl, who points to the two men; the Policeman nods knowingly.*

Sammy [*leaning over towards the Woman*]. We often plastered the roads with policemen, 'n left them thryin' out how they were going to get themselves together again!

Woman [*scornfully*]. Oh, you did, didja?

Sammy [*mockingly, to the Woman*]. Yes, we did, didn' we; we did did did didja, didn' we!

Policeman [*coming over and standing near the two men*]. Now, then, do what you have to do, 'n go about your business.

> [*The two men look round and see the Policeman. They stare at him for a few moments, and then turn their faces away, fixing their attention on the form. There is dead silence for a time, for the near presence of a Policeman is a great discomfort and very disconcerting.*

Jerry [*almost in a whisper*]. Just there on the line, Sammy. Samuel, first name, see? Lead off with a big ess. A big ess, man, a big ess. Shape it into a big ess — capital ess — don't you know what a capital ess is? Here, I'll show you — give us a hold of the pen for a minute.

> [*Jerry takes the pen from Sammy and makes the necessary correction, and returns the pen to Sammy.*

Jerry. There y'are now.   No, on ahead, cautious : a, m, u — I think — yes, u, double e, l — no, one e 'n two double ells — good God, what am I sayin' — only one double ell, only one double ell, man ! You're not listenin' to me, Sammy.   There's nothin' to prevent you doin' it right, if you'll only listen.   You've nearly a dozen of ells down.   Show it to me for a second.

[He takes the pen and removes roughly the unnecessary letters.

Jerry [*warningly*]. Now the next name, Adams ; 'n make the letthers a little smaller, or you'll be a mile away from the form before the last one comes in sight.

Sammy [*in a weary voice*]. Aw, I've had enough.

Jerry. You're too far ahead to give up now, man.   T'other name, now.   A big A for a start.   Not as big as an elephant, now — you know what an ordinary capital A is.   Oh, why did you let your hand slip ?   It'll have to do now.   [*Turning and winking at the Policeman*] He's got a few up, but he's sawl right.   [*To Sammy*] Now a little d, 'n a little u, 'n a little — wait a minute — I'm gettin' a little confused — a little m, a little n, 'n a little ess — a little ess, man !   Now, come on, 'n we'll give it to the young lady.

Woman [*mockingly, to Jerry*]. The poor man'll need a long rest, now.

[Jerry helps Sammy off the stool, and links him over to the counter, both of them trying to appear as if they were indifferent to the presence of the Policeman.   He hands over the form to the Girl, who examines it, and looks at the name in the bank-book.

Jerry [*humming, and trying to look unconcerned*]. Rum tum tiddley um tum, parley voo ; rum tum tiddley um tum, parley voo ; rum tum——

Girl [*interrupting Jerry's humming*]. Couldn't give you a pound on demand with this signature. The signature on the form doesn't correspond with the signature in the bank-book in any way.

Jerry. It's his writin', isn't it, miss? An' both of the names is Adamsususes, aren't they?

Girl. They don't correspond. Sorry; but I car. let you have the money. I don't even know that the gentleman is really Mr. Adams.

Jerry [*wild*]. Didja ever hear such consequential nonsense! [*To Sammy*] She says you're not Mr. Adams. [*To the Girl*] Of course he's Mr. Adams. Who else could he be, only Mr. Adams? Isn't he known all over the district where he lives, woman?

Girl. Why, then, didn't he go to the Post Office in his own district?

Jerry [*impatiently*]. Because it's too busy an office, 'n we decided to come to a place where he could do what he wanted to do in comfort, 'n fill in his name at his ease.

Girl [*with decision*]. I'm sorry; but I can't let the gentleman have the money.

Jerry [*horrified*]. 'N what's he goin' to do, then?

Girl. Better call back again to-morrow, or the next day.

Jerry. He wants the money now, girl.

Girl. I can't give it to him.

Jerry [*to Sammy*]. She says she won't give you the pound on demand.

Sammy. Wanna pound on demand.

Jerry [*to the Girl*]. Hear what the depositor says? He's gotta get it.

Sammy. I've gotta get it.

Jerry [*to Sammy*]. Of course you have. After the agony of gettin' things ship-shape, we're not goin' to stand any denial of our rights.

Policeman [*coming near*]. Hasn't the young lady said she can't give it to you ? So go on home, now, like decent men, an' forget all about it.

Jerry [*to the Policeman*]. The man has gotta get his money, hasn't he ?

Sammy [*dreamily*]. 'Course I've gotta get it.

Policeman [*importantly*]. Since he hasn't complied with the necessary preliminaries, he isn't entitled to withdraw his pound.

Jerry [*indignantly*]. The only preliminary was the signin' of his name, wasn't it ? 'N he signed his name, didn't he ? Y'awl seen him signin' his name, didn't you ? [*A pause.*] Are yous all afraid to speak — did yous, or didn't yous ?

Policeman. G'on now, g'on. [*To Jerry*] Y'ought to see that your comrade's incapable of discretion in withdrawin' anything from a Government corporation. G'on, now, like decent men.

Jerry [*appealingly*]. He wants that pound special, I'm tellin' you. [*To Sammy*] Don't you, Sammy ?

Sammy [*dreamily*]. I gotta get it.

Jerry [*to the Policeman*]. Hear that ? Mind you, it's a serious thing to keep a man from gettin' his private property.

Policeman [*a little angry*]. Here, g'on the pair of yous, before I lose me temper ! You've been shown every leniency ; so go home, now, like sensible, decent men, before I lose me temper.

Jerry. Give us back the bank-book, then.

Girl. Mr. Adams might lose it — I'll post it on to him to-morrow.

Jerry [*frightened*]. He doesn't want you to post it. He wants it now — don't you, Sammy ?

Sammy [*wearily*]. I've gotta get it.

Policeman [*peremptorily*]. Now go on home, like decent men, before I have to resort to exthremes. Go on 'n sleep over it, 'n to-morrow, after a wash 'n brush up, you'll be able to apply for your pound in an ordherly 'n sensible manner.

Jerry [*wildly*]. 'N are we goin' to get nothin' out of all our efforts ? Mind you, there'll be throuble about this.

Policeman [*roughly*]. Ay, it'll start now if the two of yous don't bounce off 'n be well on your way home in a minute. [*He gently pushes them towards the door.*] G'on, now, you know your way.

Jerry [*sorrowfully*]. 'N we thravelled miles to find this quiet place, so that he could sign his name in peace.

Woman [*mockingly, as they go out*]. Isn't it a pity to disappoint the poor little children !

Sammy [*as they go out*]. I've gotta get it.
   [*They go slowly and sorrowfully out. The Policeman holds the door open for them, and closes it when they have gone. The Woman goes over to the counter with her letter.*

Woman. Registered, please.

> [*The Girl takes the letter, registers it, and hands receipt to the Woman, who puts it in her bag and goes out.*

Girl [*to the Policeman*]. Glad you hunted that pair of money philanderers out of the place.

Policeman [*taking her hand into his as he reclines over the counter*]. You're lookin' fit 'n fair 'n sweet 'n rosy to-day, so you are.

Girl [*coyly*]. Am I?

Policeman [*shyly*]. Yes, y'are, so y'are.

> [*The door opens a little way then closes again. The Policeman lets go the Girl's hand and stands stiff, while the Girl pretends to be busy with a document.*

Girl. Thought that was someone.

Policeman. Same here. [*He takes her hand again.*] Y'are, really, lookin' fit 'n fair 'n sweet 'n rosy to-day, so y'are.

Girl [*archly*]. Am I?

> [*The door suddenly swings open again, and Sammy appears, with Jerry steadying him from behind. They stand in the doorway, keeping it from closing with their shoulders. The Policeman and the Girl move away from each other.*

Jerry [*encouragingly to Sammy*]. Go on, give them your ultimatum : tell them straight that you're goin' to write to the Postmaster-General before you settle down for the night. Go on, now — give them your ultimatum !

> [*They both come in towards the centre of the office.*

Sammy [*pointing a finger towards the Girl and the Policeman, which shakes and wanders from the floor to the ceiling as he points*]. I have yous taped, two of yous 'n Postmaster-zheneral ! Taped, well taped I have, Postmaster-zheneral !

Jerry [*trying to cover up Sammy's vagueness*]. Mr. Adams, the depositor, has made up his mind to send a bitther complaint to the Postmaster-General about the way he's been shunted about by public servants durin' his application for a pound on demand. [*To Sammy*] Haven't you, Mr. Adams?

Sammy. I'm tellin' them, once for all, I've gotta get it.

Jerry. There y'are, you see; can't say I didn't warn you. Somebody will be made to sit up for this.

Policeman [*loudly and ominously*]. If the pair of yous aren't gone for good in two ticks of the clock, yous'll spend the night in a place that'll give the two of you plenty of time to complain to the Postmaster-General. [*He makes a move towards them.*] Be off, I'm tellin' yous, yourselves an' your pound on demand!

[*The two men are frightened by his move towards them, and Jerry manœuvres Sammy swiftly to the door, and both of them leave as quick as Sammy can travel.*

Jerry [*as they reach the door*]. Somebody 'll be made to sit up for this, I'm tellin' you!

[*As the doors swing shut, they open again partly to show Jerry's face glaring savagely into the office.*

Jerry [*shouting in from the partly opened door*]. That's the last penny of our money the Government 'll ever get from us!

[*His face disappears, the door swings shut, and the curtain comes down.*